GANDHI AND THE FUTURE
OF ECONOMICS

Dignity Press
World Dignity University Press

Howard Richards
Joanna Swanger

GANDHI AND THE FUTURE OF ECONOMICS

Dialogues with Some Indian Intellectuals

Edited by Ivo Coelho

Dignity Press
World Dignity University Press

Copyright © 2013 Howard Richards and Joanna Swanger

This work is licensed under the Creative Commons Attribution-Share-Alike 3.0 Unported License.
To view a copy of this license, visit:
http://creativecommons.org/licenses/by-sa/3.0/.
Please note: This license allows free use of the material with the restrictions that the authors have to be mentioned as the originators and that works making use of it have to stay open under the same license.

Published by World Dignity University Press, an imprint of Dignity Press
16 Northview Court
Lake Oswego, OR 97035, USA
www.dignitypress.org
Book website: www.dignitypress.org/gandhi

Book design by Uli Spalthoff
Printed on paper from environmentally managed forestry:
www.lightningsource.com/chainofcustody

ISBN 978-1-937570-29-3
Also available as EPUB: ISBN 978-1-937570-30-9
and Kindle eBook: ISBN 978-1-937570-31-6

Contents

Foreword	9
Introduction	13
Gandhi and the Future	19
Jawaharlal Nehru	51
Jayaprakash Narayan	91
Tariq Ali	129
Vandana Shiva	153
Amartya Sen	189
Arundhati Roy	221
Manmohan Singh	251
Authors	302
Acknowledgements	304

Foreword

I have never had the pleasure of meeting Joanna Swanger, but I did meet Howard Richards at a Lonergan Conference we both attended in Naples. Richards is a man who straddles worlds: North America and South America; academia and administration; East and West. He read philosophy at Yale and the University of California, law at Stanford Law School, education at Oxford and the University of Toronto, and retired as professor of Philosophy, Education and Peace and Global Studies at Earlham College, Richmond, Indiana. Joanna Swanger is, in fact, his successor in that position. He has served as a volunteer lawyer for Cesar Chavez, and, at the other end of the spectrum, as advisor to the Ministry of Education, Chile and program evaluator in Costa Rica, Ecuador and Bolivia for the Organization of American States and the International Development Research Center, Ottawa. At our meeting in Naples, however, I learned all this only in bits and pieces. What I did understand very clearly was that Richards was deeply interested in Gandhian economics, so interested that he was in the process of going through the hundred or so volumes of Gandhi's Collected Works in order to test his hypotheses against them. It was in Naples that we decided to collaborate on a serial publication of the chapters that became the present book. Quite aware that I am not a Gandhian scholar, I make bold to say that I have never come across such a fresh and compelling interpretation of that much controverted topic, Gandhian economics. Even ardent Gandhians balk at having to defend what is commonly regarded as one of the Mahatma's idiosyncracies. Here then is a book that gently, persistently and, I think, solidly makes a case for incorporating Gandhi's insights into mainstream economics.

Gandhi and the Future of Economics is not meant to be a research study of Gandhian economics. It is rather that kind of felicitous publication that breathes new life into a known theme, and, in doing so, brings out its implications for praxis. Even better is the fact that it does all this in dialogue with a set of contemporary thinkers and actors from the Indian sub-continent – and in the process, sometimes turning received wisdom on its head, as when it proposes that there is not as big a gap between Bapuji and Nehru as is usually imagined. The crowning piece is the final chapter on Manmohan Singh: with this the past meshes securely into the present, and our authors take a stand on the much-discussed topic of the Indian economic miracle. Given that that stand emerges out of the dialogue between someone who is considered the Father of the Nation and another who enjoys the unique privilege of being not only actually at the helm of affairs but also a renowned economist, and given further the endless debates about the merits and demerits of Singh, Gandhi and the Future of Economics is as topical as it is surprising in the thesis it defends.

I have said that I met Howard Richards at a conference dedicated to the work of the Canadian philosopher, theologian and economist Bernard Lonergan. Richards enjoys some familiarity with Lonergan's economics, a familiarity that surfaces at least in the introduction if not in the rest of the present book. Would it be too much to hope for a future dialogue between Gandhi and Lonergan? Both, for one, were deeply dharmic persons; and neither, on the other hand, was a professional economist; with the expected result, therefore, that the economic theories of both have been roundly neglected and relegated to the sidelines. So perhaps the dialogue might not be as strange as it first sounds. The following quote, in fact, sounds Gandhian, but is actually from Lonergan:

> *Nor is it impossible that further developments in science should make small units self-sufficient on an ultramodern standard of living to eliminate commerce and industry, to transform agriculture into a super-chemistry, to clear away finance and even money, to make economic solidarity a memory, and power over nature the only difference between high civilization and primitive gardening.*[1]

The way to the gardening is, however, at least in Lonergan's thinking, the way of science. If Lonergan could contribute a spine of hardcore economic theory to Gandhi's basic intuitions, perhaps not only India but also the world might stand to gain.

---

1 Bernard Lonergan, For a New Political Economy, Collected Works of Bernard Lonergan 21, ed. Philip J. McShane (Toronto: University of Toronto Press, 1998) 20.

But that is a wish for the future. At the moment, I am very happy to present Richards' and Swanger's wonderfully accessible and lively resurrection of Gandhi's economic ideas to the public.

Ivo Coelho
15 August 2012
Divyadaan: Salesian Institute of Philosophy, Nashik

INTRODUCTION

"The twenty-first century will be the century of Gandhi."
—Nelson Mandela

In 1908 Mohandas K. Gandhi wrote in Hind Swaraj that modern 'civilization' could not possibly last. By 2008 it was increasingly clear to a growing number of people (although unfortunately not yet to everybody) that even though it had lasted a hundred years after Gandhi predicted its eventual collapse, Gandhi was not mistaken when he wrote that it could not possibly last indefinitely.

In India, a spate of terror attacks (Mumbai most recently) raised the question whether the root cause is deeper, larger, historical anger, as did the persecution of Christians in Orissa.

Economic disparity was becoming intolerable. Why so much misery when there is so much abundance? And at what price the abundance in terms of ecology and the environment?

Are we destroying ourselves for the short term prosperity of a minority? In India as elsewhere ordinary people were taking refuge in anti-modern fundamentalist religion, finding in an irrational faith a fount of meaning in a meaningless world; and in many cases finding in irrational faith a practical survival strategy in a world shredded by family disintegration, drugs, alcohol, violence, and poverty.

The thesis of this book is partly that Gandhi correctly predicted that modern 'civilization' would prove to be unsustainable. Our thesis is also that he correctly identified the principal reasons why it is unsustainable. Writing in the Gujarati language, he characterized modern 'civilization' as adharma. As without dharma. We will be treating adharma modern thinking and modern institutions as equivalent to (or at least as closely intertwined with) economic thinking and today's prevailing economic and military institutions. Economics and power politics (what David Harvey calls the logic of accumulation and the logic of territorial control) can be regarded as the metaphysics or as the religion (or perhaps as the anti-religion) of what Gandhi referred to as modernity.

In a paper probably written in 1933, but only published posthumously in 1998, the Canadian Jesuit theologian Bernard Lonergan made a similar prediction for a similar reason. 'Liberalism' (a term that for Lonergan names the economic side of what Gandhi called 'modern') came to dominate western and then world institutions in the nineteenth century. It would necessarily self-destruct and would threaten to destroy humanity because in practice it neglected the inner discipline of the will. Lonergan's proposed 'metaphysics of solidarity,' like Gandhi's truth and nonviolence, envisions self-restraint as a prerequisite to social transformation. It warns that in the absence of self-restraint homo sapiens is not a viable species.

Lonergan attributed the extreme violence of the twentieth century to the liberalism of the nineteenth. He characterizes the philosophical and literary mind of the nineteenth century as for the most part centred on virtue and beauty, while in practice the mind of the age was dominated by political economy. The mainstream of nineteenth century thought was a disastrous combination of good intentions and bad thinking, for which the twentieth century paid a tragic price.

Borrowing a distinction from Nietzsche, we regard Gandhi and Lonergan as among those who offer *diesseits* (this side) critiques of political economy, as distinct from *jenseits* (the other side) critiques of political economy. The former critique its premises. The latter critique its consequences.

Jenseits critiques are abundant in contemporary social science. David Harvey and Giovanni Arrighi, for example, bring to the analysis of contemporary history concepts of accumulation, of debt, of sales, of currency devaluations, of taxation, of markets and market dynamics, that derive from the institutional framework of the modern world-system. Adam Smith and David Ricardo pioneered the mirroring of the liberal institutional framework in the premises of the classical political economy. Karl Marx employed them even as he deplored the consequences he drew from them. Today David Harvey analyzes many of the consequences of contemporary neoliberalism as 'accumulation by dispossession.' The dispossession of tribal peoples by flooding their lands when big dams are built, for example, is, on Harvey's view, a part of larger historical processes whose driving force is a combination of capital accumulation and power politics.

Gandhi's religious diesseits critique is not so much about what happens if one accepts the premises of economics as it is about what to do if one does not accept them. If one does not accept as a premise what Nassau Senior says explicitly and many economists assume implicitly, that accumulating wealth is the general motive of production; and if one instead supposes that shoemakers, farmers, and carpenters produce shoes, lentils, and houses for the use of others primarily because serving others by meeting a specific need is their role in society, their calling, their dharma, even though they are indeed paid for what they do, then one will see society differently. If one is like Gandhi, one will act differently, and one will recommend that others act differently.

Other premises make other worlds possible. A diesseits critique opens up more possibilities than a jenseits critique because it treats more parameters as variable.

It will not be easy for us to make our case. Every word we use is subject to multiple interpretations. Every claim we make is obviously false on some plausible assignment of meanings to our terms. We know in our own minds what we mean, but that is cold comfort. We want to persuade the world, not privately to reaffirm our beliefs. Even the most intelligent reader cannot read our minds to see what we mean by a word, and even the most charitable reader will not agree with us when (as far as she or he can judge) the facts do not agree with us.

Our strategy for communicating with readers in order to place before them what we mean and why we mean it, will be to imagine dialogues. They will be dialogues not just with Gandhi in general but especially with the gems of insight we find in Gandhi. We will take the reader over and over the same ground from different perspectives, hoping that after multiple views from multiple viewpoints what we are saying will painlessly fall into place in the reader's mind, as a crown for a tooth painlessly falls into the place prepared for it by a skilled dentist. We will interpret Gandhi by comparison and contrast with perspectives suggested by selected other Indian intellectuals: Jawaharlal Nehru, Jayaprakash Narayan, Tariq Ali, Vandana Shiva, Arundhati Roy, Amartya Sen, and Manmohan Singh.

Our Gandhi, unlike Plato's Socrates, will sometimes be wrong. It is far from our purpose to show that he was always right. It is close to our purpose to show that conversations with him facilitate finding solutions to problems (such as, for example, poverty, war, financial crisis, inflation, environmental degradation…) that are otherwise intractable.

If our strategy works, then at the end of the book the reader will appreciate the underlying pattern of thought and action out of which we speak when we make the claims that (1) Gandhi correctly predicted the collapse of modern 'civilization,' and that (2) he correctly identified some main causes of its collapse. If our strategy works then at the end of the book the reader will know that these claims are not pessimism. They are guides to transformative action. They can be put into practice; quite as Gandhi himself never remained at the level of unapplied thinking, but always acted on his ideas.

* * *

CHAPTER 1

GANDHI AND THE FUTURE

I.G. Patel, a distinguished Indian civil servant, once remarked that economics always overtakes cleverness in real life.[1] One might be tempted to suspect that Gandhi could have been one of the clever people Patel had in mind. What has triumphed in India has been economics, while what has been discarded is Gandhian thought. The success of neoliberal nuclear-armed India, boasting an eight percent annual growth rate, might be regarded as proof that Gandhian ideas do not work, while economic orthodoxy does.

We shall be arguing, to the contrary, in favour of Aldous Huxley's assessment of Gandhi: "Sooner or later it will be realised that this dreamer had his feet firmly planted on the ground, and that the idealist was the most practical of men."[2] There is something that does work in Gandhi's critique of modernity that sooner or later must be acknowledged and acted upon, as humans work persistently to find sustainable solutions to the intractable problems that plague modern commercial societies.

---

1 I.G. Patel, Glimpses of Indian Economic Policy (New Delhi: Oxford University Press, 2002) 170.
2 Aldous Huxley, quoted in Shanti S. Gupta, The Economic Philosophy of Mahatma Gandhi (Delhi: Ashok Publishing House, n.d.) 126.

Gandhi is sometimes given credit for having been right in ways different from what we have in mind. He is said, for example, to have anticipated what is now a standard teaching of development economics: where labour is abundant and capital is scarce, labour-intensive technologies should be preferred over capital-intensive technologies.[3] Perhaps it is true that Gandhi was in this respect an early proponent of ideas that others accepted later. But to look at his advocacy of labour-intensive technology as a precocious discovery of an economic theorem is to overlook that it was part and parcel of a normative framework quite different from the normative framework in which economics lives, and moves, and has its being. Gandhi's premises were different, even when his conclusions were the same, as those of an orthodox economist.

Gandhi was an outsider with respect to the social framework of economics. His thought is important mainly because he carried out a fairly consistent critique of that framework. Perhaps because he was an outsider, all or most of his practical dreams and projects are in the end not feasible. They are too far out of sync with the institutional framework that, for better or worse, has constituted today's social reality. Yet it is precisely because

---

3 See, e.g., Ajit Dasgupta, Gandhi's Economic Thought (London: Routledge, 1996). A passage from another work is also illustrative: "In modern economic terminology, he [Gandhi] saw that the 'shadow price' of labour in the village sector was zero and the 'shadow price' of capital embodying modern techniques was extremely high. His 'khadi economics' was therefore socially rational." Amritananda Das, Essays in Gandhian Economics, ed. Romesh Diwan and Mark Lutz (Delhi: Gandhi Peace Foundation, 1985) 148.

his is a body of thought which denies the premises of the mainstream that modernity can turn to him for keys to problem-solving that it cannot obtain from any of its insiders.

It is the view of the present writers that Gandhi's outsider critique of modernity is shaped by an idealized vision of the Indian village before the British conquest. As Bertell Ollman has shown that Marx's concept of alienation cannot be understood just as a critique of capitalism, but must be understood in the light of an alternative not-alienated society imagined by Marx, we hope to show that Gandhi's imaginary ideal Indian village gave meaning to his concept of dharma and to his critique of the fallen adharma social disorder he saw around him.[4]

Gandhi's ideal Indian village was not wholly imaginary. Even early in the nineteenth century an eyewitness could say that "the Village Communities are little republics, having nearly everything they want within themselves. They seem to last where nothing else lasts. Dynasty after dynasty tumbles down, revolution succeeds to revolution, Hindu, Pathan, Moghal, Mahratta, Sikh, English are masters in turn, but the Village Communities remain the same.... The union of the Village Communities, each one forming a separated little State in itself, has, I conceive, contributed more than any other cause to the preservation of the people of India through all revolutions and changes they have suffered, and it is in a high degree conducive to their happiness, and to the enjoyment of a great portion of freedom and independence."[5]

---

4 Bertell Ollman, Alienation: Marx's Concept of Man in Capitalist Society (Cambridge: Cambridge University Press, 1994).
5 Sir Charles Metcalfe's Minute, dated 7 November 1830,

These words are not Gandhi's. They are quoted from a minute dated 7 November 1830, written by a British colonial officer. Many other witnesses could be called to testify to the high degree of social integration and functional adjustment to the environment found in India before it was compelled to join what Immanuel Wallerstein has called the expanding European world-system.[6]

The destruction of traditional ways of life by advancing modern commerce happened throughout the world. Marx cites the cheap goods produced by European factories as solvents dissolving the social fabric of traditional societies, but it was usually the case, as Marx also notes, that it was not just the charms of European commodities that inducted the natives into the European world-system, but also violence. Traditional peoples rarely joined the Europe-centred global system voluntarily. Whether it was the conscription of labourers for the tea plantations of Sri Lanka or the rubber plantations of the Congo, or imposing a monetary tax to compel Africans to work for wages in the mines, or using soldiers to prevent the pre-Columbian peoples from running away from the European missions and plantations in Spanish and Portuguese America, or the resettlement of native North Americans on reservations, or compulsory 'settlements' redefining land tenure in India to make it fit the categories of British law so land could be taxed, the plot of the story was the

---

quoted by Romesh Dutt in India in the Victorian Age (London: Kegan Paul, Trench, Trubner & Co., 1904) 197. Dutt is one of the authors recommended by Gandhi in the bibliography he appended to Hind Swaraj.
6 Immanuel Wallerstein, The Modern World System, Vols. 1-3 (San Diego: Academic Press, 1989).

same: a conflict between people who preferred the way of life they were used to, and Europeans who forced them to comply with whatever their economic projects required.

Having observed that initiation into the institutions of global commerce was generally imposed by force in the sixteenth through nineteenth centuries, we should also observe that when the peoples of Africa and Asia emerged from colonialism after World War II their leaders generally—Gandhi being one of the notable exceptions—did not propose to go back and pick up the threads of their interrupted traditional ways of life. They aspired on the whole rather to transform their nations into prosperous social democracies along Scandinavian or British lines. Why their post-colonial nations in many cases ended up neither with a culturally appropriate version of Swedish social democracy, nor with a culturally appropriate version of networks of Gandhian villages; but instead with regimes marked by corruption, persistent social problems, and persistent violence, we will try to explain, in part, by arguing that Gandhi's message has not been sufficiently or properly understood.

Our argument about Gandhi's message is about the ideal traditional Indian village, even though we thought it necessary to mention the real traditional Indian village that lent credibility to it. Our argument may, of course, be mistaken. It may be that (1) Gandhi has not been misunderstood, but that instead on the whole subsequent Indian thinkers have understood him well enough, but have sometimes disagreed with him and sometimes agreed with him. Or it may be (2) that Gandhi's alleged hitherto insufficiently understood concepts are in fact false, in which case nothing has been lost by misunderstanding them; or that (3) we will be reading concepts into Gandhi's texts that are not there; or that (4) the failure of Gandhi's projects was not at all due, as we shall be claiming, to the legal framework of modern society of which Gandhi was insufficiently critical, but entirely to some other cause or causes, and, finally: (5) it might be that even if Gandhi had been properly understood, and corrected by implementing the necessary transformation of jurisprudence, it would have made little difference. Gandhi's thought might still have been overwhelmed by other factors—say, population growth, the influence of international aid agencies exacting ideological conformity as the price of funding, the inherent selfishness of human nature, great power imperialism, the laws governing capital accumulation, the partition of India and the ensuing arms race with Pakistan, the irresistible appeal of automobiles and other modern consumer goods—and so on—so that in the end, Indian history since Gandhi would not have been better.

In the following pages we shall try to rule out the first two of these five reasons why our theses may be false. Our strategy will be mainly to discuss two aspects of Gandhi's thought (one concerning caste, the other concerning Hind Swaraj) that have these characteristics: (a) they are puzzling, likely to be misunderstood, and as far as we know regularly have been either not understood or misunderstood; (b) the better and hitherto insufficiently understood meanings that we will attribute to Gandhi after offering solutions to the puzzles are undoubtedly true.

The third of the above five reasons why our theses may be wrong—that we may be attributing to Gandhi views that are actually our own or someone else's—concerns us less. We might claim Gandhi's own approach to reading texts as precedent for reading into Gandhi what he should have said rather than what he did say. That was his own approach to reading the parts of the Rig Veda which, when literally read, justified untouchability as punishment bad souls deserved for their sins in prior incarnations. He made no bones about deliberately reading the Vedic texts as saying what they should have said. But we do not think we need to follow the method Gandhi himself used to interpret the Rig Veda in order to justify our interpretations of him. We think the better meanings we find in Gandhi are part of what he did say, not just part of what he should have said, and in fact they are not in our opinion exactly what he should have said. In any case, we are ultimately more concerned with whether ideas more or less akin to Gandhi's can save humanity and the biosphere, than we are concerned with pinning down exactly what Gandhi thought. Indeed we do not consider the latter possible.

Ruling out the fourth and fifth sources of possible invalidity listed above, concerning why Gandhi's projects failed, and concerning whether India and the world would have turned out better if Gandhi had been better understood, will be attempted in various ways, but not so much in this chapter as in the following ones. The later chapters will also add more reasons for ruling out the first three sources of possible invalidity listed above.

1. Caste

Gandhi is famous for his lifelong struggle against one aspect of caste, untouchability. He was, however, long in favour of the general principle of the caste system, Varnashram. Jawaharlal Nehru reported of him that toward the end of his life Gandhi did make some general statements against caste, but what is puzzling is not that Gandhi eventually condemned caste. What is puzzling is that a person who in other respects was sane could seriously propose in the twentieth century that young people, instead of choosing their occupations, should do what their parents did.

Gandhi wrote, for example:

Varna is intimately, if not indissolubly, connected with birth, and the observance of the law of varna means the following on the part of us all the hereditary and traditional calling of our forefathers in a spirit of duty. Those who thus fulfil the law of their varna can be counted on one's finger's ends. This performance of one's hereditary function is done as a matter of duty, though it naturally carries with it the earning of one's livelihood. Thus, the function of a Brahmana is to study and teach the science of Brahman (or spiritual truth). He performs the function, as he cannot do otherwise, as it is the law of his being. That secures him his livelihood, but he will take it as a gift from God. A Kshatriya will perform the function of protecting the people in the same spirit accepting for his livelihood whatever the people can afford to give him. A Vaishya will pursue wealth-producing occupations for the welfare of the community, keep-

ing for himself enough for his own maintenance and rendering the balance to the community in one shape or other. A Shoodra will perform physical labour in the same spirit of service.

Varna is determined by birth, but can be retained only by observing its obligations. One born of Brahmana parents will be called a Brahmana, but if his life fails to reveal the attributes of a Brahmana, when he comes of age, he cannot be called a Brahmana. He will have fallen from Brahmanahood. On the other hand, one who is born not a Brahmana, but reveals in his conduct the attributes of a Brahmana will be regarded as a Brahmana, though he will himself disclaim the label.

Varna thus conceived is no man-made institution but the law of life universally governing the human family. Fulfilment of the law would make life liveable, would spread peace and content, end all clashes and conflicts, put an end to starvation and pauperisation, solve the problem of population and even end disease and suffering.[7]

First, before a more general comment on Gandhi's reasons for supporting Varnashram, one sentence should be underlined: "This performance of one's hereditary function is done as a matter of duty, though it naturally carries with it the earning of one's livelihood."

---

7 Mohandas K. Gandhi, Harijan (26 September 1934) 260, reproduced in Economic Thought of Mahatma Gandhi, ed. J.S. Mathur and A.S. Mathur (Allahabad: Chaitanya Publishing House, 1962) 573. In a part of this same article not here reproduced, 'dharma' is explained in parentheses as 'law.'

Gandhi held—in what was perhaps a stubborn clinging to an imaginary ideal village in the face of all the real misery he knew and saw—that in a well-organized society (which, obviously, no actually existing society was), producing the basic necessary material requirements of life for everyone would be easy to do.[8] He also held that to have more would be an impediment to the good life. These two premises favour the conclusion that one should not waste time and effort on a minor question (i.e., on what would be a minor question in a well-organized society), namely the question how one is going to earn one's livelihood, but should instead get on with the major business of life, the spiritual quest for Moksha, for seeing God face to face. The premises do not imply the conclusion, but they make it more eligible than it otherwise would be. The conclusion exemplifies Gandhi's belief that what is really important is moral progress, and it also exemplifies Gandhi's belief that moral progress will bring as a logical consequence the solution to material problems.

Someone who holds the common belief that traditional India devoted too much attention to the religious and aesthetic aspects of life, and now must emphasize the economic and material aspects in order to overcome poverty, and who wishes to find texts in Gandhi to support, or at least not oppose, such a view, might cite a hundred passages where Gandhi says things like to the famish-

---

[8] For example, in his 1916 talk on morality and economics at Muir College, he stated that acquiring the necessities of life was a rather simple performance for which the theories of economics were not needed. The whole text of the talk is reprinted as an appendix to the Cambridge reprint of Hind Swaraj, edited by Anthony J. Parel, cited in note 20 below.

ing man God takes the form of a piece of bread, or that the reason for being of the Congress Party is to struggle against poverty, and so on. Our reading is that in such passages Gandhi is not saying that for the poor material progress must come before moral progress. His whole philosophy was to the contrary. Rather, in social relationships to which poor people are parties material progress is moral progress: moral progress is material progress.[9]

Speaking more generally, Gandhi's defence of caste makes sense (to the extent that it makes sense at all) in the context of an ideal Indian village. For Gandhi such a village was an imagined historical realization of an ideal that was spiritual and at the same time and by the same token functional. But to make this claim we must also say that there is something about an ideal Gandhian village that makes it Indian. In other words, the Indian concept of caste, together with related ideas in which it is embedded, adds something characteristically non-Western and non-modern—or perhaps just non-modern, for Gandhi sometimes says that there is no important difference between Western and Eastern traditions, although there is an important difference between non-modern and modern. The ideal village must be more than and in some way better than a Western modern village that would

---

[9] "Hunger is the argument that is driving India to the spinning wheel. The call of the spinning wheel is the noblest of all. Because it is the call of love." M.K. Gandhi, Young India (13 October 1921), reprinted in his Economics of Khadi (Ahmedabad: Navajivan Press, 1941) 54. Passages like this one show that for Gandhi material progress was not prior to moral progress but inseparable from it.

already be ideal as an implementation of liberté, egalité, and fraternité.

Unlike any real caste system, the caste system of Gandhi's ideal village accords everyone equal respect, granting everyone the same human dignity regardless of caste or calling. In this respect Gandhi echoes the eighteenth century European ideals most famously formalized by Immanuel Kant. For Kant every rational being has inherent dignity as an end-in-itself. But obviously Gandhi did not need to support caste in order to support an ideal of human dignity. He could have just endorsed Kant. On their face caste distinctions are violations of human dignity. Gandhi's caste-without-rank appears to be more a concession to Western ideals to make caste acceptable than a positive case for caste. The question remains what it is about Varnashram that makes it worth keeping—or seem to Gandhi to be worth keeping—after it has been amended to delete rank and insert equal respect for all. With reason Gandhi said that his concept of Varna "has nothing in common with caste as we know it today," but the puzzle remains why he endorsed the purified concept of caste that he did endorse.[10]

One way to look for a solution to the puzzle would be to hypothesize that Gandhi finds something in caste which makes it possible to implement the same human ideals the West in principle holds, but better than the West itself has implemented them. Gandhi is famous for having said that Western civilization would be a good idea. He often pointed out that the West is notoriously unfaithful to its own moral norms, both its eighteenth

---

10 Gandhi, Young India (17 November 1927) and (20 October 1927), quoted in Gupta, Economic Philosophy 170.

century humanist norms and its Judeo-Christian norms. For example, freedom, the most prominent of the Western norms, conceived as the autonomy of the individual, would be greater in Gandhi's ideal villages than in the West. Perhaps there was even more freedom than in the West in the historically existing Indian villages prior to the British conquest and the dissolution of village life under the pressures of modern commerce and industry. The appropriate technologies of the ideal village would be controlled by individual workers who owned their own tools; or by small groups of workers; or by village panchayats which would make decisions at best by consensus and at worst by grassroots democracy—never by decree or by force. Instead of the modern world described by Anthony Giddens as one where people are disciplined mainly by fear of losing their jobs, there would be a world where most people are self-employed, or working in sisterly and brotherly small groups. They would own their own tools. (Large enterprises that necessarily transcend the village level would be exceptions, as will be discussed in several chapters subsequently.) People would be freer, because they could not be fired, because they were never hired.

A similar point can be made with respect to egalité. Equal respect for everyone in the ideal village is civility, but it is not only civility. It is personal security, freedom from fear of battery, rape, or theft, but it is also more than that. It is also material equality in the sense that all the people in the village eat roughly the same quantities of rice and lentils (or of whatever, among the available foods, they choose to eat), occupy roughly the same size space for sleeping, and in general consume at the same level. Although Gandhi opposed (in theory anyway) extreme inequalities of wealth, he did not propose equalizing wealth, but instead its socially responsible use. Ownership of land and of things was to be regarded as a fiduciary relationship (of which much more later) binding the owner to the duties of a trustee. People who took advantage of their legal status as property owners to consume at a level higher than the physically healthy (and spiritually uplifting) simple living standard of the village were to be regarded as in breach of their fiduciary duties, and as thieves.

It can be concluded that (at least in some important respects) Gandhian villages (assuming that it would be feasible to organize them) would put into practice the modern Western ideals of freedom and equality more perfectly than they have been put into practice in any actually existing modern Western society. (It must be acknowledged, however, that for some thinkers, the material equality envisioned by Gandhi counts as imperfection rather than as perfection, because they measure perfection according to different standards, or even, as in the case of Robert Nozick, because they object to using any standard to measure any such thing—of which more in later chapters.) It still remains to solve the puzzle why Gandhi thought that caste would make a positive contribution to the institutional structures of the villages, rather than being an oriental blemish marring an otherwise beautiful realization of Western ideals. To continue to attempt to solve this puzzle we turn to the third of the classic ideals of the French Revolution, fraternité.

John Rawls has pointed out that of the three watchwords liberté, égalité, and fraternité, the third has been least used. While the West has had limited success in putting the first two into practice, the third has not been given any definition, much less the plethora of persuasive definitions given to 'freedom' and 'equality' in the endless debates about them. Rawls proposes that his own theory of justice as fairness at last assigns a meaning to this neglected ideal, and that it is, moreover, a meaning that is well integrated into the mainstream of Western liberal discourse. Rawls and Gandhi can both be read as holding that how a society treats its poorest members is a main criterion for deciding whether it is a just society. Yet here again we would insist that although the conclusions may be the same or similar, the premises are different. Most importantly, the efficient causes, through which the welfare of the poorest is to be maximized, are different. For Rawls they are economic; for Gandhi they are moral.

Rawls cites Jan Tinbergen and other leading economic writers for the proposition that too much equality hurts the poor, while an adequate dose of inequality helps the poor. (This proposition is not incompatible with the studies by Amartya Sen, John Wilkinson, and others—in which the Indian state of Kerala is usually Exhibit A—which show empirically that a great deal of equality helps the poor and also the whole society.) Although Rawls hesitates to cross disciplinary lines to examine the reasons why mainstream economics has come to this conclusion, he does from time to time allude to some. The phenomenon of inequality making the poor richer is attributed to incentives. Rawls calls the incentives "a concession to human nature." Material rewards are distributed by the economic mechanisms that the modern West has invented (and which in Rawls' ideal liberal world it constantly strives to improve) to those individuals who make outstanding contributions to the common good: for example, by spending long arduous years in medical school learning to do ear surgery, or by inventing a comic mouse or a two-tiered hamburger that brings pleasure to billions. If human nature were better, then talented individuals would perform such specialized feats of service to others without material incentives. As human nature is, the poorest class is best served when there is just enough inequality (but no more) to call forth those activities that will result in maximizing the poorest's welfare.

For Gandhi the efficient causes of the welfare of the poor prominently included the humane in humanity. At Gandhi's insistence the members of the Congress Party passed resolutions requiring themselves to wear clothes made of khadi, a relatively expensive cloth of relatively poor quality, for the purpose of giving employment to the poorest class. Country people had been idled and thrown into destitution when the spinning and weaving crafts they had used for generations to supplement their agriculture-based survival strategies were destroyed by the competition of cheap imports of British textiles, and to a lesser extent by the products of local Indian mills. The motive for wearing khadi was solidarity with them.

At this point we need to make a detour to add a point which detracts from the symmetry of the argument, but which is necessary background for some of the following chapters. Lurking in the background of Rawls' texts, perhaps left in the background because Rawls does not wish to trespass on the turf of his colleagues in the economics department, is the fact that the empirical data which confirm the fact that too much equality hurts the poor, are not only data about incentives for workers. They are also about incentives for investments. This is the case, for example, with Arthur Okun's Brookings Institution study Equality vs. Efficiency.[11] It is one of many studies which report on a trade-off between social justice and economic efficiency, where the efficiency in question presupposes a world in which owners must be paid for the permissive acts of allowing the use of the property they own. Thus Rawls' borrowed proposition that the poor are hurt by too much equality reflects not only a psychological fact about the need for incentives to stimulate individual effort, but also an institutional fact about property rights.

Back from the detour: Gandhi's writings discuss a variety of ways in which the poor become less poor, in which actions deliberately taken by the non-poor for the purpose of serving the poor, or to help the poor help themselves, figure prominently. Gandhians are conscious consumers, who buy products produced where there are high labour and ecological standards. The poor themselves, when they follow Gandhi's philosophy, seek ways to make use of every idle hour and every unused resource, often starting with cleaning up the village and improving sanitation. Gandhi invokes the image of the Great Annihilator from the Bhagavad-Gita. Whom the Great Annihilator annihilates is he or she who lazes around instead of devoting every waking moment to self-improvement and service to others. As in religious revivals among the poor of all faiths, there are campaigns against drunkenness. The poor band together in cooperatives and other associations for mutual benefit, often with help from

---

11 Arthur Okun's study Equality vs. Efficiency: The Big Tradeoff (Washington, DC: Brookings Institution Press, 1975).

middle-class activists. They produce as much as they can for their own use, and they share with their neighbours, through barter, through gifts, and through diverse kinds of reciprocal obligations. Like everyone else they try as best they can to sell whatever they have to sell, whether it is labour-power or something else, to get cash to meet cash expenses. Like everyone else they quarrel, for which reason learning nonviolent conflict resolution is a major part of making any collective effort succeed. Gandhi himself lived in Indian villages, and started or participated in numerous down-to-earth projects for uplifting them.

We claim that Gandhi's principle (a principle which is, in one word, service), inspired as it is by a partly imaginary history, and seasoned as it is by experience, provides a theoretical alternative that is more comprehensive, and therefore more true, than standard economic theories. Since there are so many economists, and they have written so many theories, we find it difficult to specify which theories are the standard ones in contrast to which Gandhi's principle is an alternative. We will deal with this difficulty partly by mentioning some things Gandhian commentators have had to say about the main schools of economics in subsequent chapters, and partly by commenting here on a passage which has been seminal for most subsequent writers on economics, the famous passage about Adam Smith and his dinner, found in his Wealth of Nations, first published in 1776:

> In almost every other race of animals each individual, when it is grown to maturity, is entirely independent, and in its natural state has occasion for the assistance of no other living creature. But man has almost constant

occasion for the help of his brethren, and it is in vain for him to expect it from their benevolence only. He will be more likely to prevail if he can enlist their self-love in his favour, and shew them that it is to their own advantage to do for him what he requires of them. Whosoever offers to another a bargain of any kind proposes to do this. Give me that which I want, and you shall have this which you want is the meaning of every such offer; and it is in this manner that we obtain from one another the far greater part of those good offices which we stand in need of. It is not from the benevolence of the butcher, the brewer, or the baker, that we expect our dinner, but from their regard to their own interest. We address ourselves not to their humanity but to their self-love, and never talk to them of our own necessities but of their advantages.[12]

Looking at this classic and fundamental passage from Smith helps to establish Gandhi's outsider status. It is not a text Gandhi would have written. It lays down premises that are not his. If Gandhi were forced to speak Smith's language, he would say that Smith underestimates the power of benevolence, and that Smith overestimates the extent to which human security can be achieved by relying on the self-interest of others for one's bread. Gandhi, however, does not speak Smith's language. He asks differ-

---

12 Adam Smith, An Enquiry into the Nature and Causes of the Wealth of Nations (New York: Random House, 1937) 14. Amartya Sen comments on this famous passage in his Ethics and Economics (Oxford: Blackwell, 1987), at 21-28. Sen finds that all things considered, Smith had a balanced view of human nature that recognized the importance of a number of motives other than self-love.

ent questions, gets different answers, and uses a different vocabulary. Hence with respect to Smith and the intellectual traditions Smith started, Gandhi was an outsider, as, we suppose, Smith would have been in a traditional Indian village.

Gandhi did not expect the daily rice and lentils of the villagers to be supplied entirely by benevolence or entirely by self-interest, although he surely recognized the significance of each. He emphasized a third factor, which he named 'dharma,' a word usually translated as 'duty,' 'religion,' or 'ethics,' although Gandhi himself translates it in a passage quoted above as 'law.'

While acknowledging that Vinit Haksar and others have in several ways fruitfully brought Rawlsian thought and Gandhian thought into dialogue with each other, we would claim that insofar as Rawls' implicit strategy for favouring the poor depends on standard economic ideas like those of Smith in the passage quoted, his discourse and Gandhi's are incommensurable. Dharma draws its meanings and uses from the context of villages where people are born with duties to others, and into a wide social network where others have duties to them. Gandhi's ethics of duty has been compared to the minority voice in Western ethics of Bernard Bosanquet.[13] For Bosanquet, as for Gandhi, ethics is about duty. To do one's duty is to correctly play the role one has been assigned in the social order.

We believe that these considerations tend to explain Gandhi's support of caste. In a caste society, every baby is born with a vocation, with a role to play for the good

---

13   Bernard Bosanquet, The Philosophical Theory of the State (London: Macmillan, 1899).

of the community. If the community is well organized, and if all the people therefore follow their dharmas there will be a satisfactory adjustment of culture to ecology. In Marx's terms, there will be a satisfactory exchange of matter and energy with the environment.

It can correctly be argued that when Gandhi proposed that children follow the callings of their parents, he undermined the moral autonomy of the individual that in other respects he championed. Yet there is a question prior to the question what one's vocation will be. It is the question of whether one will have any vocation at all. Caste assures that everyone is born into a vital social role meant to serve the community in some way. Faced with the tragic spectacle of adharma modern society in which babies were daily being born without having attributed to them any membership at all in a bonded community larger than a nuclear family, and with no obligation at all to serve society, Gandhi was understandably reluctant to give up the Varnashram traditions of India.

Consider the alternatives. Suppose that caste as it existed back at the time Gandhi wrote about it (the 1920s and 1930s) had some desirable qualities, some undesirable qualities, and some neutral qualities. Suppose that a better institution might exist that had only desirable qualities. Gandhi might well prefer caste to the better institution because, unlike the better institution, it did exist. Improving caste by reforming it would be a more practical way to move toward the best result than starting from scratch, and it would also be a way more respectful of the way of life that people were accustomed to, and therefore more respectful of the dignity of the people. Choosing the alternative of improving tradition by reforming it, the alternative Gandhi did choose, clearly defies Smith's worldview, or at least that part of his worldview expressed in the early pages of his Wealth of Nations. Gandhi writes: "God pervades all—animate and inanimate. Therefore renounce all and dedicate it to God and then live. The right of living is thus derived from renunciation. It does not say, 'When all do their part of the work I too will do it.' It says, 'Don't bother about others, do your job first and leave the rest to Him.' Varnadharma acts even as the law of gravitation. I cannot cancel it or its working by trying to jump higher and higher day by day till gravitation ceases to work. That effort will be vain. So is the effort to jump over one another. The law of varṇa is the antithesis of competition which kills." [14]

The principle of Gandhi's underlying thought concerning caste's desirable qualities is undoubtedly true in the sense that if it were put into practice it would describe a functional society. If every person did her or his duty in a well-organized society, then all needs would be met, insofar as meeting them was not prevented by natural obstacles beyond human control. Gandhi's principle is a tautology, A = A. Duty done equals duty done. Duty done

---

14 In an address to Christian missionaries in Madras in 1916 Gandhi connected caste with India's traditional rural villages. "The vast organization of caste answered not only to the religious wants of the community but it answered to its political needs. The villagers managed their internal affairs through the caste system...." He connects caste with Swadeshi, and therefore with the general principle that it is better to reform one's own tradition than to reject it in favour of foreign ideas. M.K. Gandhi, Economics of Khadi (Ahmedabad: Navajivan Press, 1941) 6. The quotation in the text is from Harijan (6 March 1937).

equals the deeds required by duty performed. In a well-organized society, when the deeds required by duty are performed, all of its institutions are functional and not dysfunctional. We are well aware that this platonic tautology is a recipe for the closed society trenchantly criticized by Karl Popper and others, but we do not therefore conclude either that Gandhi did not believe it or that it is not valid. We conclude that when, where, and to the extent that it is put into practice important other considerations must also be borne in mind.

The empirical findings of economics concern, in contrast, hypotheses which may and may not be true at any given place and time. Smith only hypothesized that self-interest would bring him his bread. That hypothesis might have proven true for sixty or more consecutive mornings while Smith was writing The Wealth of Nations at Kirkcaldy during a cold Scotland winter, but it was surely not true during Smith's infancy or during his dotage. Under other circumstances, however, it might empirically have been false even in mid-life. It might in other circumstances have been in the self-interest of the baker to starve Smith into submission and not to give him a crumb until Smith allowed the baker to exploit him shamefully and take all he had.

2. Topics Other than Caste

A conclusion to be drawn from the immediately preceding considerations is that although it is hard to understand why Gandhi wrote in favour of Varnashram, once his reasons are understood it should be acknowledged that they are undoubtedly true, even if not sufficient to establish all his empirical conclusions. His basic principle is a tautology. Economic research, as well as research in psychology and the other social sciences, should not be regarded as a refutation of Gandhi, and certainly not as presupposing the adoption of a more scientific and wiser worldview that supersedes Gandhi's. Empirical studies should be regarded as contributions to learning how to achieve in practice under a given set of circumstances the pro-social behaviour that Gandhi advocated in principle and with his life tried to exemplify.

We want to develop this conclusion, not just here but also in following chapters, in general and not just with respect to caste: and not just as an academic exercise but also as an analysis of something dreadfully and fatally wrong with the modern world-system in which most of us today live and move and have our being. We do not claim to be revealing a message hitherto hidden. Gandhi wrote in his autobiography that his purpose in life was to see God face to face, and that he looked upon his life as a series of opportunities for service. We are not the first readers to believe that he meant what he said. Nor do we claim that there is no word in Gandhi that can be understood without imagining an idealized traditional Indian village where every villager's ruling passion is to achieve Moksha by serving the community.

We will trace in following chapters a number of ways in which Gandhi's ideas have interacted with those of other Indian thinkers, always thinking of Gandhi as someone who came at problems from a standpoint outside of modernity even though his was a hybrid mind including many modern elements. Then, when we get to law, our argument will take a turn that we fear will be hard to follow. Having generally regarded Gandhi as a seer who saw more deeply and truly than anyone else, we will then say that he did not sufficiently carry through his principle (the same principle named in various ways—love, nonviolence, ahimsa, dharma, and others— somewhat as Kant stated the same categorical imperative in various formulations). He did not sufficiently criticize the normative framework of commercial society, the law. Having attributed a principle to him, we will criticize him for not employing his own principle consistently.

Others have criticized Gandhi for other reasons, and for good ones. We do not wish to say that once his thought is amended to include a critique of the juridical framework of the global economy it becomes one hundred percent correct. Certainly he himself would not have made any claim to be one hundred percent correct about anything. Many have made fun of Gandhi for wanting everyone to be a vegetarian and to abstain from sex. As a religious man he was haunted by the eternal curse of all religion: the temptation to sacrifice the liberty of others on the altar of one's own beliefs. Fortunately for humanity, Gandhi's desire to sacrifice himself for God took the form of a passion for social service. "Self-realization, i.e. Moksha, can be had only through the service of humanity."[15]

---

15 Gupta, Economic Philosophy 176. Gupta cites for this

Fortunately, too, Gandhi's was an ecumenical religion. He could find a room in his spiritual palace for every faith and even for a sophisticated secular humanist like the one who will be treated in the next chapter. Nevertheless, even this apostle of nonviolence, truth, and self-suffering could not fully exorcise the temptation that has tempted so many. We are afraid that this consideration will make our argument even more difficult to follow, since in addition to criticizing Gandhi for inconsistency, we will attribute merit to criticisms of the principle with which he failed to be consistent.

Next, in brief outline, here is a reading using a vision of Gandhi as a man driven by a non-modern religious passion, in order to make clear another text which is otherwise problematic. It takes Gandhi's early work Hind Swaraj to be one which: (1) is puzzling and likely to be misunderstood; and (2) can be given a clear meaning that is undoubtedly true.

Gandhi wrote Hind Swaraj in 1908 on a boat on his way back to South Africa from London. The list of recommended readings he appended to his text shows that he was not an isolated thinker whose ideas were different from everything that was in the air at the time he wrote. He was a member of a turn-of-the-twentieth-century anti-modernist school of thought. Gandhi's fellow anti-modernists included John Ruskin, Leo Tolstoy, Henry David Thoreau, Edward Carpenter, Taylor, Blount, Sherard, and Max Nordau. Gandhi also cited historians who had written about the traditional villages of India: Romesh Dutt and Sir Henry Maine.

---

proposition Harijan (29 August1936).

Many of the pages of Hind Swaraj are devoted to denying that the vaunted modernization of India lauded by the British as their great accomplishment had in fact accomplished anything worthwhile. In this vein Gandhi criticized railways, machinery in general, cities, doctors, and lawyers. It is easy to look at the book as one whose central message is an attack on the various institutions that Gandhi criticizes, of which the central one seems to be machinery.[16]

But in later life Gandhi appeared to backtrack on many of the specific points on he touched in Hind Swaraj.[17] It turned out that he did not really mean that anything the British had brought to India was per se evil, but rather that many things tended to become evil because they were not properly employed. They were employed for the wrong motives and for the wrong ends. Yet to the end of his life Gandhi never ceased to proclaim that he still stood firmly behind what he had said in Hind Swaraj.[18] He did not retract a word of it. A puzzle then arises: How can a book be wholly right if it is hard to find any specific point stated in the book that Gandhi did not modify in subsequent years?

---

16 See the essays in Hind Swaraj: A Fresh Look, ed. Nageshwar Prasad (Delhi: Gandhi Peace Foundation, 1985).

17 "Gandhi was most dynamic in his outlook. His views on machines, for example, underwent a dramatic change from 1924 onward. A sense of limits grew in him. He was deadly opposed to even the smallest 'tools' before 1924 but then he realized his mistake and agreed to use machines." Gupta, Economic Philosophy 43.

18 See Anthony J. Parel's introduction to the edition of Hind Swaraj edited by him, cited in note 20 below.

We suggest, in line with our general idea about how to understand Gandhi, that the central thread of the book, which holds its various parts together, is a passion for dharma. The central point of Hind Swaraj, which the book illustrated in several ways, was that modern so-called civilization was adharma. It had no soul. Consider the following passage in this light:

This civilization is irreligion [adharma], and it has taken such a hold on the people in Europe that those who are in it appear to be half mad. They lack real physical strength or courage. They keep up their energy by intoxication. Women, who should be the queens of households, wander in the streets, or they slave away in factories. For the sake of a pittance, half a million women in England alone are labouring under trying circumstances in factories or similar institutions. This awful fact is one of the causes of the daily growing suffragette movement.

This civilization is such that one has only to be patient and it will be self-destroyed. According to the teaching of Mahomet this would be considered a Satanic civilisation. Hinduism calls it the Black Age. I cannot give you an adequate conception of it. It is eating into the vitals of the English nation. It must be shunned. Parliaments are really emblems of slavery. If you will sufficiently think over this, you will entertain the same opinion, and cease to blame the English. They rather deserve our sympathy. They are a shrewd nation and I, therefore, believe that they will cast off this evil. They are enterprising and industrious, and their mode of thought is not inherently immoral. Neither are they bad at heart. Civilisation is not an incurable disease, but it should never be forgotten that the English people are at present afflicted by it.[19]

---

19 M.K. Gandhi, Hind Swaraj and Other Writings, ed. Anthony J. Parel (Cambridge: Cambridge University Press, 1997) 37-38. In his glossary, the editor, Anthony J. Parel, translates dharma as "duty, natural moral law; religion as ethics and religion as sect." Gandhi may have gotten the idea that modern civilization will self-destruct from reading one of the books he recommends, which, in turn refers to Morgan's Ancient Society. "Thus Morgan in his 'Ancient Society' points out over and over again that the civilised state rests upon territorial and property marks and qualifications, and not upon a personal basis as did the ancient gens, or the tribe; and that the civilised government correspondingly takes on quite a different character and function from the simple organisation of the gens. He says (p. 124), 'Monarchy is incompatible with gentilism.' Also with regard to the relation of Property to Civilisation and Government he makes the following pregnant remarks, (p. 505): 'It is impossible to over-estimate the influence of property in the civilisation of mankind. It was the power that brought the Aryan and Semitic nations out of barbarism into civilisation. The growth of the idea of property in the human mind commenced in feebleness and ended in becoming its master passion. Governments and Laws are instituted with primary reference to its creation, protection, and enjoyment. It introduced human slavery as an instrument in its production; and after the experience of several thousand years it caused the abolition of slavery upon the discovery that a free-man was a better property-making machine.' And in another passage on the same subject, 'The dissolution of society bids fair to become the termination of a career of which property is the end and aim; because such a career contains the elements of self-destruction.'" Edward Carpenter, Civilisation: Its Cause and Cure (New York, Charles Scribner's Sons, 1921 [1889])

Gandhi's point stated in this passage, which, if our interpretation is correct, pervades and informs the whole of the book, is undoubtedly true. Western and specifically British, civilization did lack the dharma that was the organizing principle of Gandhi's imaginary village. The British writers Gandhi recommends, John Ruskin, Edward Carpenter and the others, had said the same things of their own country in almost the same terms. Gandhi's comments elsewhere in Hind Swaraj on railways are meant to illustrate the main point. They underline that material progress without moral progress does not make people better. Further, when the so-called 'progress' enriches a few and impoverishes many it does not deserve to be called even material progress. In 1908 Gandhi debunked the specific ornaments of British pride. If he later said, what perhaps he never meant to deny, that in the context of an ethic of service and duty and voluntary simple living the same specific machines and professionals might be truly useful, he did not in saying so retract what he meant

---

37-38. Gandhi's idea that modern society bears the seeds of its own destruction anticipated Fred Hirsch's argument that market economies systematically destroy the moral basis without which they cannot function; see his The Social Limits of Growth (Cambridge: Harvard University Press, 1976). See also in this connection Stephen Marglin, The Dismal Science: How Thinking like an Economist Undermines Community (Cambridge: Harvard University Press, 2008). The first part of John Ruskin's Unto this Last, which cast a magic spell on Gandhi when he read it in 1904, ends with, "... the economic principles taught to our multitudes... so far as accepted, lead straight to national destruction." On Ruskin's influence see Elizabeth McLaughlin, Ruskin and Gandhi (London: Associated Universities Press, 1974).

to say in 1908. Hence Gandhi could say subsequently that he stood by the philosophy he had expressed in Hind Swaraj. He still believed that modern 'civilization' could not possibly last, and that in the long run any possible future for humanity would necessarily be a future that rediscovered dharma.

* * *

CHAPTER 2

JAWAHARLAL NEHRU

"It may be that the message which he [Gandhi] embodied will be understood and acted upon more in later years than it is today."
—Jawaharlal Nehru, 1951[1]

The modernity that Gandhi criticized in Hind Swaraj can be defined as a simplification of ethics. Monetary transactions replace kinship and community with what Georg Simmel called "a unity which eliminates everything personal and specific."[2] The normative framework of commerce replaces dense networks of subtle interpersonal obligations with a few relatively clear and relatively simple rules. Protect property rights. Comply with contracts. Castes, tribes, and patterns of feudal allegiance, are replaced by the new dominant organizing principle

---

1 Foreword to Mahatma: Life of Mohandas Karamchand Gandhi by D.G. Tendulkar, 1951, reprinted in Nehru: An Anthology, ed. Sarvepalli Gopal (Delhi: Oxford University Press, 1980) 116. This work is hereafter cited as Anthology.
2 Georg Simmel, "Money in Modern Culture," Theory, Culture and Society 8/3 (1991) 17-31, at 20. See also Georg Simmel, The Philosophy of Money (London: Routledge, 1978; first published in German in 1900).

of social relationships: the market. Its principle is buy cheap and sell dear. Caveat emptor. Because of the market's simplified ethics—an ethics stripped of personal relationships, entzaubert—Gandhi could call modernity adharma. The best-known paradigm of the coming of modernity to Europe is the enclosure movement of seventeenth century England. It evicted the yeomanry from their common lands, establishing by force the rights of landowners. It created a landless proletariat. It transformed the meaning of the land, separating its traditional tillers from it, making it into fixed assets on the account books of businesses. The enclosed and rethought land became a factor of production, producing wool to be exchanged for money in distant markets. Modernity's most famous ideology is the definition of la liberté given by Denis Diderot in the Encyclopedie of the eighteenth century French philosophes: freedom means that whatever the law does not forbid is allowed.

All this is not to deny that modern society is capable of endless complexity. On its simplified and weak foundations rambling and towering edifices have been built. In a society whose basis is commodity exchange, governed at first and in principle by simple laws of private property and private contracts, public law becomes a frail addendum and a dubious superimposition; public law ultimately becomes a towering and tottering edifice endlessly complicated by efforts to achieve the goals of public policy in a world where the exercise of private rights perennially thwarts them—for example through tax evasion, and, for another example—a famous one in India—the evasion of land reform legislation. State (public life) is distinguished from society (private life). There are interminable deliberations about the interactions of the two halves of this socially constructed dichotomy, for example about when and whether the government should intervene in the market. The contract—most importantly in the form of contracts of exchange by purchase and sale—confers legitimacy by consent; and in a society where contracts of purchase and sale have become the central practice used to organize how things relate to people, there is a tendency to make consent the only principle of legitimacy. There are endless complex debates about what is and what is not consent.

All this is not to deny, either, that some dense networks of subtle interpersonal obligations are bad. Most are mixed bags. Some, like the agape communities of the early Christians have generally enjoyed among commentators the status of an ideal for which to strive. Others, like the traditional patriarchal family, are seen by most commentators today as institutionalizations of disrespect. What is distinctive about modernity is not that its characteristic dense networks of community norms are especially good or especially bad. What is distinctive is that there is a vast area of human behaviour that is not, from the point of view of law and liberal morals, subject to any community norms at all. The marketplace where strangers meet strangers is the institutionalization of Durkheim's anomie, of Gandhi's adharma. In the words of modernity's greatest moral philosopher its transactions are ohne sittliche Gehalt (without moral content). Friedrich Engels, in his The Condition of the Working-Class in England, described the amorality of life under pure capitalism in terms as graphic as those of Gandhi in Hind Swaraj:

> [E]veryone stands for himself, and fights for himself against all comers, and whether or not he shall injure all the others who are his declared foes, depends upon a cynical calculation as to what is most advantageous to himself... all differences are settled by threats, violence, or in the law-court. In short, everyone sees in his neighbor an enemy to be got out of the way or, at best, a tool to be used for his own advantage. And this war grows from year to year, as the criminal tables show, more violent, passionate, irreconcilable.[3]

The history of India provides many examples of the simplification of ethics wrought by the imposition of modernity on the subcontinent by force of British arms. Gandhi cites historical works that describe the shredding of the social fabric of traditional life by the knives of the laws that governed commerce. To the works he cites could be added others written later, such as those of Ananda Coomaraswamy, and the detailed descriptions of the normative structures of traditional India provided by the great anthropologist Louis Dumont. When Dumont wrote his great book about Western society, From Mandeville to Marx: The Rise of Economic Ideology, he used traditional India as a foil to the West, bringing out the ethnocentric character of the norms the modern West supposes to be universal by contrasting them to those that had given form and structure to life in India, and also pointing out, as Gandhi points out, that the

---

3 Friedrich Engels, The Condition of the Working-Class in England, Marx and Engels, Collected Works (New York: International Publishers, 1845) 4:427.

pre-modern societies of the West had much in common with the pre-modern societies of the East, in those many centuries prior to what Karl Polanyi in his great book The Great Transformation called the 'disembedding' of market relationships from the matrix of interpersonal social relationships. Some of the most telling examples of the simplification of ethics are related in Asian Drama by the Swedish economist Gunnar Myrdal.[4]

Myrdal gives details on how the complex and subtle interpersonal norms that governed human relationships to the produce of land in pre-British India were forced into the straitjacket of British concepts of property rights. Somebody had to be the landlord, and somebody had to be the tenant. There had to be a 'settlement' deciding who owned what so that the British tax collectors would know on whom to levy, and who would forfeit ownership in case the taxes were not paid. Among the consequences of modernizing concepts of land tenure were disorientation, greater exploitation of the strong by the weak, and hunger. Myrdal also gives examples where the same consequences flowed from the imposition of Western concepts of contract law.

Some features of the simplification of ethics described in detail by authors Gandhi cites in his recommended readings appended to Hind Swaraj and also by Dumont,

---

4 Ananda Coomaraswamy, What is Civilisation? and Other Essays (Ipswich: Golgonooza Press, 1989); Louis Dumont, From Mandeville to Marx: The Genesis and Triumph of Economic Ideology (Chicago: University of Chicago Press, 1977); Karl Polanyi, The Great Transformation (Boston: Beacon Press, 1957); Gunnar Myrdal, Asian Drama (New York: Pantheon Press, 1968) 2:1033-1047.

Polanyi, and Myrdal, are depicted in a few words by Jawaharlal Nehru in his history of India as follows:

> *The destruction of village industries [by British manufactures] was a powerful blow to these communities [the traditional villages of India]. The balance between industry and agriculture was upset, the traditional division of labor was broken up, and numerous stray individuals could not easily be fitted into any group activity. A more direct blow came from the introduction of the landlord system, changing the whole conception of the ownership of land. This conception had been one of communal ownership, not so much of the land as of the produce of the land. Possibly not fully appreciating this, but more probably taking the step deliberately for reasons of their own, the British governors, themselves representing the British landlord class, introduced something resembling the English system in India. At first they appointed revenue-farmers for short terms, that is persons who were made responsible for the collection of the revenue or land tax and payment of it to the Government. Later these revenue-farmers developed into landlords. The village community was deprived of all control over the land and its produce; what had always been considered as the chief interest and concern of that community now became the private property of the newly created landowner. This led to the breakdown of the joint life and corporate character of the community, and the cooperative system of services and functions began to disappear gradually.*

The introduction of this type of property in land was not only a great economic change, but it went deeper and struck at the whole Indian conception of a cooperative group social structure. A new class, the owners of land, appeared; a class created by, and therefore to a large extent identified with, the British government.[5]

Nehru pointed out, as also Gandhi pointed out, and as Amartya Sen has argued in detail in a book-length study of famines, that famines in India are not caused by lack of food, but by lack of entitlement to food. The British brought hunger to India not because they destroyed agricultural production, but because they ripped up the social fabric, what Nehru in the passage just quoted called "the cooperative system of services and functions" which organized the sharing of food. The cash-nexus replaced the community. Those without money, no longer members of a community administering collectively the produce of communal land, starved. The British ruled different parts of India for different lengths of time, varying from 300 to 100 years. Nehru shows that in the 1940s (when he wrote his history of India while imprisoned

---

5 Jawaharlal Nehru, The Discovery of India (Garden City, New York: Doubleday, 1959) 217-218. It did not help that sometimes the British opted to codify and enforce the pre-existing Hindu or Muslim law. Although they diligently sought to follow the letter of pre-existing law, they failed to understand its spirit, as was acknowledged by a philosopher who was also an officer of the British East India Company, John Stuart Mill, and as was also pointed out by Nehru in The Discovery of India 244.

by the British at Ahmednagar Fort) hunger and mass poverty were worst in the parts of India that the British had governed the longest. Bengal, which had been the richest part of India, had become one of the poorest after nearly 300 years of British rule. Punjab, having been one of the poorest areas, was governed by the British scarcely one hundred years. It kept its traditional social structures longer. It was less exploited, and it emerged as one of the relatively famine-free parts of India.

From the vantage point of the world of 2009, Gandhi's 1909 critique of modernity, which he continued and elaborated until his assassination in 1948, and which has been in important ways corroborated by the writings of others, might be seen as a plea for what is today called 'social capital.' And so it is. Like Gandhi, World Bank studies and other studies of social capital advocate dense networks of reciprocal obligations. They demonstrate empirically the role of 'social capital' in coping with what is called 'the crisis of governability' and in furthering 'human development.' Dharma might perhaps be regarded as an early precursor of 'social capital,' or perhaps 'social capital' might be regarded as a late echo of dharma. We want to claim the empirical evidence showing the positive contributions to development made by social capital as a belated vindication of Gandhi. However, somewhat ungenerously, we want to suspend judgment, and to take up later in following chapters, the question as to whether the favour should be returned. In terms of a Venn diagram, we say that the facts brought to light by the study of social capital tend to prove Gandhi's case, but we do not say that everything Gandhi meant by dharma is appropriately included under the conceptual umbrella today called social capital.

In spite of his intimate acquaintance with Gandhi, and in spite of his knowledge of Indian history, Jawaharlal Nehru took a very different view of modernity and modernization. It was not that Nehru was unaware that traditional societies often had denser and more binding sets of social obligations than modern ones. It was rather that he conceived history differently. He viewed it through a different lens. He formed his concepts with a different gestalt.

Nehru was convinced that the direction in time of the arrow of history was from feudalism to capitalism to socialism. Somewhat pathetically, as we see Nehru looking back at him now, he looked upon capitalism as out of date and destined to be superseded by a forward march of socialism that would wipe every tear from every eye. Religion pointed backward, toward feudalism. Science pointed forward, toward socialism. For Nehru, "every civilization which resists change declines."[6] 'Change' meant moving in the directions that science and technology were driving history. Although he never had occasion to say so, Nehru would have agreed with Peter Berger's definition of modernity as "the institutional concomitants of technologically induced economic growth."[7]

---

6 Nehru, Discovery of India 194.
7 Peter Berger et al, The Homeless Mind (New York: Random Press, 1973), quoted by Menachem Rosner and David Mittelberg, "The Dialectic of Alienation and De-Alienation," in Alienation Theories and De-Alienation Strategies, ed. David Schweitzer and R. Felix Geyer (Northwood, Middlesex, UK: Science Reviews Ltd., 1989) 150.

When you have technology and economic growth you get modernity. If one wants technology and economic growth—which Nehru certainly did want, because he saw them as indispensable to end the poverty of the masses, and because he saw them as indispensable to prevent India from being a weak nation that would be conquered by strong neighbours—then one welcomes the modernity that goes with them.

Nehru criticized Gandhi often, sometimes harshly. In his 1936 Autobiography Nehru wrote:

He [Gandhi] is an extraordinary paradox. I suppose all outstanding men are to some extent. For years I have puzzled over this problem: why with all his love and solicitude for the underdog he yet supports a system which inevitably produces it and crushes it; why with all of his passion for non-violence he is in favour of a political and social structure which is wholly based on violence and coercion? Perhaps it is not correct to say he is in favour of such a system; he is more or less of a philosophical anarchist. But as the ideal anarchist state is too far off still and cannot easily be conceived, he accepts the present order.

Sometimes he calls himself a socialist, but he uses the word in a sense peculiar to himself which has little or nothing to do with the economic framework of society which usually goes by the name of socialism. Following his lead a number of prominent Congressmen have taken to the use of that word, meaning thereby a kind of muddled humanitarianism.[8]

---

8 Jawaharlal Nehru, An Autobiography (London: John Lane,

In such passages Nehru attributed to Gandhi an aversion to class conflict, while he attributed to himself, Nehru, greater realism and stronger support for the working class and peasantry. Nehru accepted the inevitability of class conflict. He wrote in a letter to Gandhi that he accepted very little of what the latter had written Hind Swaraj.[9]

One might take the view that Nehru understood Gandhi well enough, but disagreed with him. We will try to make a case that in spite of their long and close association the two did not fully understand one another, at least with respect to two important subjects, religion and economics. If we are right, then even if one finds that Nehru had valid reasons for wanting to industrialize and modernize India, one should also find that Nehru did not fully take into account, because he did not understand, important aspects of Gandhi's critique of modernity.

It is a puzzle why Gandhi supported Nehru so much. In 1929 Gandhi designated Nehru as President of the Congress. In 1936 he was the decisive influence in making Nehru Congress President and titular head of the movement. In 1946 it was again Gandhi, this time contrary to the recommendations of the Congress provincial committees, who made Nehru the presiding head of the Congress movement, which virtually guaranteed that he would become prime minister when independence was attained.[10] Nehru described himself as irreligious,

---

1936) 515-516.
9 Letter from Nehru to Gandhi, 11 January 1928, reprinted in Gopal, Anthology 99.
10 B.R. Nanda, Jawaharlal Nehru: Rebel and Statesman

and explained in detail why he cast his lot with secular humanism and not with any form of spirituality. If Gandhi really was religious through and through, one might have expected him to choose a lead disciple and political successor with a philosophy closer to his own. If Gandhi really cared about religion, one might have expected him at least to reply to Nehru's arguments against it with some sort of defence of his faith.

There is a solution to the puzzle that does not oblige us to conclude that Gandhi was not thoroughly religious and did not care about religion. It is that Gandhi did not consider his religion at all affected by Nehru's arguments for preferring a scientific worldview to a mythical worldview. Gandhi's religion was truth. He believed in science every bit as much as Nehru did, and he was fond of using images from geometry or chemistry to illustrate his ideas. Nehru's criticisms were directed at someone else's religion, not at Gandhi's. The only defence of his faith Gandhi needed was, "[M]y life is my message."[11] For similar reasons Gandhi could designate Nehru as his political successor. That one of the two was 'irreligious' and the other 'religious' was a verbal quibble. Both believed in truth.

A problem with this solution to the puzzle is that it is consistent with seeing no reason at all for Gandhi to be religious. He could have just adopted Nehru's scientific worldview, period. Sometimes Nehru himself, when he describes Gandhi's religion, makes excuses for Gandhi by disassociating him from the features of religion which

---

(Delhi: Oxford University Press, 1995) 179-180.
11 This is a quotation attributed to Gandhi on signs at his Sabarmati ashram.

modern liberals condemn: Gandhi is not prejudiced against people of other faiths than his own; he is not prejudiced against atheists or agnostics; he does not imagine supernatural causes for natural events (with occasional lapses); he does not want to make India a theocracy. Gandhi worships truth. The same might perhaps be said of Auguste Comte, of John Stuart Mill, or of Nehru's favourite Bertrand Russell. One is then left to wonder what there might be in Gandhi's religious truth that would distinguish it from Nehru's scientific truth.

Professor R.G. Gupta in his dictionary of Gandhian moral terms offers definitions of ahimsa, satyagraha, and many other words, but when he gets to truth he gives up. He finds Gandhi's use of the term too protean. He offers no definition of it.[12] We will suggest that Professor Gupta gave up too soon. There are some core elements in Gandhi's conception of truth that Nehru and others have not sufficiently appreciated or understood. Today they make Gandhi's ideas even more defensible than 'science,' 'scientific method' and 'truth' generally—three ideas that have been thoroughly deconstructed in the half century that has elapsed between Nehru's time and our own. They give a meaning to Gandhi's faith different from the merely negative meaning of deleting from religion everything that liberals do not like about it. Erik Erikson came close to articulating them when he wrote:

Gandhi commits himself only to "the relative truth as I have conceived it," but he also clings firmly to the dictum that only insofar as we can commit ourselves on selected occasions "to the death" to the test of such

---

12 R.K. Gupta, A Dictionary of Moral Concepts in Gandhi (Delhi: Maadhyam Book Services, 2000).

truth in action—only to that extent we can be true to ourselves and to others, that is, to a joint humanity.... [T]here is no reason to question the fact that the sudden conviction that the moment of truth had arrived always came upon him as if from a voice which had spoken before he had quite listened. Gandhi often spoke of his inner voice, which would speak unexpectedly in the preparedness of silence—but then with an irreversible firmness and an irresistible demand for commitment.... That is, the moment of truth is suddenly there—unannounced and pervasive in its stillness. But it comes only to him who has lived with facts and figures in such a way that he is always ready for a sudden synthesis and will not, from sheer surprise, frighten truth away. But acting on that inner voice means to involve others on the assumption that they, too, are ready—and when Gandhi listened to his inner voice, he often thought he heard what the masses were ready to listen to. That, of course, is the secret of all charismatic leadership, but how could he know it was "the truth"? Gandhi's answer would be: Only the readiness to suffer would tell.

Truthful action, for Gandhi, was governed by the readiness to get hurt and yet not hurt—action governed by the principle of ahimsa.... With all respect to the traditional translation of ahimsa, I think Gandhi implied in it, besides a refusal not to do physical harm, a determination not to violate another person's essence. For even where one may not be able to avoid harming or hurting, forcing or demeaning another whenever one must coerce him, one should try, even in doing so, not to violate his essence, for such

> *violence can only evoke counter-violence, which may end in a kind of truce, but not in truth. For ahimsa as acted upon by Gandhi not only means not to hurt another, it means to respect the truth in him.... a man should act in such a way that he actualizes both in himself and in others such forces as are ready for a heightened mutuality.... Gandhi made a similar assumption when he viewed Satyagraha as a bridge between the ethics of family life and that of communities and nations.... Truth in Gandhi's sense points to the next step in man's realization of man as one all-human species, and thus to our only chance to transcend what we are.[13]*

Let us agree to amend Erikson's words by making the pronouns inclusive rather than masculine, and by replacing 'essence' with the 'status as a member of a Habermasian ideal speech community,' or some other phrase which makes the self to be honoured and nurtured relational. Then one might paraphrase, and perhaps extend, Erikson by saying that for Gandhi a core element of truth was fidelity in human relationships. Facts and figures are important because one must be true to the people who are counting on one to be truthful.

This interpretation accords with Gandhi's own account of the beginning of his fascination with truth in his Autobiography. He writes that as a child he was persuaded by a young companion to take up eating meat, to become strong and to become the kind of Hindu who could rise up and throw out the British. But he could never tell his

---

13   Erik Erikson, Gandhi's Truth: On the Origins of Militant Nonviolence (New York: W.W. Norton, 1969) 411-413.

pious mother that he was eating meat, nor could he lie to her. Truth meant being true to his mother and that meant not eating meat, however much he might want to do so, and however much he might rationally be persuaded that it was the right thing to do.

What we take to be another core element of Gandhi's concept of truth, or perhaps the same element viewed from another angle, is found in the source that Gandhi credits with having inspired his concept of Satyagraha, Leo Tolstoy's The Kingdom of God is Within You. Tolstoy wrote:

> *The condition of men is the result of their disunion. Their disunion results from their not following the truth which is one, but falsehoods which are many. The sole means of uniting men is their union with the truth. And therefore the more sincerely men strive toward the truth, the nearer they get to unity.*
>
> *But how can men be united in the truth or even approximate to it, if they do not even express the truth they know, but hold that there is no need to do so, and pretend to regard as truth what they believe to be false?*
>
> *And therefore no improvement is possible so long as men are hypocritical and hide the truth from themselves, so long as they do not realize that their union and therefore their welfare is only possible in the truth, and do not put the recognition and profession of the truth revealed to them higher than everything else.*[14]

---

14 Leo Tolstoy, The Kingdom of God is within You (Lincoln: University of Nebraska Press, 1984 – reprint of an 1894 edi-

Truth, conceived as Gandhi conceived it, is about religion, since for him God is Truth and Truth is God. Although Gandhi says that both of these convertible terms are so rich in meaning that a lifetime is not long enough to plumb the depths of what they mean, at the core of the meanings that Gandhi does succeed in plumbing there are human relationships which are functional and not dysfunctional. People respect each other and work together for the common good. Gandhi's is a scientifically respectable view of religion. For him religion works, as it works to bind society together in Emile Durkheim's sociology of religion, and as it works according to the many scholarly accounts of religious phenomena which focus on what religion does.[15]

From Gandhi's point of view, Nehru's critical remarks on religion in his Autobiography and elsewhere were

---

tion) 341-342. Tolstoy had particularly in mind the Russian Christians who did not speak the truth they professed to the power of Russian landlords and army officers who violently repressed the poor.

15   Sir James George Frazer, The Golden Bough: A Study in Magic and Religion (New York: Macmillan, 1922). Emile Durkheim, The Elementary Forms of the Religious Life (New York: Macmillan, 1926). It should be mentioned, however, that in a respect not directly relevant here, Hinduism is a hard case for Durkheimian theories of religion, since such theories postulate a dichotomy of the sacred and the profane, while the tendency of Hinduism is to make everything sacred. For an interesting Marxist account of the social and ecological functions of the Hindu institution of the sacred cow see Marvin Harris, Cows, Pigs, Wars and Witches: The Riddles of Culture (New York: Vintage Books, 1975).

indeed largely beside the point. It is true that religions have myths and cosmologies, but it is not true that their principal function is to explain natural phenomena for people who desire explanations but lack science. Sir James Frazer in The Golden Bough proposed such a theory of religion, but hardly anyone supports Frazer's theory today. Our forbears who invented the great traditional belief-systems had more important issues to deal with than explaining natural phenomena. Survival, for example, was one such concern. Survival depended on community, and, in Thomas Berry's words, "There is no community without a community story."[16] While Nehru's attacks on religious belief were not relevant to what Gandhi believed, Nehru's excuses for Gandhi's religion, which cleared him of charges of bigotry, missed the positive core of Gandhi's faith. Nehru had, of course, good reasons for his opinions: he witnessed religious intolerance at its worst in communal violence and he saw in action any number of foolish and irrational religious beliefs that served wicked purposes or none. It is understandable that he, like many members of the middle class throughout Asia, saw secularism as the hope of the future.[17]

To say that Gandhi and Nehru also talked past each other regarding economics would not be quite right, since there was no common object of discourse called 'economics' about which they disagreed. Gandhi talked

---

16 Thomas Berry sometimes made this remark during seminars he conducted in the summers during the 1980s at the Holy Cross Centre in Port Burwell, Ontario, Canada.

17 See generally Huiyun Wang, Discourses on Tradition and Modernization (Delhi: Maadhyam Book Services, 2001).

in terms of a 'constructive programme,' which he once summarized as follows:

> *The constructive programme is a big undertaking including a number of items: (1) Hindu-Muslim or communal unity, (2) Removal of untouchability, (3) Prohibition, (4) Khadi, (5) Other village industries, (6) Village sanitation, (7) New or basic education, (8) Adult education, (9) Uplift of women, (10) Education in hygiene and health, (11) Propagation of Rashtrabhasha, (12) Cultivating love of one's own language, (13) Working for economic equality. This list can be supplemented, if necessary, but it is so comprehensive that I think it can be proved to include items appearing to have been omitted.[18]*

Gandhi's constructive program is not economic in any reasonably narrow sense of the term 'economic.' It is not oriented toward establishing favourable conditions (what some scholars call a 'regime of accumulation') so that money can profitably be invested. It does not mention savings and investment at all. It does not offer scientific explanation of economic phenomena, as David Ricardo offered explanations of the division of revenues among the social classes. Its interest is entirely in righting wrongs and pursuing goals. It does not suppose that welfare is maximized when people get as much as possible of what they prefer. On the contrary, it supposes that people should do their duty, not what they prefer to do. It does

---

18 Harijan (18 August 1940) 252, reprinted in Economic Thought, ed. J.S. Mathur and A.K. Mathur (Jaipur: Arihant Publishing House, 1994) 606.

not suppose that investment is needed to create jobs. On the contrary, it urges every idle hand in the village to set to work immediately.

Nehru did think in economic terms. As an activist prior to independence he tended to think in Marxist terms, and as prime minister he tended to think in the categories of mainstream economics. As an activist he was often upset with Bapu (Gandhi) because he thought Bapu was on the side of the rich, in spite of the fact that Gandhi lived among the poor and personally embraced voluntary poverty out of solidarity with them, and in spite of the fact that he spent every waking moment promoting khadi and other anti-poverty programs, and in spite of the fact that Nehru himself wore khadi and supported Gandhi's programs as far as they went. Nehru distrusted Gandhi's proposal that the rich be declared trustees of their wealth for the benefit of the poor. He thought it amounted to asking the ruling class to give up power voluntarily, and since they would never do that he thought it amounted to leaving them in power. Much as Nehru loved Bapu, he thought Bapu was on the wrong side in the class struggle. Bapu did not understand reality, or else, as Nehru sometimes suspected, he deliberately turned a blind eye to reality because he was not fully committed to the cause of the poor.

We have introduced the word 'reality' even though neither Gandhi nor Nehru uses it because we want to use it to say that the two of them thought in different realities. As Nehru said of Gandhi, "I could never understand the background of his thought.... [H]e was a very difficult person to understand; sometimes his language was almost incomprehensible for an average modern."[19]

For Nehru the simplification of ethics had already happened, and could not be reversed. It was already clear who owned what. It was already clear that economic actors entered into contracts in pursuit of bargains favourable to themselves. For Gandhi the world where traditional interpersonal obligations customarily meant more than legal title or the deals of the day had not yet disappeared. Its tendency to fade away could be reversed. The road to village uplift ran by way of the restoration of dharma. Although Nehru recognized the role that dharma had played in India's history, he saw the world of the mid-twentieth century in terms of the great social forces depicted by Marxist and Fabian theory. Those modern forces created for all peoples the opportunity to move through capitalism toward socialism. Rather than emphasizing India's idiosyncrasies, he emphasized its participation in the global struggle for human emancipation. From Nehru's point of view Gandhi could be faulted for waffling on the main issue: the ownership of the means of production. Gandhi, Nehru said, thought industrialization was the problem not the solution, but Gandhi was wrong. The problem was not industrialization per se, but rather capitalist industrialization. Without industrialization India would be forever condemned to poverty and weakness. Gandhi could be faulted for being lukewarm concerning the two instruments most required for industrializing in a way that would lead to the sharing of the

---

19 Jawaharlal Nehru, Nehru on Gandhi: A Selection Arranged in the Order of Events from the Writings and Speeches of Jawaharlal Nehru (New York: John Day Company, 1948) 32, 52.

wealth and the abolition of poverty: public ownership and planning.

Nehru in office as prime minister and as perpetual chairman of the Planning Commission retreated rightward from the positions taken by Nehru the militant leftwing activist. He took office in the period immediately after World War II when the civil servants of the third world were learning the language of the recently coined password to first world largesse: development. To understand how that language arose, Antonio Escobar has written, one must understand "why so many countries started to see themselves as underdeveloped in the early post-World War II period, how 'to develop' became a fundamental problem for them, and how, finally, they embarked upon the task of 'un-underdeveloping' themselves by subjecting their societies to increasingly systematic, detailed, and comprehensive interventions."[20] The result of the sudden dominance of this new discourse was that, "Even those who opposed the prevailing capitalist strategies were obliged to couch their critiques in terms of the need for development, through concepts such as 'another development,' 'participatory development,' 'socialist development' and the like."[21]

Nehru joined the newly prevailing discourse by claiming that the Soviet Union had demonstrated that a development could be achieved by a path different from that of the United States and the West. If two paths to development were possible, then so was a third, distinctively

---

20 Antonio Escobar, Encountering Development: the Making and Unmaking of the Third World (Princeton: Princeton University Press, 1995) 6.
21 Escobar 5.

Indian, path, one that would be socialistic and democratic at the same time. As to how to achieve rapid industrialization in a populous poor country India had much to learn from another populous poor country, Russia. The statistical adviser to the Planning Commission, Professor P.C. Mahalonobis, went to Moscow to study planning. India's first and second Five Year Plans (1951-1956 and 1956-61) drew on Soviet experience, as well as on the Bombay Plan proposed by a business group, the People's Plan proposed by a labour group, and other sources.

There was bad news for the poor. Planned development in India turned out to be a capital accumulation process, as had been, according to conventional wisdom, the unplanned development of the USA and the planned development of the Soviet Union. In a capital accumulation process the surplus (what was left over after subsistence needs were met) had to be turned over to the upper classes. It made little difference whether the upper classes were private capitalists, landlords, or government officials. It was the upper classes who invested savings to make the economy grow. As studies like those of Simon Kuznets claim to show, the real prospect for an increase in wages is a long run prospect for productivity increases so great that some portion of the benefits of increased productivity reaches wage-earners.[22] For the foreseeable

---

22 Simon Kuznets, Growth, Population, and Income Distribution (New York: Norton, 1979). Amritananda Das has written: "…a strategy of forced accumulation of capital has much the same consequences practically whether the ideology behind it is capitalist or socialist. It means taking from the poor (who inevitably bear the brunt, in a poor country, of a policy of consumption restraint) and putting the proceeds in the hands

future in India, the poor must necessarily—according to this logic—stay poor. Further, since there was never enough capital to invest to create enough jobs to employ everybody, many of the poor would be not just underpaid, they would be unemployed. Nehru—not the old militant Nehru but the new prime minister Nehru—explained:

> *We cannot have a welfare state in India with all the socialism or even communism in the world unless our national income goes up greatly. Socialism or communism might help you to divide your existing wealth, if you like, but in India there is no existing wealth for you to divide; there is only poverty to divide. It is not a question of distributing the wealth of the few rich men here and there. That is not going to make any difference in our national income. We might adopt that course for the psychological good that might come of it. But from the practical point of view, there is not much to divide in India, because we are a poor country. We must produce wealth, and then divide it equitably. How can we have a welfare state without wealth?*[23]

Whether the bad news for the poor is definitive, or whether the news for the poor can be made better, or whether perhaps the bad news for the poor apparently

---

of whatever class happens to control the means of production (capitalists, state officials, or a combination of both) so as to enable them to accumulate more rapidly." Amritananda Das, Foundations of Gandhian Economics (Delhi: Centre for the Study of Developing Societies, 1979) 7.

23 Jawaharlal Nehru, speech of 22 January 1955, reprinted in Gopal, Anthology 311.

implicit in the truism that wealth must first be produced before it can be distributed is an entirely bogus ideological construction, are questions that will be addressed in the following chapter and subsequently.

Nehru's experience as head of state made it harder for him to answer some of the questions Gandhi used to ask, although since Gandhi was assassinated (on 30 January 1948) just four months after Nehru became prime minister (on 15 August 1947), Gandhi was not present to continue his dialogue with Nehru. Nehru had criticized Gandhi for being on the wrong side on the crucial issue of the ownership of the means of production. Gandhi took a different approach. He had called on owners to act as trustees for the benefit of the poor. He had called on them to adopt a frugal lifestyle, in order to free up resources to meet the basic needs of the poor, and in order to set a good example. Although Nehru had rejected Gandhi's approach in theory, in the long years of struggle before independence he had to a considerable extent followed it in practice. Jawaharlal, together with the other members of the Nehru family, had heard Gandhi's call and followed it in the years just before and after 1920 when they first came under Gandhi's influence. Luxury was banished from Anand Bhavan, their family residence in Allahabad. The building was converted from an elegant Victorian mansion to a one composed of modest rooms housing a secretariat for the Congress movement. They dressed in khadi. But they never surrendered their properties. They administered them, for the benefit of the poor, for the benefit of India. Now that Nehru was prime minister, one could ask again, in a different context, whether, if the Nehru family could become trustees, why could not other families do likewise? Why not the Tatas and the other big business pals of Gandhi? And if Jawaharlal Nehru could not be a faithful trustee of his family's private fortune, then how could he be a faithful trustee of the public purse as prime minister of India?

While Nehru had insisted on socialism understood as public ownership, Gandhi had always insisted that everything depended on moral progress. With moral progress the poor could benefit even from business activity conducted in the private sector. Without it they would not benefit even from business activity conducted in the public sector. Now the shoe was on the other foot. Nehru himself was the presiding officer of the entity that owned more of India's financial and industrial resources than any other entity, the Government of India. The proposition that everything depended on who owned the means of production was being tested by experience.

It is worth remembering, in the course of this dialogue imagined as having been conducted by a still living Nehru with a recently deceased Gandhi, that—contrary to what some commentators have assumed—Gandhi did not recognize a distinction between a compulsory legal obligation of the public servant to serve the public interest, and a purely voluntary choice of a private sector owner or executive to act as a fiduciary charged with serving the public interest. Trustees have compulsory legal obligations too. Courts enforce trusts. Gandhi spoke of owners of wealth becoming "statutory trustees."[24] As a public

---

24 Harijan (31 March 1946) 63, reprinted in Economic Thought, ed. Mathur and Mathur 619-621; see also 628-630. According to Gandhi, the right to decide who should succeed to the trusteeship of the trust property after the trustee's

sector civil servant can be held to account for defalcation of public funds, so a trustee can be held to account for defalcation of trust funds. Gandhi's concept was like the equitable concept of fiduciary duties from which it was derived. It was a concept of duties that the duty-bearers could be required to perform.

Gandhi had proposed that the members of Congress should not form the Government of India at all, but instead continue after independence their catalytic work as change agents building cultures of peace and solidarity in civil society. He might have reminded Nehru of that. He might have said that the construction of social democracy depended more on the details of work among the masses than on the principles of government policy. It is more a work of ants than a work of elephants. But maybe not. He might have taken a different tack and questioned the overarching principles that framed Nehru's worldview. As Nehru drifted rightward from socialism to developmentalism, he remained always imprisoned within an adharma economic paradigm. From a militant socialist position heavily influenced by Marx's mistaken claim that

---

death, "should be given to the original owner who became the first trustee, but the choice must be finalized by the State. Such arrangement puts a check on the State as well as the individual." Harijan (16 February 1947), quoted in Gupta, Economic Philosophy 96. In response to a question, Gandhi said, "I would be very happy indeed if the people concerned behaved as trustees, but if they fail, I believe we shall have to deprive them of their possession through the State with the minimum exercise of violence." M.L. Dantwala, Gandhism Reconsidered (Bombay: Padma Publications, n.d.) 57; quoted in Gupta, Economic Philosophy 99.

the cause of the exploitation of labour was to be found in the relations of production, Nehru moved to a version of development planning heavily influenced by the mistaken claims of John Maynard Keynes and Gunnar Myrdal that technocratic mandarins could macro-manage the economy for the benefit of all with no need for cultural transformation. He never questioned what J.R. Hicks called the social framework of economics. But maybe Gandhi would have taken both tacks. There is nothing inconsistent about advocating both a paradigm shift and careful attention to the details of life at the grassroots.

To justify calling Gandhi's constructive program a paradigm, to which one might shift, we need to specify how it could be taken as an exemplar. What we mean by 'paradigm' (substantially following Thomas Kuhn) is a concrete particular achievement, which becomes an exemplar for the practice of others, which eventually defines normal practice (as the previous paradigm, prior to the shift to the new paradigm, used to define normal practice). Gandhi's work for his constructive program was a concrete particular achievement, even though, as will be discussed in other chapters, his constructive program was not entirely successful. It remains to specify what made Gandhi an example of practices different in principle from an adharma economic paradigm.

We have already listed several features of Gandhi's program that make it an example of something different from economics. Gandhi himself sometimes endorsed a general principle he called 'the law of nonviolence,' or, alternatively, 'the law of love,' which, he said, was "the law of our species as violence is the law of the beast." One might then (mistakenly, we think) think of Gandhi as denying what Adam Smith affirmed. Smith affirmed that self-love was stronger in the human species than love for others. But we do not think that Gandhi did directly disagree with Smith on this point, or at any rate we do not think he had to disagree with Smith in order to justify what he did and to advocate that others act similarly. In connection with trusteeship, for example, Gandhi admitted that acting as a true trustee was not likely to happen in the cases of most property owners. He said, nevertheless, that human life would be much better than it is at present if people would adopt trusteeship as a principle and try to "act up to it." Our interpretation is consistent with Gandhi speaking of the 'law of love.' He does not speak of acting from the 'motive of love' (what Kant might call the Neigung, inclination, of love) but rather of love as a 'law.' 'Law' is a word Gandhi sometimes uses to translate dharma. We think it is reasonable to take Gandhi to mean that what people should do is their duty, and what duty accomplishes, if it is done in a well-organized society, is what the love of a mother and father accomplishes for their children, namely, meeting their every need (including their need to develop autonomy and self-reliance) insofar as it is possible to do so with the resources available.

One might ask how this principle, acting up as best one can to the law of love, for which Gandhi's life serves as a paradigmatic example, comports with economics as it already is, or as it is already becoming. One might begin to answer this question by noting that in its beginnings economic science stood in the shadow of Newtonian mechanics, a shadow cast by people like Adam Smith's beloved friend David Hume, who explicitly proposed to "introduce the experimental method of reasoning into moral subjects," by which he meant introducing Newton's method. In terms of Aristotle's classification of causes, in the eighteenth century a great goal of scholars was to banish final causes from science, and to explain the regularities of phenomena only through efficient causes. A science, so conceived, could not serve any final end at all, and a fortiori not the end of acting up to the law of love, or, as Gandhi sometimes said, "wiping every tear from every eye." However, over the years and decades, economics has become more a policy science. It is defined less by analogy with mechanics and more as the study of how to make rational choices. In the twenty-first century, final causes are once more part of science, now in the form of policy objectives. Gandhi's law of love might be interpreted as a call to social scientists to take a pro-social and pro-environment point of view when evaluating the rationality of policy choices. The late Mahbub ul Haq, a Pakistani economist, might be said to have taken a step in a Gandhian direction when he invented the Human Development Index. The index measures not just how much the world, and each nation, is developing in terms of measures of goods and services produced, but also how much human values are being served by development. Ul Haq's index, and other indices invented by progressive economists, might be regarded as tools promoting Gandhian aims because they measure the extent to which ethical goals are achieved. A Gandhian paradigm shift might be regarded as nudging modern economic society to keep moving in some directions it is already moving in.

The concept that tools of economic analysis might be employed in policy sciences aiming at all-round human development does not imply that they always will be. Economics is sometimes defined as the study of the allocation of scarce resources. Looking at economics through the lens of this definition makes it easy to see that anybody might allocate any resources she, he, or it controls for any purpose, including wicked purposes. Tolstoy identified economic science, in a book whose perusal Gandhi recommended, as a weapon which the rich use to dominate the poor by systematic lying; Tolstoy wrote, "Hypocrisy, which had formerly only a religious basis in the doctrine of original sin, the redemption, and the Church, has in our day gained a new scientific basis and has consequently caught in its nets all those who had reached too high a stage of development to be able to find support in religious hypocrisy."[25] Another way to define economics, or at least to define classical political economy, is to call it the systematic ideology which develops out of and reinforces bourgeois common sense. At the level of common sense (of what Marx called 'false consciousness'), that is to say, at the level of everyday buying and selling by ordinary people, Gandhi proposed a series of moral reforms, which, like ul Haq's proposal to define true development as human development, will be sympathetically received and taken as guides for action by some people and ignored by others. Gandhi wrote, for example, "Humanity does not search for low prices in a spirit of bargain. The humane in people even in purchases seeks opportunities for service, and therefore wants to know first not the price of the article of purchase but the condition of its producers, and makes purchases in a manner

---

25 Tolstoy, The Kingdom of God is within You 336.

that serves the most needy and the most deserving."[26] Somewhere in the middle, more systematic than common sense, but less systematic than the professional economists who do theory-based research and advise governments, are the bookkeepers, the accountants, and the managers who also allocate scarce resources. Some of them will do social audits and keep track of volunteer hours donated to nonprofits, while others will develop clever schemes to cheat on taxes, defraud investors, and make insiders rich. Some will draft and follow mission statements that commit their enterprises to social and environmental responsibility, while others will hire goons to beat up striking workers. A paradigm shift in Gandhi's direction might be defined as a qualitative change in society which will result from a gradual quantitative increase in the number people using ethically all the tools of economic analysis, at every level of sophistication from the personal budget to the global input-output model.

But there might also be another way to talk about the differences in principle between the forms of thought that Nehru employed as prime minister and chairman of the Planning Commission, on the one hand, and Gandhi's constructive program on the other. The incommensurability of the paradigms might be not just a matter of how ethically the tools of economic analysis are used, but also a matter of the tools themselves and the conceptual and institutional frameworks that provide the contexts for their use. Indeed if the only defining quality of a Gandhian paradigm were commitment to an ethic of service, then any misunderstanding between Gandhi

---

[26] Gandhi, Harijan (30 November 1945), reprinted in Economic Thought, ed. Mathur and Mathur 166-167.

and Nehru would not be fundamental. One of the tools of economic analysis in question—a key one if one follows Lionel Robbins in defining economics as the study of the relationship between ends and scarce means which have alternative uses—is the concept of 'opportunity cost.'

'Opportunity cost' is one of the reversals of common sense through which science leaps into abstraction, constructs a conceptual apparatus in a world of its own, and then returns to the real world with analytic power that leaves common sense far behind. It reverses the common sense assumption that the cost of something is a property belonging to that thing, viz its price. For common sense the price of a suit could be, for example, 500 rupees. From an opportunity cost point of view, the cost of the suit is the opportunities foregone by acquiring it. Assuming that the choice actually made is the best choice, its cost is the next best among all of the alternative sets of purchases one might have made if one had not spent the 500 rupees on the suit. More abstractly, the cost of allocating any scarce resource is the benefit that might have been obtained by allocating the resource elsewhere. Even more abstractly, the optimum choice is a rejection for good reasons of the entire gamut of courses of action not chosen. In principle, there can never be a rational allocation of scarce resources until all alternatives have been canvassed. In practice it is only possible to consider the alternatives that are made conceivable and salient by the conceptual and institutional framework of thought—although the illusion of having considered all possibilities can sometimes be achieved by maximizing or minimizing a mathematical function where the key variables can take on any value.[27]

---

27 For an example where it might falsely appear that all alter-

The dependence of opportunity cost analysis on considering all alternatives suggests a way in which Gandhi was more rational and scientific than Nehru, or, perhaps better, a way in which a third person might adopt a wider concept of the possible alternatives, and thus become more rational, because of selecting a course of action after considering more options. Gandhi thought outside the box, compared to the people Nehru dubbed the 'average modern,' because his context was the ideal Indian village. The simplification of ethics had not yet happened, or if it had happened it could be cured, or perhaps superseded by a future ethic better than anything found in the present or the past. A life like Gandhi's own, consisting of 'opportunities for service,' and 'experiments with truth' was still possible.

For Nehru, on the other hand, the limits of the possible are circumscribed by property law and contract law as they were imposed on India by the British. For him they are, according to one of Peter Berger's ideas that we think Nehru would endorse, among the institutional concomitants of the modern technology that promises (and, Nehru thought, alone promises) to end India's

---

natives have been considered: the optimal decision might be to choose a value of x that maximizes the value of y, where $y = 4x - x2$, where x and y are natural numbers. Then $x = 2$ will be the optimum, since for that value of x, $y = 4$, and for any other value of x, y will be smaller. All possible alternatives are considered in the sense that all possible values of x are considered. However, in a larger sense all possible alternatives have not been considered because the real-world problem in question might be conceived in terms of concepts other than x and y, or in terms of another equation.

poverty. Their circumscription of the possible remains even when the workings of the market are modified by what Richard Peterson has called "state policies which take market abstractions for granted."[28] It remains even when legal title to resources passes out of private hands and into government ownership; it remains even when a series of public laws superimposed on private law prescribes minimum wages, maximum hours, and collective bargaining. It remains as the horizon of the endless debates about nationalization vs privatization and free markets vs planning. Gandhi opens up a wider rationality because his viewpoint is one that generates additional alternatives.

On the eve of India's independence, Gandhi generated an alternative no one else known to history thought of, although if Gandhi was as much in tune with the mentality of the Indian peasant as Nehru said he was there were probably some unknown peasants somewhere in India who also thought of it. Gandhi proposed that the Muslim League be invited to form the Government of India. The League's leader, M.A. Jinnah, made it clear that he would regard such an invitation as the British returning India to the Muslim Mogul Empire from which (on Jinnah's view of history) they had stolen it.

In Gandhi's mind, his proposal made perfect sense. The young boy who gave up what he most desired, surreptitious carnivorous feasts with his friend, for the sake of his relationship with his mother, had become an elderly

---

28 Richard T. Peterson, "Alienation and Intellectual Practices," Alienation Theories and De-alienation Strategies, ed. D. Schweitzer and R.F. Geyer (Northwood, Middlesex, UK: Science Reviews Ltd., 1989) 229.

man willing to give up twenty five years of struggle for the independence of India for the sake of the love that ought to exist between Hindus and Muslims. Gandhi's alternative was not rejected for good reasons in the course of the deliberations that ultimately led to partition and to mass murder. It was not considered. It made no sense—it was not on the conceptual map—for the minds of Nehru, Lord Mountbatten, and the other principal decision-makers.

Gandhi once wrote,

> "Recall the face of the poorest and weakest man you have seen and ask yourself if the step you are contemplating is going to be of any use to him. Will he gain by it?"[29]

In the following chapters there will be further elaboration of the idea of a paradigm shift which shifts not only in favour of willingness to evaluate one's actions by the criterion Gandhi suggests in the lines just quoted, and shifts not only in favour of right means following Gandhi's precept that means become ends, but also shifts the framework of scientific thinking about social problems. We have suggested that in principle Gandhi's outsider's critique of modernity opens the way to thinking that is more rational because it conceives of more alternatives to choose among. We plan to discuss several ways to make this general idea specific and practical.

Jawaharlal Nehru served for seventeen years (1947-1964) as prime minister of India. His top priority

---

29 Gandhi, quoted in the introduction to The Meaning of the Mahatma for the Millennium, ed. Kuruvilla Pandikattu (Delhi: Maadhyam Book Services, 2001) 1.

objective was to end the poverty of India's masses. He did not succeed. There was modest industrial growth. There were many plans and programs designed to end poverty that failed to do so. Agricultural production fell from 63.3 million metric tons of rice, wheat, and other food grains in 1954 to 60.9 million metric tons in 1956 to 58.3 million tons in 1958, while population increased. After 1958 there was a temporary improvement, but by the mid-1960s per capita availability of food-grains had fallen back to the levels of the mid-1950s. In 1964, the year Nehru died, government programs to stave off famine depended on importing 7.5 million metric tons of grain made available to India by the United States under Public Law 480, a figure that went up to 10.5 million metric tons the following year.[30]

Some say (1) that Nehru failed because he was too capitalist. His economic plans amounted to subsidies for the rich by giving them protection from foreign competition, exclusive permits, and cushy jobs in the public sector. Labour remained as oppressed as ever. His attempts to empower the rural poor and to redistribute land achieved little and left most of the poor and landless worse off than they had been before. (2) Others say that Nehru was too socialist. The smuggler, the blackmarketeer and the tax-evader were produced by statist policies contrary to human nature and to the laws of economics. Useful work was not rewarded, while spending time and money

---

[30] Shalendra D. Sharma, Development and Democracy in India (Boulder: Lynne Rienner Publishers, 1999) 129-130. For further data on the lack of economic improvement for the masses under Nehru see Myrdal, Asian Drama 1:570 and the sources there cited.

currying favour with politicians was. (3) Some say he was too Gandhian. He threw money at community development, village uplift, and cottage industry schemes that should have gone to progressive industrialists and farmers who took full advantage of modern technology. Many other hypotheses concerning Nehru's failure have been mooted, some of which will be mentioned in later chapters, where, also, the tension between Gandhi as saint and Gandhi as lawyer, which is now rumbling ominously in the depths of the subtext, will appear on the surface as an explicit theme. The next chapter will consider the relationship of Gandhi's ideas to those of Jayaprakash Narayan, who in the first days of Nehru's tenure as prime minister held the first of the three hypotheses mentioned here.

* * *

CHAPTER 3

JAYAPRAKASH NARAYAN

"Looking back, it seems clear that he [Gandhi] had already begun to lay the foundations for his future course of action. But the significance of what he was doing was entirely lost upon me, as perhaps upon many others."
—*J.P. Narayan, 1957*[1]

In 1936 Jayaprakash Narayan (also known as J.P.) wrote:

The answer will be found in the origins of unemployment under capitalism. What do we find there? We find that production has been curtailed ruthlessly; factories are lying idle; credit is frozen; warehouses are glutted. At the same time we find people who are in dire need of all the things that are locked up in warehouses or wantonly destroyed by the State and the capitalists. On the one hand, there is said

---

1 Jayaprakash Narayan, letter of resignation from the Praja Socialist Party, 1957, reprinted as chapter 18 of Bimal Prasad, ed., A Revolutionary's Quest, Selected Writings of Jayaprakash Narayan (Delhi: Oxford University Press, 1980) 196. This work is hereafter cited as Selected Writings.

to be overproduction; on the other, an appalling underconsumption.

Can there be anything more contradictory than this? Yet it is one of the most persistent characteristics of capitalism. It is clear that in a world where the vast majority of people live in dire need there can be no overproduction. All that can be produced today, and a thousand times more, can be consumed without any difficulty. But, then, where is the rub? The rub is in the fact that the poverty of the people, their lack of purchasing power, does not allow them to buy the goods that are lying idle or being dumped into the sea or thrown into the bonfire. The purchasing power of the great majority of the people in capitalist countries comes from the wages they receive; and the latter are kept down as low as possible by the capitalists so that their profits may be the highest possible. Thus a vicious circle is drawn. The capitalist goes on manufacturing goods so that by selling them he may draw his profit, at the same time he restricts the consuming power of the community by his policy of wages. Naturally, there is maladjustment between production and consumption; and he periodically finds that he has produced "too much." Then he restricts production and throws his workers out of employment.

Now, it should be clear that if goods were produced for consumption and not for the profit of a few, all that was produced would be consumed. There would be no limit to the purchasing power of the people except the supply of good itself, because "wages" would represent under those conditions the sum total of consumption goods produced. Overproduction would arise only when the needs of the community have been satisfied, and these, as I have already indicated, are almost insatiable. Restriction of production and de-mechanization would not be necessary till that point has been reached.[2]

Narayan wrote in the depths of the world depression of the 1930s, and in the following pages other references will be made to it. However, there are always involuntarily unemployed people, many with unsatisfactory employment, a great deal of underutilized capacity, and many unmet needs that could be met if underutilized resources were mobilized to meet them. In what follows the depression of the 1930s is to be understood as a convenient and dramatic symbol standing for social arrangements that are always dysfunctional, even when there is no depression.

Narayan asserts that the cause of unemployment, which is an aspect of the larger problem of simultaneous overproduction and underconsumption, is the lack of

---

[2] Jayaprakash Narayan, in chapter 3 of Why Socialism? as extracted in Selected Writings 49-50. We have corrected a misprint where 'are' should have been 'or.' We will sometimes refer in the singular to the inter-related set of problems Narayan poses as 'the problem,' even though in another context we might use the plural and make a list of what the separate problems are. We do not share the bias of those who consider it to be always or nearly always more scientific to speak of a series of distinct problems. We agree with those who see capitalism as having a central contradiction, which can be named as the contradiction between the accumulation of profits and the production of use values. It creates obstacles to solving many problems. Hence one can also speak of a single problem containing sub-problems, inasmuch as each sub-problem is exacerbated and partly caused by the same central contradiction.

purchasing power of the workers. The lack of purchasing power, in turn, is caused by exploitation. The workers are the producers, but the owners own the products of the workers' alienated labour. The owners sell the products, and pay the workers who make them whatever the law of supply and demand compels them to pay, keeping the rest of the revenue for themselves. (Marx, following Ricardo and Smith, thought workers would get only enough to subsist on, but the argument does not depend on whether wages are at a subsistence level or higher.) If, Narayan reasons, the producers were also the owners, so that there would be no deduction from their incomes to pay for what Paul Baran called the 'permissive acts' performed by owners who charge for allowing the use of the assets they own, then worker purchasing power would be higher. There would be no underconsumption because workers would have more money to buy things. There would be no overproduction because everything that could be produced could be sold.

Narayan's 1936 account of the cause and cure of simultaneous overproduction and underconsumption can be criticized from Marxian, Keynesian, and Gandhian viewpoints. Of the three, the Gandhian is the most fundamental. It is the one which brings into focus the basic structures of the modern world which are at the root of the causes, and which must be transformed to effect a cure.

From a Marxist viewpoint it must be said, contrary to Narayan, that even when the means of production are owned by the producers, the proceeds from the sale of all the goods produced will not go to wages. Narayan allows for this by specifying that wages would equal only the sum total of consumption goods produced, recognizing that some goods are production goods which cannot directly be consumed, but only indirectly consumed through their role in augmenting future production. The percentage of productive effort devoted to making consumption goods may be rather small if a Stalin or a Nehru is intent on major investments in heavy industry in order to industrialize a backward country rapidly. Regardless of whether or not consumption goods production is deliberately restricted to promote saving and investment, however, wages will not be equivalent to the sum total of consumption goods produced. There are several reasons why the workers will not receive as wages the equivalent of all they produce, even when the capitalists have been dispossessed and the workers are the owners. In 1875, when the German social democrats proposed that workers should be paid the undiminished proceeds of what they produced, Karl Marx explained that before the workers could be paid, there had to "be deducted" the following:

- First, cover for the replacement of the means of production used up.
- Secondly, additional portion for expansion of production.
- Thirdly, reserve or insurance fund to provide against mis-adventures, disturbances through natural events etc.

These deductions from the 'undiminished proceeds of labour' are an economic necessity, and their magnitude is to be determined by available means and forces, and partly by calculation of probabilities, but they are in no way calculable by equity.

After the above deductions, there are other, social, deductions:
- First, the general costs of administration not belonging to production. . . .
- Secondly, that which is destined for the communal satisfaction of needs, such as schools, health services, etc. . . .
- Thirdly, funds for those unable to work etc. . . .[3]

If, then, even when the producers own the means of production, the money the workers are paid still has a value less than what it would cost to purchase their products, then there is still a tendency toward simultaneous overproduction and underconsumption. This tendency might be reduced by purchases by those unable to work, as under capitalism it is reduced by purchases by the profit-making classes. Narayan in the passage quoted properly assumes that where the bulk of the people live on wages the purchases of the non-working classes will not be enough to stabilize the system. The situation is not likely to be different when there are fewer non-workers. A socialist dictatorship might solve the problem by force. If there is enough surveillance and enough discipline, then people might be compelled to continue producing even where there are no willing buyers with enough money to buy their products. Or as Ché Guevara proposed, people might be persuaded to engage in economic activity when it is not profitable or in their self-interest to do so by moral suasion. Or by some combination of force and moral suasion. If production does not depend on profit, or on people thinking it worth their while to work, but

---

3 Karl Marx, Critique of the Gotha Programme (New York: International Publishers, 1938) 7.

can instead by motivated by other motives—including but not limited to fear of punishment—then factories need not lie idle for lack of effective demand. Nor need the products lie in warehouses unused for want of buyers. They could be given away free, or they could be allotted through a rationing system in which money plays a reduced or even negligible role.

In 1936 Narayan offered the Soviet Union as proof that his argument was true. He pointed out that all the capitalist countries were mired in the depths of the Great Depression, in which idle hands, idle lands, and idle factories coexisted with unmet needs. Only the Soviet Union, he said, had full employment and a stable economy. He was not, by the way, quite right to single out the Soviet Union in this way, since there was also full employment and a stable economy in another country which disregarded the laws of capitalist economics and made the economy run with other motives, Hitler's Germany.[4] In any case, if the reflections made here are valid, the Soviet Union

---

4 See Peter Drucker's study of Hitler's economy, The End of Economic Man (New York: John Day, 1939). Drucker explains in detail how Nazi Germany was not run on the basis of investment for profit, but nevertheless was made to run by enlisting other motives. Hitler demonstrated that an economically successful alternative to capitalism is possible, although he did not demonstrate a desirable alternative to it. Amritananda Das has argued that a Gandhian economy must appeal to nationalism, which is perhaps neither the best nor the worst of human motives. Das, Foundations of Gandhian Economics (New York: St Martin's Press, 1979) 72. Das thinks historical experience shows that a desire to benefit the poor is not a strong enough motivation for the sacrifices necessary to secure the benefit of the poor.

did not prove Narayan's point. The problem to be solved was harder than Narayan thought it was. If the Soviet Union solved it, it did not do so by making wages equal to the sum total of consumption goods produced. It had to use other means. After 1936, as credible evidence of atrocities poured in, Narayan gradually changed his mind about the Soviet Union. He ended up concluding not only that the Soviet experience represented a cure worse than the disease, but also that its evils were not simply due to sociopathic personalities like Stalin, but were inherent in its principles. The case of the Soviet Union does not demonstrate the validity of Narayan's 1936 solution to the problem of simultaneous overproduction and underconsumption. If it demonstrated a solution to the problem at all, it did not demonstrate a desirable one.

John Maynard Keynes attributed the problem to a different set of causes. He proposed a different cure. At a practical level, Keynes consciously sought an alternative to Marx. He wanted to find ways to stabilize an economy and to promote social justice (at least to a limited extent) without major changes in the ownership of the means of production. At a theoretical level, he did not need to add anything to the criticisms of Marxian theory that had already been written by others. Keynes was initiated into the profession in the heart of an economic orthodoxy that had already decided, beginning at the first publication of Capital and continuing forward from there, that Marxism was more metaphysics than science. His father John Neville Keynes was a professor of economics; he studied economics at Cambridge under Alfred Marshall and became editor of the Economic Journal, the leading British academic journal in the field. His theoretical concerns were those of a community of scholars that had already decided that Marx was wrong. Keynes could take it to be assumed in his milieu that the sort of thing he was doing was more scientific than anything Marxists were doing. That put Gandhi two down, for reasons we will now explain.

The passage we quoted at length above from Jayaprakash Narayan was taken from a chapter in Narayan's book Why Socialism?, which was written as a refutation of Gandhi. Narayan there argued that Gandhi's approach was merely ethical and religious, which was equivalent to saying that it did not provide valid explanations of the cause and effect relationships that determine what happens in the world. Narayan contrasts Marxism with Gandhian thought by claiming that Marx was scientific. Exhibit A of Narayan's proof that Marx was scientific and Gandhi was not is in the passage quoted. Marx could explain simultaneous overproduction and underconsumption. Gandhi could not. Narayan attributed to Gandhi the naïve view that the cause of unemployment was machinery. The true cause had been proven by Marx (according to Narayan) to be the exploitation of labour rooted in the private ownership of the means of production. If the weight of opinion of the majority of the economics profession, including Keynes, was that orthodox economics is more scientific than Marx, and if Marx is more scientific than Gandhi, that makes orthodox economics very much more scientific than Gandhi. Gandhi was two down.

For Keynes the context of finding a scientific explanation for the same Great Depression of the 1930s that Narayan explained in Marxist terms, was that of an economics profession that had long ago left Marx far behind, or at least thought it had. For Keynes, the lack of sufficient purchasing power to buy the products of industry, and the consequent idling of industry and laying off of workers even while needs were not being met, was not a problem defined in terms of what Marx would call relations of production. The problem was defined in terms of what Marx would call the level of circulation. According to the labour theory of value, as Marx applied it, the secret of profit-making (and also, according to Narayan, the secret of simultaneous overproduction and underconsumption) could only be discovered by going deeper than the level of circulation to analyze the exploitation of labour at the level of the relations of production. But for orthodox economists the law of supply and demand was science while the labour theory of value was not science. The latter was metaphysical nonsense.

The problem, for Keynes, was to explain why the law of supply and demand did not bring about a satisfactory equilibrium. The Depression was equilibrium of a sort. Prices were fixed at the levels people were willing and able to pay. The amount currently produced (disregarding unsold amounts left over from prior overproduction) was the amount the market effectively demanded. If more were produced it would not be sold; if prices went down it would not be worthwhile to produce as much and supply would decline; if prices went up people could not or would not pay the higher prices. In these respects the law of supply and demand was working just as it was supposed to work. But, as Narayan said, "factories are lying idle; credit is frozen; warehouses are glutted. At the same time we find people who are in dire need of all the things that are locked up in warehouses or wantonly destroyed by the State and the capitalists. On the one hand, there is said to be overproduction; on the other, an appalling underconsumption." According to Say's Law, supply produced its own demand. Therefore, if there was a supply of workers willing and able to work, then there must be a demand for them. Demand for investment capital was supposed to be a function of the price of money—i.e., of the interest rate. Yet in the Depression, interest rates went down to one percent, and sometimes neared zero percent, and still nobody wanted to take the risk of borrowing funds to put them to work to earn profits. The valiant efforts of classical economists to massage the data and tweak the theory to make them fit each other were in vain.

Keynes took large notice of the fact that in any given society for any given period, total purchases must equal total sales. This is an accounting identity. (We mention that it is an accounting identity partly in order to point out that economics is not always social physics; it does not always take concepts from mechanics like elasticity, equilibrium, and so on and postulate equivalents to them in the social world that can be treated with the same mathematical tools.) The accounting identity must be true because each exchange transaction is a purchase from one party's point of view and a sale from the other party's point of view. All the money spent is the same as all the money taken in as receipts. (We think this general point holds up well enough when it is complicated by considering three party transactions, delivery of goods to be paid for at a later date, and so on….)

Yet people do not in fact spend all they earn. Already, Alfred Marshall, Keynes' father's teacher at Cambridge, had written in a critique of John Stuart Mill's version of the supposed law that supply creates its own demand: "But though men have the power to purchase, they may not choose to use it." [5] For Keynes, "[W]hen our income increases, our consumption increases also, but not by so much. The key to our practical problems is to be found in this psychological law.... This analysis provides us with an explanation of the paradox of poverty in the midst of plenty. For the mere existence of an insufficiency of effective demand, may, and often will, bring the increase of employment to a standstill before a level of full employment has been reached." [6]

Because of the psychological law, as Keynes called it, that people prefer not to spend all they earn, there will always be a certain amount of savings, except perhaps in the extreme case where everybody is living from pay check to pay check. This is a good thing if you want there to be funds available for investment. It is a good thing if you want people to postpone consumption and put their money in banks, and stocks, and bonds, and insurance, and corporate retained earnings, and government budget surpluses and the like in order to bring into play what Ludwig von Mises called "roundabout methods of production." Savings make possible a world where instead of living from hand to mouth people can enjoy the benefits of incomparably more efficient roundabout production methods, which can only be enjoyed after long lead times needed for research and development and/or long lead

---

5 Alfred Marshall, quoted by John Maynard Keynes, in The General Theory of Employment, Interest, and Money (New York: Harcourt Brace, 1936) 19, note 2.
6 Keynes, General Theory 29-30 and 30-31.

times needed for the installation of expensive equipment, such as, for example, dams, hydroelectric generators, long distance transmission lines, and the wiring for electricity of all the buildings in all the neighbourhoods of a large city.

Yet the inevitability of savings is not necessarily a good thing from the point of view of the accounting identity noted above. If business equals production for profit, and production for profit depends on sales and every sale is someone else's purchase, then it is not clear how business is supposed to continue from one time period to another. If all the money spent is all the revenue, and if some of the revenue is set aside for savings, then there will be less money spent the next time around. And therefore less revenue.

All would be well if all the money saved were invested. Then all the money would be spent the second time around. It would not all be spent by consumers, but it would be spent by someone; it would be spent by consumers and investors combined (leaving aside as not essential to the present point government spending and foreign trade).

Keynes locates the problem in the tendency of investment to lag behind savings. Differing from Narayan's focus on worker purchasing power, Keynes locates the problem in total purchasing power, also known as aggregate demand. If there is plenty of investment, then the circulation process can continue indefinitely, with there always being enough revenue in somebody's hands to carry on a steady stream of sales transactions producing for ever and ever steady streams of revenue. This reasoning, this mindset, this institutional framework, leads to the imperative for 'economic growth.'

Whatever other reasons a modern economy may have for wanting to grow; there is an accounting identity that compels it to grow. There has to be enough investment to sop up savings and thus ward off what is called a 'downturn' where goods cannot be sold and workers cannot be employed. Investment only happens, however, when investors rationally believe that at some future date they, or the enterprise they are investing in, will be the owners of some product that can be sold at a profit. Hence more and more products must be brought to market for the sake of the stability of the system, independently of the ethical or ecological reasons which may or may not justify bringing to market more products or bringing to market any particular product. The government can prohibit the production of products it might deem harmful, such as cigarettes or sport-utility vehicles or pornography or violent television shows seen by children, but if it prohibits them it makes compliance with the growth imperative harder to achieve. Then some other profitable ways to invest capital must be found to make up for the prohibition against making money by means the legislature deems harmful.

Keynes and Keynesians have generally not been notably concerned with weeding out undesirable businesses. Keynes himself frankly admitted that the health of the economy required vice, not virtue. Their efforts have been devoted to keeping economies stable by using some combination of policy instruments to avoid overproduction. They advise governments to pump money into the system, or encourage others to pump money into the system, so that there will be enough purchasing power to avoid major gluts of unsold products and thus keep productive processes humming along at some reasonable more or less normal level. In his General Theory, Keynes argued against his neoclassical colleagues that the low-level equilibrium of the Great Depression was not a freak. It was not something that was going to go away by itself. To make it go away, governments and reasonable people in the private sector had to do something about it.

To stabilize the economy, Keynes advocated a number of measures that defied the common sense of people brought up to believe that the purpose of business was to make money by producing some useful product or service, and that the measure of business success was the accountant's balance sheet. Deficit spending by the government in hard times is one of the most famous. He identifies the problem using a kind of reasoning that follows out what happens when account books are kept.

In important ways Keynes identifies being able to move beyond an accounting mentality as the solution to the problem. It is better to put people to work doing something useful than to leave them idle, regardless of what the bookkeepers say about it. Keynes asked people to see the physical and human realities that sometimes became invisible when the world was viewed through the conceptual lenses of accountancy: *"The nineteenth century,"* he wrote,

carried to extravagant lengths the criterion of what one can call for short "the financial results" as a test of the advisability of any course of action sponsored by private or by collective action. The whole conduct of life was made into a sort of parody of an accountant's nightmare. Instead of using their vastly increased material wealth and technical resources to build a wonder city, the men of the nineteenth century built slums; and they thought it right and advisable to build slums because slums, on the test of private enterprise, "paid", whereas the wonder city would, they thought, have been an act of foolish extravagance, which would, in the imbecile idiom of financial fashion, have "mortgaged the future"— though how the construction to-day of great and glorious works to-day can impoverish the future, no man can see until his mind is beset by false analogies from an irrelevant accountancy.[7]

Keynes located the problem of simultaneous overproduction and underconsumption at the level of circulation. His solution to the problem consisted of a series of policies designed to stimulate consumption and investment. He alleged that the real world results to be expected were more important than any paper losses that might have to be written off. Unlike Narayan's solution of the same date, Keynes' solution did not call for a change in the ownership of the means of production. Like Nehru, Keynes did not have the luxury of protecting himself from empirical refutation by clinging to a counterfactual argument that the world would have been better if his ideas had been applied, because to a large extent his ideas were applied. They were orthodox from the mid-1930s to the mid-1960s. Although some, like Gunnar Myrdal, thought that "the Keynesian revolution" had changed economics

---

7 John Maynard Keynes, "National Self Sufficiency," The Yale Review 22/4 (1933) 765.

forever, the general consensus is that mainstream economics has now reverted to something very like pre-Keynesian economics. The age of Keynes is over.[8] On a practical level, managing national economies with the tools of macroeconomics has proven to be impossible in the era of globalization, leaving in the lurch social democrats who used to favour Keynesian policies to bring about full employment, equity, and inclusion of the marginalized.[9] A.M. Huq is one of those who has pointed out that Gandhi had a better analysis than Keynesian ideas provides with respect to India's basic problem of massive

---

8 "The marriage between interests and values that liberalism neatly underwrote in the nineteenth century, with its simple but elegant view of the world, is in the process of being repeated—a process perhaps embraced with more fervour in Britain than anywhere else." Will Hutton, The Revolution That Never Was: An Assessment of Keynesian Economics (London: Longman, 1986) 15. "In the middle 1940s, the Keynesians felt superior and triumphant. During the 1950s they were mostly losing their confidence…. In 1963 I thought that the clear academic retreat from Keynesianism had already been accompanied by a retreat in policy." William H. Hutt, The Keynesian Episode (Indianapolis: Liberty Press, 1979) 415, 419, in Keynes, Uncertainty, and the Global Economy (Beyond Keynes, vol. 2), ed. Sheila Dow and John Hillard (Cheltenham UK: Edward Elgar, 2002). Recently, Paul Krugman has argued that a series of financial crises have shown that Keynes was right after all. Paul Krugman, The Return of Depression Economics (New York: W.W. Norton, 2009).
9 See, e.g., Mark Latham, Civilising Global Capital: New Thinking for Australian Labor (Sydney: Allen & Unwin, 1998); and Robert Reich, The Work of Nations (London: Simon and Schuster, 1991).

rural poverty: "[H]e [Gandhi] had a better perception of the nature of massive rural unemployment than he is given credit for. That type of unemployment is structural, seasonal, and technological, rather than cyclical. Deficiency of aggregate demand has very little to do with that type of unemployment." [10]

Gandhi's thought suggests an explanation of simultaneous overproduction and underconsumption that is in principle different from those discussed so far, and also different from the explanation of unemployment Narayan attributed to Gandhi when he associated him with the view that unemployment is caused by machines. The explanation is that modern society is adharma. This comprehensive and somewhat flexible word, rich in connotations, can serve as an emblem of several aspects of Gandhi's thought and practice, which suggest creative ways to think about the problems Narayan posed in 1936 when he asked, "Can there be anything more contradictory than this?"

Gandhi questions the constitutive principles of economic science laid down by Adam Smith, when he attributed the origins of its subject matter to the human

---

10 A.M. Huq, "Welfare Criteria in Gandhian Economics," in Essays in Gandhian Economics, ed. Romesh Diwan and Mark A. Lutz (New Delhi: Gandhi Peace Foundation, 1985) 68. Although developing nations after World War II generally accepted the idea of macroeconomic planning of a more or less Keynesian sort, they often did not accept the idea that in poor country contexts Keynes' concept of effective demand being an obstacle to growth was valid. See Amartya Sen, Employment, Technology and Development (Delhi: Oxford University Press, 1999).

propensity to truck or barter: "Give me that which I want, and you shall have this which you want." Gandhi questions Smith's confidence that he can find security in relying on the self-interest of the butcher, the brewer, and the baker to bring him his dinner. Much historical evidence shows that indeed Smith's confidence in the efficacy of self-interest is not a principle of general validity. In the Depression of the 1930s it was in the self-interest of employers to lay off their employees. It was in the self-interest of bankers to foreclose on people's houses and farms. In Argentina in 2001, it was in the self-interest of entrepreneurs to abandon their enterprises, leaving the workers without work, the government without taxes, and consumers without products. One might regard such well-known and frequently occurring situations where self-interest does not function to meet human needs as bugs in the system that can be corrected by redesigning institutions to harness self-interest more effectively. Or, like Gandhi, one might consider another alternative: that people ought, in principle and as a matter of duty, make themselves useful to their fellow human beings, and, indeed, to all life.

Gandhi's solution to the problem of simultaneous overproduction and underconsumption is not a sentimental humanitarianism. It is not sentimental because it is about duty, not about feelings. It is not a humanitarianism because it is primarily about serving family and neighbours, not about trying to serve all of humanity at once. Gandhi wrote, "Pure service to one's neighbours can never, from its very nature, result in disservice to those remotely situated. 'As with the individual, so with the universe,' is an unfailing principle, which we would do well to take to heart."[11] Gandhi locates the problem not at the level of the legally constituted relations of ownership at the level of production, nor at the level of interruptions of the flow of money in the circuits of buying and selling, but at the level of personal morality and interpersonal relationships. Gandhi's viewpoint is, in principle, the most fundamental of the three, because production relations and circulation relations are subsets of interpersonal relations.

Over the years, Jayaprakash Narayan came to see the paradox of poverty in a world where there could be enough for all more and more as Gandhi saw it. J.P. was never tempted by the theory that the supply of labour and the demand for labour would come to a satisfactory equilibrium if only the free market were left alone to work its magic. Nor was he ever tempted to believe that poverty could be abolished without making any changes in the ownership of the means of production. He came to believe, instead, in "new values and ideas... so chosen that they have a direct bearing on some major social problem and their acceptance and practice are expected to lead to a solution of that problem and incidentally to a radical change in society."[12] His evolution away from Marx was an evolution from Marx to Gandhi, much to the delight of his wife Prabhavati, who had been a Gandhian all along.[13]

---

11 M.K. Gandhi, Young India (18 June 1931).
12 Narayan in the resignation letter cited in note 1 above, at 205.
13 The gradual shift of Narayan's thought from Marx to Gandhi is recounted by his close friend Minoo Masani in Minoo Masani, Is J.P. the Answer? (Delhi: Macmillan, 1975) 10-33.

By 1959, Narayan was echoing what Gandhi had written in 1909:

Modern industrialism and the spirit of economism that it has created, a spirit that weighs every human value on the scales of profit and loss and so-called economic progress, have disintegrated human society and made man an alien among his fellow men. Not only has the community been disintegrated, even the family is languishing in the West, and the mother, the woman, who was the centre and soul of the family, is losing her womanhood.

The problem of present day civilization is social integration. Man is alone and bored, he is 'organization man.' He is man ordered about and manipulated by forces beyond his ken and control –irrespective of whether it is a 'democracy' or a 'dictatorship.' The problem is to put man in touch with man, so that they may live together in meaningful, understandable, controllable relationships. In short, the problem is to recreate the human community.[14]

---

14 Jayaprakash Narayan, "A Plea for Reconstruction of the Indian Polity," Selected Writings 218-219. Narayan gives an explanation of the meaning of dharma: "The concept of dharma was of great importance in ancient India. It prescribed and regulated individual and group behavior in all walks of life. This concept of dharma and its role in Indian polity and the wider life of society is another example of that synthetic, organic, communal organization of Indian society which has been discussed above. Communities, territorial or functional, had developed laws and codes of behavior to regulate the internal life of their communities and groups and their relations with the rest of society. There were in addition codes and laws

In Narayan's proposed socialist Gandhian grassroots communities, there can be no unemployment. People follow the norms that prescribe their roles in families and communities in a spirit of service. Earning wages is not the purpose of working. Finding someone willing to pay for work is not the condition that must be met in order to start work. Cessation of pay is not an event that implies that one must stop work. This does not mean, as Gandhi, with whom Narayan presumably agrees, explained, that there can be no money changing hands. The primary and decisive motivation for work is a spirit of service, but money may be received, as well as other benefits, in association with service.

An example is provided by the work of the Congress members who worked under Gandhi's leadership to organize the khadi movement that promoted the spinning of cloth by hand. In order to qualify for a staff position people had to demonstrate so much commitment to the cause that they would work as volunteers even if they were not paid. Having joined the movement because they believed in it, some staff members (not the ones who had other incomes and did not need it) were supported by the movement.[15]

---

that were common to and excepted by all of them that made up the universal social ethics. The ensemble of these social ethics exercised a powerful influence over the State." Selected Writings 217.

15 "Those who are engaged in this voluntary organization not only derive no pecuniary advantage from it but are expected, if they can, to give their labour free of any hire." Gandhi, Economics of Khadi (Ahmedabad: Navajivan Press, 1941) 542.

Another example is discussed by Gunnar Myrdal in Asian Drama. Myrdal pointed out that even villagers who had become modernized to the extent that they took work for wages in cities, often chose to go back to the village some of the time to do agricultural work in order not to forfeit their traditional right as a member of an extended family to share in the harvest. They wanted to remain in good standing as community members lest their community membership lapse from disuse. In this system there is no unemployment within a kinship network because anybody who shows up and participates in the work also participates in the benefits of the work. Myrdal had a low opinion of this system because more people were employed than were needed for the tasks done. If five people did work that three could have done just as well, then the extra two added nothing to the product. Society would have been better off if the extra two had been employed elsewhere doing something else. Gandhi too took large notice of the surplus of labour in Indian villages, and it was partly to put to work the labour power that was left over after all necessary agricultural tasks were done that he promoted hand spinning and other village crafts. Gandhi, like Keynes, was concerned with what we may call social efficiency broadly defined as meeting a basket of desirable goals with the resources available. He was concerned with finding some honourable and respected work for everybody to do and with giving everybody a legitimate claim to receiving the necessities of life.

Churches provide other examples. Churches usually have many volunteers and some paid staff. In between there are many people who perform many roles which they would never perform if they were motivated just by market incentives and/or which they would never be assigned if the purpose were to make a profit by employing them. They are supported in various ways and to various degrees by the community of the faithful and by endowment income.

Examples could be multiplied indefinitely. Parents often have the social role of taking care of children, and children often have the social role of taking care of aging parents, where the primary motivation for the work is service, but the workers are supported and helped by other family members, and sometimes also by non-profit or governmental institutions such as child care centres, hospitals, and schools. In every walk of life, in the public, private, and non-profit sectors, there are people who feel called to a vocation, and there are organizations that write mission statements declaring pro-social goals. The transition from a money-dominated economy to one where dharma is taken more seriously than it is now is not a brusque shift from one single model to another single model. It is gradual sarvodaya, moral awakening. To the extent that a spirit of service and social responsibility pervades society, unemployment becomes a non-concept, because there is always something to do, and there is always somewhere to turn in time of need.

In Narayan's proposed socialist Gandhian grassroots communities there would, in principle, be very little overproduction. The problem is solved by redefining its terms; by taking its analysis to a deeper level where the very categories of economic analysis, which are the institutional framework of modernity, are reconsidered. This, we think, is what J.P. meant by his rather confusing slogan, "Total Revolution."[16] It does not mean destroying everything and starting over; quite to the contrary, it is a constructive process. It means reconsidering every aspect of life, and constantly striving to improve life in all its aspects. Overproduction, by definition, means the production of goods that are not sold, which remain unsold because there are no willing buyers for them. It is a problem that dissolves for the most part when selling ceases to be the be-all and end-all of production.

For classical economics, before it was, in Paul Sweezey's words, freed from "the tyranny of Say's Law" by John Maynard Keynes, overproduction meant that the producers had produced the wrong things.[17] They should have made something else. Instead of making what consumers wanted, they had blundered and made something consumers did not want, or made too much of something because although consumers did want that thing they did

---

16 Narayan explains his concept of total revolution in Selected Writings 369-371. "There are four aspects for the work for total revolution: struggle, construction, propaganda, and organization. In the present situation we should concentrate on the constructive aspect.... Total revolution is permanent revolution. It will always go on and keep changing both our personal and social lives." Selected Writings 369. The concept is analyzed by the Gandhian economist Romesh Diwan in "Total Revolution and Appropriate Technology," which is chapter 12 of Diwan and Lutz.

17 Paul Sweezey, "The First Quarter Century," Keynes' General Theory, ed. Robert Lekachman (New York: St Martin's Press, 1964) 305. Sweezey writes, "[H]is greatest achievements were freeing economics from the tyranny of Say's Law and exploding the myth of capitalism as a self-adjusting system which reconciles private and public interests."

not want that much of it. If the market were left alone, producers would of their own accord re-allocate resources in response to price signals. Overproduction would go away as supply and demand came into equilibrium.

Keynes made clear in theory what had always been clear in practice. The inability to sell something often meant not that people did not want it and need it, but that people did not have the money to buy it. Traditional thinking provides a solution to the problem encountered by someone who has produced something that cannot be sold, which is needed by people who cannot afford to buy it. Give it away. There is an example in the bagel shop where part of this is being written. Every evening at closing hour the unsold bagels are put into a large bag. A little old Hispanic lady in tennis shoes arrives and takes the bag of unsold bagels to the Salvation Army. She does not speak much English and does not have a car. But she does not need to know English to know that God wants her to move the bag from the bakery to the mission. God speaks to her in Spanish, as God speaks to the masses of India in their many languages and dialects. She does not need the aid of modern automotive technology, and she does not need wages, to accomplish her task. Whether the baker's act in giving the bagels, the lady's work in moving them, or the eating of the bagels by the homeless people at the shelter is reflected somewhere in books of account or economic statistics we do not know. We do know that it happens every day.

The Government of India, in several recent years, has had a larger problem. Instead of a sack of unsold bagels, the government has millions of metric tons of grains stored in warehouses.[18] The government is afraid to give it away, because the availability of so much free food would depress prices. Lower prices would depress production. They might throw India, which has slowly and laboriously achieved food self-sufficiency, back into dependence on imports. In some cases the depressed prices would throw farmers, who have been slowly and laboriously climbing out of poverty, back into poverty.

In Narayan's proposed socialist Gandhian grassroots communities, the Government of India's problem would not arise. There would be no accumulation of power, or of grain, at the Centre. Decision-making and grain surpluses would be widely dispersed in thousands of villages. What to do with the grain would be rationally decided by ethical people—no wonder they called J.P. a dreamer!—in ways that would keep going both ecologically sound production processes and fair distribution that met everyone's needs, including shipping grain to other areas that might have a shortage. Instead of the quasi-mechanics of supply curves intersecting demand curves, and instead of business people making decisions with what Keynes —optimistically!—called 'irrelevant accountancy' there would be what Cyert and March called 'satisficing.'[19]

---

18 "Fifty million tons of foodgrain are rotting while people cannot afford to buy food. Stocks of rice have increased from 13 million tons to 22 million tons, while wheat stocks have gone up from 8.72 million tons to 24.11 million tons between 1994-95 and 2000-01." Vandana Shiva in Sustainable Agriculture and Food Security, ed. Vandana Shiva and Gitanjali Bedi (Delhi: Sage, 2002) 460.
19 Richard Cyert and James March, A Behavioral Theory of the Firm (Oxford: Blackwell, 1992). The authors show that

'Satisficing' means that the decision-makers would find a satisfactory solution to the problems that would solve everybody's problems to some reasonable degree and leave nobody abandoned, rather than trying to maximize profit, and, indeed, rather than trying to maximize any single variable (except perhaps a composite variable that might be constructed as a measure of satisfying many different needs, interests, social goals and ecological goals).

The self-governing local community would solve the problem of how to distribute the unsold product without depressing production by talking about it together. The local community would be aware of the several interests that need to be synthesized. It would have the wisdom that comes from what Clifford Geertz calls 'local knowledge.'[20] As Gandhi wrote, when you "concentrate production in particular areas," then "you would have to go in a round-about way to regulate distribution, whereas if there is production and distribution both in the respective areas where things are required, it is automatically

---

business people in practice often do not follow the precepts of classical economic theory. Instead of maximizing returns, they 'satisfice' by finding solutions to problems that do not leave anyone terribly unhappy. More recently, Pierre Calame has argued in favour of a vector accountancy that facilitates pursuing not a single goal, but several goals at once. Pierre Calame, Essai sur l´oeconomie (Paris: Éditions Charles Leopold Mayer, 2009). It is important to add that the survival of the firm at all costs should not be a goal. Firms should cease to exist when they are no longer useful, taking suitable measures to protect the human persons who survive the death of the legal fiction that is the firm.

20 Clifford Geertz, Local Knowledge: Further Essays in Interpretive Anthropology (New York: Basic Books, 1985).

regulated, and there is less chance for fraud, none for speculation."[21] We think 'automatically' was not quite the word Gandhi was looking for, and that what he meant was matching production to distribution would be "easily regulated by the local people."

For the same reasons, the local communities would contribute in practice to solving a problem Keynes did not need to solve in theory, because the classical economists had already solved it in theory: how to avoid the technical blunder of making what is not needed instead of making what is needed. The modern world is beset by the constant failure to materialize the economists' utopia of competition among producers, no single one of whom is large enough to set prices, leading to a social maximum. The economists' utopia's failure to materialize leads to numerous attempts to correct the failings of in-practice-non-ideal markets through the technocratic workings of large governmental bureaucracies, and those of private and hybrid bureaucracies. Anyone can tell a dozen stories of such bureaucracies making the sorts of dumb mistakes which tend to show that the bureaucratic cure is worse than the market disease: like ordering the production of two hundred thousand rear wheels for bicycles, and only one hundred thousand front wheels for bicycles. Critics of the Soviet Union made lists of such mistakes, and pointed out that they would never have happened in a market economy. In India some of the dumb mistakes of large bureaucracies have been in mega-dam projects,

---

21 Gandhi, Economic Thought, ed. J.S. Mathur and A.K Mathur (Jaipur: Arihant Publishers, 1994) reprinted from Harijan (2 November 1934) 301.

as will be discussed further in the chapter on Vandana Shiva.

J.P.'s Gandhian proposals are anti-statist and anti-bureaucratic. They entrust decision-making to people who are on the front lines, on the ground, who know the exact details of each small problem. J.P.'s solution to the problem of how to organize social cooperation is in its own way similar to the market solution advocated by Adam Smith and his Austrian followers von Hayek and von Mises. J.P. offers another solution to the problems of allocation and re-allocation of resources that in orthodox economics price signals are supposed to solve. Smith's famous example was the pin. No high-level bureaucrat with a general overview of the whole problem knows how to make a pin. And yet pins get made, in production processes organized by markets, because each participant in the complex social process of pin making has learned from experience how to carry out her or his specialized task.

J.P.'s proposed version of participatory democracy corrects the insightful but exaggerated faith of Adam Smith in the market in a different way than statist bureaucracy—a way we will not attempt to summarize in a phrase because it has many facets, being, as J.P.'s admirer Bimal Prasad says, a synthesis of Marxist, Gandhian, and Western Democratic ideals. J.P.'s solution does not eliminate the possibility of overproduction altogether. Overproduction does not become a non-concept as unemployment does. Mistakes and injustices might still happen. But under J.P.'s proposed Gandhian decentralism there will be less overproduction because the conceptual frame of reference within which production is harmonized with meeting needs is more comprehensive. There are more options to choose from because the institutional framework is reconsidered. The simplified ethics of modernity is re-complicated again as flesh and blood people with all their foibles and failings work within institutional frameworks they are constantly re-inventing to wrest a decent living for all in the face of the physical realities of their bio-region. The difficult problem of distributing products fairly without depressing prices and discouraging producers remains. It is more likely to be solved because it is broken down into many specific local problems, in which more people's wisdom contributes to the search for solutions. It is addressed with the wisdom and the good will (Narayan's optimism again!) of people with on-the-ground detailed knowledge of each situation. Needless to say, also, when more people 'own' a solution because of having contributed to planning it, that solution is more likely to be implemented.

Gandhi, and Narayan following Gandhi, suggests an idea which provides in principle a solution to underconsumption and to poverty, even though neither expressed the idea explicitly, or at least not explicitly using exactly the words we shall use. The idea is unconditional love. The cause of poverty in the midst of plenty is not precisely in the ownership of the means of production. It is in conditionality. It is in the fact that owners only employ the means of production they own to produce things people need when it is profitable for them to do so. The condition is the check. Unless they can truck and barter, giving this which they have in exchange for that which they want, they sit on their property and exclude others from it as trespassers, rather than putting it to use. Nor is the cause of poverty precisely the lack of aggregate demand that keeps factories and workers idle. It is the condition that is the fundamental check. Demand only counts as effective demand when people have money to pay, because the condition without which providers will not provide them with what they need is that they must give money in exchange. The fundamental problem is neither at the level of production relations nor at the level of circulation relations, but at the level of the constitutive rules of modern society. Workers do not work, and owners do not invest, unless there is compliance with the condition that they get money for their work, or for their granting permission to use their property.

Although Gandhi never spoke of 'eliminating conditionality,' he came close, and he clearly implied the idea. He wrote, for example:

The worker will not only be spinning regularly, but will be working for his bread with the adze or the spade or the last, as the case may be. All his hours minus the eight hours of sleep and rest will be fully occupied with some work. He will have no time to waste. He will allow himself no idleness and allow others none. His life will be a constant lesson to his neighbours in ceaseless and joy-giving industry. Bodily sustenance should come from bodily labour, and intellectual labour is necessary for the culture of the mind. Division of labour there will necessarily be, but it will be a division into various species of bodily labour and not a division into intellectual labour to be confined to another class. Our compulsory or voluntary idleness has to go. If it does not go, no panacea will be of any avail, and semi-starvation will remain the eternal problem that it is. He who eats two grains must produce four. Unless the law is accepted as universal, no amount of reduction in population would serve to solve the problem. If the law is accepted and observed, we have room enough to accommodate millions more to come.[22]

In one of many passages where Gandhi assured his readers that he was not against technology, just in favour of what J.P.'s friend E.F. Schumacher later came to call intermediate or appropriate technology, Gandhi wrote:

... I am socialist enough to say such factories [one for making Singer sewing machines] should be nationalised, or State-controlled. They ought only to be working under the most attractive and ideal conditions, not for profit, but for the benefit of humanity, love taking the place of greed as a motive. It is an alteration in the conditions of labour that I want. This mad rush for wealth must cease, and the labourer must be assured, not only of a living wage, but a daily task that is not a mere drudgery. The machine will, under these conditions, be as much a help to man working it as to the state, or to the man who owns it. The present mad rush will cease and the labourer will work (as I have said) under attractive and ideal conditions. This is but one of the exceptions [to being against machinery] I have in mind. The sewing machine has love at its back. The individual is the one supreme consideration. The saving of labour of the individual should be the object,

---

22 Gandhi in Mathur and Mathur 291, reprinted from Harijan (31 August 1934) 229.

and honest humanitarian considerations, and not greed, the motive.[23]

If all the people on earth, freed from the check of conditionality, made their best effort to utilize their talent and treasure for the common good, then there would be no poverty, except insofar as nature made poverty inevitable, and except insofar as lack of knowledge on how best to use resources produced mistakes. This hypothetical state, characterized by much more good will than there is now, need not be one in which there would be no markets. Even the pure in heart whose only desires are to serve God, neighbour, and biosphere (not to mention the less pure in heart who are capable of the relative non-violence, decency, and efficiency elicited by market transactions, but not of altruism) may be grateful for price signals telling them what is wanted when, where, and how much. This hypothetical state of good will and accurate knowledge, which we will imagine as employing accountable markets to do the things markets are good at, sets a standard by which less desirable states can be measured. There would be no poverty if everyone did the right thing. There would be less poverty if more people did the right thing. These things would be true as long as people did the right things, i.e., those things that meet human needs and preserve the environment, regardless of what motives they might have for doing them, and regardless of what beliefs they might hold. Unconditional service to others is a perfect standard relevant to an imperfect world.

Gandhi did not use the language of 'unconditional' and 'conditional.' He wrote sometimes of the law of dharma,

---

23 Gandhi in Mathur and Mathur 475-476, reprinted from Young India (13 November 1924) 378, interpolations added.

sometimes of the law of love, and sometimes of the law of non-violence, or ahimsa. The three are synonyms in that they all prescribe unselfishly using right means to attain right ends. 'Dharma' has the drawback that it is identified with tradition. It needs to be corrected with reminders that duty today might not be the same as duty yesterday, and even that duty yesterday might have been wrong even then but the people back then, or some of them, did not know it. 'Love' has the drawback that it sounds sentimental. It needs to be corrected with reminders that one ought to do the right thing whether or not one feels like it. 'Non-violence' has the drawback that it brings to mind as its supposed opposite physical and emotional violence, more than what Johan Galtung christened structural violence, such as the violence of the jurisprudence that excludes millions from the benefits of property ownership, and the violence of economic institutions that leave in penury whoever has no marketable commodity to sell.

J.P.'s non-violent campaigns of the 1970s featured the slogan 'total revolution.' That slogan tended to be identified in the public mind with J.P.'s call for the resignation of the government of Bihar, his native state, and with the larger project of bringing down the government of Prime Minister Indira Gandhi. But we think 'total revolution' is better understood as a consistent effort to put into practice Gandhian ideals, as interpreted and modified by J.P. The revolution had to be 'total,' because it affected everything, both ends and means, and because it would never be over. Existing institutions will always be judged as failures in the light of what in principle they could be.

J.P. came to believe that social transformation could not be achieved by government action, certainly not by the actions of central governments in a country as vast as India. In his Marxist days he had written that the key to socialism was state power. Once in control of the police and the army, the socialists could change the economy by legislation and by coercion. Later, as a Gandhian, he came to believe that social change had to begin at the grassroots, or as his friend Minoo Masani said, at the rice-roots. There had to be a transformation of civil society, by civil society, for civil society. J.P. resigned from the socialist party he had founded, and joined Vinoba Bhave's sarvodaya movement. (He could not join Gandhi because Gandhi was already dead by the time Narayan was finally won over by his ideas.) J.P. had several opportunities to become Prime Minister of India. He declined them each time. He declined not from personal humility but from theoretical consistency. He believed that governments could not bring about the needed changes. Sarvodaya could. However, in his last years he had some third thoughts, tending to see the need for complementary government action and grassroots work.

As it turned out, the Bhoodan sarvodaya movement, led by Vinoba Bhave and followed by Jayaprakash Narayan, succeeded to a limited extent, but it did not transform the system.[24] It collided with what is called economic reality. Its main effort was to facilitate the self-organization of Gandhian villages on donated land. Landlords pledged in public meetings to donate some of their land, but when it came time to hand it over many of them balked and refused to sign the transfer deeds. Gandhi himself

---

24 On the accomplishments of Bhoodan, see T.K.N. Unnithan, Gandhi and Free India (Groningen, Holland: J.B. Wolters, 1956) 127-131.

had collided with another aspect of economic reality in his efforts to promote the spinning of khadi cloth in the 1930s. No matter how hard he tried to secure a living wage for the spinners, he could not succeed because the people buying the cloth were themselves living at so low a level that they could not pay enough—even if they wanted to—to provide a living wage for the spinners.

If the thesis of this book is correct, then Gandhi, if we imagine him smiling down from heaven on those of us still struggling on this earth, can still speak to us with the counterfactual luxury of saying that the world would be better if his philosophy were more widely practiced. In picturing him smiling down at us, urging us to follow his lead, we do not picture him as trying to justify everything he said, wrote, or did, which in any event he could not do because he contradicted himself so often. We do not picture him as proposing another school of economics. Rather, he advocated a traditional ethical framework by whose standards the work of economists of all schools can be evaluated. His ethical framework has not been tested and disproved just because some experiments failed. The limited success of the Bhoodan sarvodaya movement that J.P. joined, need not lead one to see "the JP movement as yet another form of Indian populism, and his ideas as a subspecies of that latter-day Gandhism which promises much, but delivers little or nothing—except a constantly reiterated and impotent moral outrage at the many iniquities of modern India."[25] Instead, one can take

---

25 David Selbourne, "A Political Morality Re-examined," In Theory and in Practice: Essays on the Politics of Jayaprakash Narayan, ed. David Selbourne (Delhi: Oxford University Press, 1985) 181. The phrase quoted expresses an attitude the author

the failures of Gandhism so far as evidence that both it and the economic realities with which it has collided require further examination.

The next chapter will compare Gandhian thinking to revolutionary socialism, as it is advocated in the writings of Tariq Ali. Ali is a contemporary intellectual who was born in India and spent his childhood there, although the city he came from later became part of Pakistan.

* * *

---

attributes to his former self, of which he later repented.

CHAPTER 4

TARIQ ALI

"Gandhi was not so much a peasant as a fox."
—Tariq Ali

There are at least two ways to think about achieving a classless society.

(In speaking of two ways to 'achieve' a classless society we do not claim to have an airtight case that a one hundred percent classless society would be desirable, although we are inclined to think it would be. We do assume that achieving a society much more nearly classless than those that prevail today is a goal worth striving for. It is not the only goal worth striving for, and there is some danger that in striving for a classless society one may contribute to evils as great as or greater than those of a class-divided society. We beg the reader to understand that when we speak below in shorthand of 'classless society' as a goal we always do so with these reservations.)

One way to think about achieving a classless society would be to think in terms of starting with a class-divided society in which members of an upper class own the means of production. No distinction need be made whether those means of production are agricultural, industrial, knowledge-based, or something else. The upper class lives from profits, interest, rents, and other forms of income from property.[1] The members of a lower class are compelled to live by selling their labour power, or if they are unable to sell their labour power, or unwilling to do so on the terms offered, they live by crime, begging, or prostitution.

This two-class model of a class-divided society was regarded by Marx, and has been regarded by most people who have employed it since, as a simplification useful for analytic purposes. It is not intended to reflect the historical complexities of class relationships at any given time and place.

Starting with such a conception, a way to achieve a classless society would be for the workers to take power, motivated by their collective self-interest. Here it does no harm to identify the lower class, the one that does not own the means of production, with the workers, provided that it is remembered that some members of the lower class are marginal. The marginal members of the lower class are called 'workers' even though they do not work, or do not work regularly. (We retain the term 'marginal' because of its connotation of exclusion from the benefits of organized society. But we acknowledge the validity of Paulo Freire's objection to the use of the term. Freire points out that the homeless, the unemployed, the

---

1 These three are Marx's 'holy trinity' which he conceived as portions of the surplus value extracted from labour. Karl Marx, Capital, vol. 3 (New York: International Publishers, 1970). In the model here assumed it is not necessary to assume that the ultimate source of property income is exploited labour; it could also be a rent from property, where property is itself conceived as itself a factor of production that generates value.

rejected, the people who eke by on seasonal and irregular work, are in an important sense not marginal to the present order of society. In fact, their existence is a central and essential consequence of the dominant institutional framework.[2])

When the workers take power, they will use their power to take away from the ruling class its ownership of the means of production. This is a tautology. The reason why the upper class is a ruling class is that it owns the means of production. Taking their power and taking their property is the same thing. This does not mean, by the way, taking houses and barber shops. It is the big stuff that counts. The effect of the workers seizing the means of production will be to make everyone a worker, or everyone an owner, depending on how one looks at it: a classless society.

The workers, motivated by collective self-interest, would do three good things in the classless society they would establish. They would abolish an inherently unjust division, the division of society by accident of birth into haves and have-nots. They would make society's institutions for producing and distributing goods and services function to meet their needs, which would mean meeting everyone's needs, because everyone would be a worker. In order better to meet needs, they would fully develop the forces of production.

Karl Marx can be read as emphasizing the last of these three. He defines capitalism as a form of society whose

---

[2] Paulo Freire, Pedagogy of the Oppressed (New York: Continuum, 1975). We will also sometimes use 'workers' to mean 'people,' as the term 'people' (or 'popular class[es]') is sometimes used to refer collectively to workers, peasants, and whoever else is conceived as not in the ruling class.

wealth appears as a vast collection of commodities, that is to say, of goods produced for sale. Socialism would be a form of society where goods would be produced for use. There would be no unemployed people. No resources would be withheld from production just because their owners think they can make more money waiting for the price to rise than by putting them to use. No patents would be acquired for the purpose of preventing others from working them. The only limit put on the development of the forces of production would be the exhaustion of human needs and wants, except perhaps some limits set by a desire to preserve the environment for future generations. Checks on production imposed by lack of consumer purchasing power would cease to be obstacles. Hence the classless society would also be the one capable of the most rapid and complete development.

Advocates of capitalism argue the contrary.[3] They say a class-divided society is required for development. There must be an upper class which is not living hand to mouth, so that somebody will be able to save. Without saving, no investment. Without investment, no development.

---

3   W.W. Rostow, Stages of Economic Growth (Cambridge: Cambridge University Press, 1960); Albert O. Hirschman, The Strategy of Economic Development (New Haven: Yale University Press, 1992); Simon Kuznets, Growth, Population, and Income Distribution (New York: Norton, 1979). Amritananda Das writes, "Since the strategy involves a rapid rise in monetary savings, the conclusion is inevitable that (as workers save a smaller portion of their incomes than capitalists) accelerated accumulation of capital needs a shift of the income distribution away from workers to capitalists." Amritananda Das, Foundations of Gandhian Economics (New York: St Martin's Press / Bombay: Allied Publishers, 1979) 6.

The purpose of investment is to take out more money than was put in; in other words capital accumulation. Given an undeveloped and therefore poor society, the lower class must work for low wages, since otherwise there could be no upper class with enough revenue to accumulate capital. (This last point is not usually made in precisely these terms. Instead, since owners of the means of production can usually pass on wage increases to consumers as higher prices, and since they can also usually shut down their operation and establish a business elsewhere, the argument for low wages takes different forms. Wage increases are inflationary. Wage increases make the nation less attractive to mobile capital.)

There is a second way to think about achieving a classless society.

One might think in terms of starting with a class-divided society in which there is an upper class, a middle class, and a lower class. The middle class grows by whittling away at the privileges of the upper class, both through voluntary whittling accepted by members of the upper class who choose to be socially responsible, and through involuntary whittling by legislation that restricts the statutory prerogatives of the upper class to own many things and to do as they please with them. More people come to enjoy the benefits of property ownership as the concentration of wealth decreases. Meanwhile, the marginal members of the lower classes—the impecunious felons, the addicts, the drifters, the chronically unemployed, the mentally ill, the disabled and the unskilled—are progressively integrated into the disciplines and benefits of organized social life. Working people progressively acquire the status of stakeholders in their particular firms and in the wealth of society as a whole. Workers are made secure by pensions and by health care benefits, and made powerful by invitations to participate in lifelong education and in governance at every level. When there is no more upper class and no more lower class, everyone will be middle class: a classless society.

Introducing the idea that the middle class, instead of or in addition to the working class, might be the universal class which will usher in the classless society, involves some conceptual shifts away from the criterion used in the two-class model of society stated above. It will be recalled that the criterion for class membership in that model was owning or not owning the means of production.

It is awkward to use the ownership criterion to adjust the two-class model to provide a conceptual slot for a third class. The best one can do is to separate out a part of the owning class as petit bourgeois. They are the ones who own means of production, but only small ones. In place of the neat binary disjunction, owns or does not own means of production, there is a quantitative continuum of the amount of means of production owned, in which at some cut-off point a person's assets become too small to make that person a member of the haute bourgeoisie and that person is defined as a member of the petite bourgeoisie. The question of motivation to push for social change is also awkward. The very definition of the proletariat as not owning the means of production implies that its members are dispossessed, frustrated, unsatisfied. They are defined as people who have a motive for changing the status quo. But the middle class, defined according to the ownership criterion as people who own something but not much, can be expected to be at least partly satisfied with the status quo. The growth of the middle class might be seen, as often it has been seen, as an insurance policy for capitalism, assuring that socialism will never come about because fewer people will find it to be in their interest to bring it about. For this second way to a classless society, it remains to ask why and whether anyone would want to whittle away at the privileges of the upper class, or incorporate marginal people into the benefits of society, and why anyone, except for the working class itself, would promote the security and the empowerment of the working class.

Mainstream social science goes part way toward showing what it might mean to define a middle class. Some speak of socio-economic status, SES, as a surrogate for class. Educational attainment as well as income and wealth are counted. Apart from SES, many studies measure quantitatively and/or depict ethnographically a variety of characteristics that can plausibly be called markers of class.[4] Such studies counter any tendency there might

---

4 Thomas J. Fararo and Kaiji Koska, Generating Images of Stratification (Boston: Kluwer Academic Publishers, 2003); Gordon Marshall, Repositioning Class: Social Inequality in Industrial Societies (Thousand Oaks: Sage Publications, 1997); Mel Bartley, Health Inequality: An Introduction to Theories, Concepts, and Methods (Cambridge UK: Polity Press, 2004). Apart from the two ways to a classless society mentioned here, but still using its simple concepts, one might imagine a society where machines did all or most of the work, and all the people shared ownership of the machines. In this case it would be the upper class that would be the universal class, ushering in a classless society where everyone's income was rent, interest, and profit. J.P. Narayan thought along such lines at one point,

have been to privilege ownership of the means of production as the single criterion for mapping social class. They show that whatever criterion one uses there are people in the middle who are not at either end.[5]

If the two-class model is as simple and clear as anything gets in social science, and if empirical research shows social reality to be complex and confusing, a middle class model might seek to precipitate back out of the world's complexity and confusion (without losing the insights of the two class model) another criterion which is (relatively speaking) simple and clear. This can be done by associating the idea of 'middle class' with the related idea of 'middle-class values.'

In eighteenth century England there was a middle class (or at least a fragment of a class large enough to produce a literature) that was self-defined by its values. They were the Whigs. Their claim to be the rightful governing class of England was founded on self-ascribed virtue. The boundaries which separated the middle class from the allegedly dissolute aristocracy and the allegedly dissolute masses were moral boundaries. In that environment the

---

as did Fourier and Saint Simon.

5 The point here is that empirical studies show that there are ample reasons for having conceptual categories to put people in whose scores are moderate on class measures. It should also be mentioned that there are in some cases fewer and fewer people to put in those categories. Neoliberalism has brought with it a dramatic decline of middle class status in many countries. See Branko Milanovic, Decomposing World Income Distribution: Does the World Have a Middle Class? (Washington DC: World Bank, 2001); Larissa Lomnitz and Ana Melnick, Chile's Middle Class: A Struggle for Survival in the Face of Neoliberalism (Boulder: L. Rienner, 1991).

Methodist movement was one that sought to uplift the working class into the middle class by teaching a method for acquiring virtue, and by providing a faith community of brethren who upbraided each other when someone backslid. In sociology the locus classicus for associating a middle class with adherence to norms is the work of Emile Durkheim. He claimed that his empirical studies showed that anomie was produced by the easy life of the upper classes and by the hard life of the lower classes, as compared and contrasted with the life of the solid middle.

What 'middle-class values' means in the many cultures and globalized hybrids of today is a long story we are not prepared to tell.[6] Let it be enough to assert that there are good historical and sociological reasons for including conformity to conventional norms in the mix of indicators used to define who is in what class. Who is in a middle class depends only partly on property ownership.

If it be granted that a class can be identified by a set of socio-economic indicators that includes looking for a relative absence of Durkheimian normlessness, then it still remains to ask whether such a class can have any motivation to change the status quo. Indeed, on a worst case scenario the middle class is the class from which the fascists are recruited who put down constructive change with a hatred and a bigotry that exceed those of the principal beneficiaries of the status quo, the upper class. An important part of this remaining question asks whether an ethical appeal that tries to bring out the best in existing

---

6 See Howard Richards, "Middle Class Values," Gandhi Marg 24/4 (Jan-March 2003) 389-400; and Howard Richards and Joanna Swanger, The Dilemmas of Social Democracies (Lanham, MD: Lexington Press, 2008) ch. 13.

conventional norms and to raise them to a higher ethical level can be a dynamic force which changes the course of history. Enter Gandhi.

Tariq Ali is a firm advocate of the first of the two ways here mentioned to think about achieving a classless society. He belongs to a revolutionary socialist subset of those who propose to achieve a classless society through working class power. He holds rather specific political beliefs mainly associated with the tradition founded by Leon Trotsky. The revolution will come through the revolutionary action of the working class. That class will learn the necessity of revolution from its own experience of class struggle. The end of the desired process must be democratic because without democracy the workers would have no power. It must be a deeper democracy than the familiar bourgeois representative democracies, including besides parliaments and parties also strong independent trade unions and works councils in which the workers themselves direct the operations of the enterprises.

Ali has given a consistent series of explanations of why revolutionary mass action by the working class so far has almost always failed. The mass action of students and workers in France in early 1968 might have overthrown the system if a collaborationist Communist Party had not struck a deal with President De Gaulle in which capitalism was allowed to survive in return for increased wages and benefits.[7] Similarly, the socialist government of Salvador Allende in Chile might have survived in 1973 if Allende had accepted the far left's demand to arm the

---

7   Tariq Ali, 1968 and After: Inside the Revolution (London: Blond and Briggs, 1978) 18-19, and generally 10-31. (Hereafter Inside the Revolution).

masses and had used his electoral victory to construct organs of direct people power in the factories, in the farms, and in the neighbourhoods.[8] Earlier, in late 1968, on the other side of the Iron Curtain, the democratization of Czechoslovakia might have survived if President Dubcek had called for mass revolutionary action by the working class, instead of foolishly believing that he could compromise with the Russians. Ali remarks that Allende and Dubcek faced essentially the same choice, namely whether to appeal to the masses to fight back.[9] In the summer of 1975 the Portuguese revolution failed because the far left failed to win over the masses to the side of revolution, while the Communists, as usual, did not trust the masses, and the Socialists, under Mario Soares, carried out what was in effect a campaign against socialism in the name of democracy.[10] In Britain the working classes are ready for revolutionary socialism, but they are betrayed by a so-called 'Labour' Party which is intent on proving to the ruling class that it can keep the workers in check better than the Tories.[11] In Iraq and Syria the Ba'athist Party had the potential to be a revolutionary socialist party, but it degenerated in both countries into the tool of a few power-seeking families and cliques.[12] The continuing inability of the Arab world to resist foreign capitalist domination is a series of self-inflicted wounds,

---

8   Ali, Inside the Revolution 66-67.
9   Ali, Inside the Revolution 79.
10 Ali, Inside the Revolution 109-10.
11 Ali, Inside the Revolution 139-82. See also Tariq Ali, The Coming British Revolution (London: Cape, 1972).
12 Tariq Ali, Bush in Babylon: The Recolonisation of Iraq (London: Verso, 2003) 103-12.

brought about by its internal divisions. Tariq Ali's views on all of the above are shaped by his readings of Leon Trotsky's and Isaac Deutscher's accounts of the betrayal of the Russian Revolution and the Stalinization of Russia.[13]

The pattern is similar in Tariq Ali's works of historical fiction. Several of them concern the fall of Islamic civilization in Spain, and Sala-al-Din's success in driving the Christian crusaders from Jerusalem in 1186. Force is the ultimate arbiter. Unity is the key to having superior force. The victories of the Christian barbarians are blamed on divisions among the Muslims. The worst enemies of the cause of the Believers are the self-seekers who collaborate for gain with the enemy. Sala-al-Din spent most of his career as sultan fighting the collaborationists among his own people, always with the ultimate purpose, which near the end of the book he achieves, of retaking Jerusalem.[14]

Fitting the pattern, according to Ali India might have gone socialist if it had not been for Gandhi. It was Gandhi who, more than anyone else dissuaded Nehru from leading a frankly socialist independence movement when the direction of the movement was decisively shaped between 1933 and 1936. Gandhi and Sardar Patel persuaded rebellious elements within the military to surrender at a point where revolution might have been possible in 1946.[15] It was Gandhi whom the big business backers of the

---

13 See especially Leon Trotsky, The Revolution Betrayed (New York: Merit Publishers, 1965); and Isaac Deutscher, The Unfinished Revolution: Russia 1917-1967 (New York: Oxford University Press, 1971).
14 Tariq Ali, The Book of Saladin (London: Verso, 1998).
15 Tariq Ali, The Nehrus and the Gandhis: An Indian Dynasty (London: Chatto & Windus, 1985) 50-56, 72.

Congress relied on to tame Nehru.[16] Their backing sealed the class character of the Congress.

Jawaharlal Nehru could never understand why Gandhi unilaterally called off the non-violent civil disobedience campaign for the independence of India in 1922 after an incident in the village of Chauri Chaura in which an enraged crowd set fire to a police station, burning to death the policemen inside. He did not understand why the acts of an excited mob in a remote village should put an end to the nation's struggle for freedom. Ali offers an explanation. Chauri Chaura was a pretext. The real reason for calling off the movement was that throughout India the peasants and workers were making class demands. The movement was cancelled to prevent a socialist revolution.[17]

Ali also has an explanation for a puzzle discussed in Chapter 2: why Gandhi, who was so religious, promoted the career of Nehru, who was so irreligious. Ali's explanation is that by making Nehru the President of the Congress, Gandhi could better maintain some control over him, and thus prevent him from leading revolutionary mass action.[18]

Within Tariq Ali's worldview, Gandhi can only be understood as a spoiler. To portray Gandhi to Ali as a messenger who embodies a message which, if understood, would make a good society possible, it would be necessary not only to complete the historical record by bringing into evidence other things Gandhi said and did, but to change Ali's worldview. Notoriously, a person's

---

16 Ali, Dynasty 85.
17 Ali, Dynasty 28.
18 Ali, Dynasty 43.

worldview is formed by the thoughts and experiences of a lifetime. Rather than try to engineer a quick conversion, we think it better to offer a contribution to a dialogue of worldviews in which alternate ways of viewing the same facts enter into conversation with one another. No one will convince anyone quickly.

Like Leon Trotsky, in the same country and nearly in the same time period, Gandhi's mentor Leo Tolstoy was made sick at heart by the terrible suffering of the working classes, and by their terrible repression at the hands of the upper classes and the state. Like Tariq Ali, Tolstoy was an educated scion of a landed aristocratic family who became a partisan of the dispossessed. His analysis of the causes of oppression, and his strategy for social change, were somewhat different.

Tolstoy recounts his experience conversing with soldiers and officers on a troop train.[19] They were on their way to kill and torture poor peasants accused of rebellion. They were ordinary people who thought they were doing their duty. They were ordinary people who were deaf to the voice of conscience. They were ordinary people who did not think clearly. They were mostly members of the working class who were being utilized to terrorize fellow members of their own class, motivated not so much by an opportunity to vent savage instincts as by blind obedience to conventional authority.

On Tolstoy's analysis (as on Marx's), the upper classes like to believe that their privileges result from voluntary

---

19 Leo Tolstoy, "The Kingdom of God is Within You," The Kingdom of God and Peace Essays, The World's Classics (London: Oxford University Press, 1951, first published 1893) 445:334-372.

agreements and from economic laws, while the real cause of privileges of the upper class, and of the corresponding oppression of the working class, is violence.[20] Tolstoy was himself born into a military caste, whose raison d'être was conquest and the defence of conquests made by one's ancestors. Like the characters in Tariq Ali's historical novels, Tolstoy was born into a world where social structure was created by brute force, reinforced by lies.

The solution to the problem follows from the analysis of its causes. Truth and non-violence.[21] Truth will unite the oppressed.[22] Truth will bring the oppressors face to face with the reality of what they are doing. Ruling out violence as a legitimate way to resolve conflicts will—and no other way will—change social structures. Refusing to obey orders when they are contrary to conscience will dissolve the principal cause of the oppression of the poor.

Tariq Ali's worldview is not as different from Tolstoy's as it might first appear to be. Ali is not in general an advocate of violence. The revolutionary action he advocates

---

20   Tolstoy 343-344.
21   Gandhi expressed his agreement with Tolstoy when he wrote, "Those who seek to destroy men rather than their manners adopt the latter and become worse than those they destroy under the mistaken belief that the manners will die with the men. They do not know the root of the evil." Young India (17 March 1927), reprinted in Gandhi, Economics of Khadi (Ahmedabad: Navajivan Press, 1941) 206.
22   Tolstoy 410. "The miseries of men are due to their discord. And their discord results from their not following the truth which is one, but falsehood which is legion. The only means by which men can be united is by union in the truth. And therefore the more sincerely men seek the truth the more nearly they will approach to union."

is mostly mass demonstrations, general strikes, electoral campaigns, education, the relatively peaceful takeover of factories and other buildings, and the building of alternative institutions that create the new society in the shell of the old. Where other means are open, war is not the people's means of struggle. War is regularly forced upon the workers by a ruling class that regularly resorts to military violence when it is unable to retain power by legitimate means. When civil war comes, Ali wants the preponderance of military force to be on the side of the workers, not on the side of reaction.

Like Tolstoy, Ali believes that truth will unite the oppressed and unmask the ideologies of oppression. He does not believe that the truth was finally revealed by Marx, so as to render superfluous the critical search for truth by independent scientists and scholars after the revolution. He agrees (in this respect) with David Hume, John Stuart Mill, and Karl Popper that truth is always tentative, and that the best guarantee of anyone's claim that a theory is true is the freedom of everyone else to refute it if they can. In Ali's vision of a democratic socialist society, freedom of speech, freedom of the press, and other liberal freedoms are preserved and deepened, without the tyranny of money over the media, politics and the academy that currently makes a mockery of liberal values.

For Tolstoy, truth (not all truth, but truth) is found in the message of Jesus Christ, regarded not as a set of mystical beliefs but as a practical guide to life.[23] Similarly, Gandhi found truth in his social gospel version of Hindu-

---

23 See, for example, Tolstoy 435-436. The subtitle of the essay is "Christianity not as a mystical doctrine but as a new understanding of life."

ism and in what might be called his ecumenical spirituality. Ali will have none of this. Ali complains that in India secularism has come to mean accepting all religions when it ought to mean accepting no religion.

Tolstoy's worldview suggests an alternative reading of Tariq Ali's basic texts, Leon Trotsky's The Revolution Betrayed and Isaac Deutscher's The Unfinished Revolution. The Stalinization of Russia can be read as a story about hypocrisy and violence. It can be claimed that the recipe for the antidote to the Stalins of the world, slow but more certain than any other, is truth, non-violence, and conscientious disobedience.

Tolstoy's analysis of the causes of social oppression might have been true even if it were the case that all appeals to conscience are fruitless. It could be that social structure has always been determined by violence and lies and always will be. The validity of Tolstoy's analysis does not depend on whether he is able to offer a hopeful alternative. On the other hand, Tolstoy's proposed solution, to live a life of truth and non-violence as a contribution to improving society, requires the premise that ethics can have some efficacy as a cause of historical change.

In 1900 Tolstoy's concept of ethical politics could have been regarded as a speculative theory, although even then historical research would have disclosed numerous precedents for it.[24] After Gandhi put Tolstoy's principles into practice in South Africa in 1910-14, it became a tested theory. It and variants more or less akin to it have been tested since then in enough places at enough times that

---

24 For accounts of pre-Tolstoyan anticipations of Tolstoy's philosophy see Sanderson Beck, Guides to Peace and Justice (Ojai, California: World Peace Communications, 2003).

the reports of them fill many volumes. In Russia, when the Soviet dictatorship finally fell in 1989, it was more because of Tolstoy than because of Trotsky.

There is therefore not any doubt at this point in history that rational appeals, ethical appeals, and non-violent methods in general can have important impacts on historical events, including influencing major institutional changes. In the light of the proven power of non-violence, we need to take another look at the series of failures to achieve democratic socialism by the revolutionary action of the masses that Tariq Ali has analyzed. We shall add to this reconsideration failures to build social democracy and responsible capitalism, which might have resulted, if they had continued long enough, in what we have called achieving a classless society by the second way. If ethics works, then why is the world today awash in neoliberalism and irresponsible globalization?

The tendency of Tariq Ali's explanations, some of which were mentioned above, is to say that socialism fails because the workers are let down by their leaders. This is not just a trend in the data that Ali has discerned in the data by the logic of induction. The structure of modern society, what Karl Popper calls its situational logic, plus the conceptual lenses Ali uses to view modern society, create a Gestalt in which failure of revolution caused by failure of leadership is a recurrent pattern. It is all about power. Capital has more power. Labour has less power. For the workers to have more power, they would have to unite in revolutionary action. They do not do so (on Ali's view) because at crucial moments their leaders make the wrong choices.

But Gandhians have a different worldview. If they are right, then it is not all about power, or at least not all about power narrowly conceived. Truth and non-violence also can change society. The dismal historical record, however, is that a classless society is not coming about either by the first way, by the second way, or by any other way. The revolutionary socialists fail, either because they do not bring off the revolution at all or because when they do bring it off the revolution does not lead to the desired free and democratic classless society. The Gandhians also fail. The social democrats have either failed or have become so indistinguishable from conservatives that their success brings a classless society no closer. We are not against consoling oneself by taking note of the good news and genuine social progress that can be found here and there in the history of the twentieth century and in what has so far transpired of history of the twenty-first, but we do think that more explanation of failure is needed. The factors emphasized by Ali and by Tolstoy go some distance toward explaining the phenomena observed, but they do not fully explain the persistence and intensification of class divisions.

High on the list of additions needed to the roster of obstacles to making a transition to a classless society one must place what might be called the functional requirements of the system. As already mentioned, advocates of capitalism point out that somebody has to save and invest. Inflation must be kept in check. The international competitive position of the nation must not be eroded by provoking capital flight, or by pricing exports above what foreign buyers are willing to pay.

The systemic imperatives imposed by the functional requirements of a modern society are little changed by changing the ownership of the means of production. Tariq Ali writes concerning the negotiations between Czech technocrats and Russia in the 1968 crisis: "The technocrats and Moscow tended to agree on one aspect of the economy: they both saw the choice (though not in these words) as being between bureaucratic centralisation or the 'market economy.' They deliberately ignored the third and Marxist choice, namely the transferring of all power to a nationally elected congress of workers' councils, which would make the final decisions regarding planning and investments."[25] Ali explains that the councils would consider the advice of professional economists, and then make the final decisions. There is no doubt, however, that the professional economists would have advised that somehow there had to be saving and investment, that inflation had to be kept under control, and international competitiveness maintained. They would have pointed out that the worker-controlled factories in Yugoslavia went into debt and failed to keep costs low enough and sales high enough to turn a profit, just like capitalist firms.

The need to comply with the functional requirements of the system remains, even when ownership changes hands, because the system is a circulation system, not just a production system. But this does not mean that the systemic imperatives of circulation are neutral. Far from it. Nothing triggers capital flight so much as a threat of nationalization. With a few exceptions, the global market acts as a homeostatic mechanism that reacts negatively to

---

25 Ali, Inside the Revolution 42.

transfers of wealth from the rich to the poor, thus restoring society to its normal practice of transferring wealth from the poor to the rich. Efforts to do without the market, and to coordinate the overall economic processes of a society through political control of the system, trigger another threat, that of marching down what Friedrich von Hayek called the road to serfdom.[26]

In practice, a socialist-leaning government which has not lost its sincerity, which has not given up and decided to devote itself only to managing capitalism, a government which still wishes to find ways to move an inch or two toward a classless society, is hemmed in by the need to comply day by day with the functional requirements of the system. Globalization narrows the options even more, as national governments find that decisions are out of their hands. Globalization appears to be irreversible, and the band of options open to peoples and governments appears to consist of ways to adjust to it, not of ways to

---

26 Friedrich von Hayek and another distinguished Austrian economist, Ludwig von Mises, have shown that the tendency to lose political freedoms when market economies are replaced by planned economies is a threat inherent in the logic of the situation Although there may be ways to avert and solve the problem, it cannot be averted or solved simply by weeding out psychotic personalities like Stalin and Hitler, or simply by putting in charge of the process people like Tariq Ali who believe in freedom. See Ludwig von Mises, Socialism: An Economic and Sociological Analysis (New Haven: Yale University Press, 1951); Friedrich von Hayek, The Constitution of Liberty (Chicago: Regnery, 1972); Friedrich von Hayek, Economic Freedom and Representative Government (London: Institute of Economic Affairs, 1973); Friedrich von Hayek, The Road to Serfdom (Chicago: University of Chicago Press, 1944).

transform it. Their hands are tied by international markets, by the World Trade Organization (WTO), and by the International Monetary Fund (IMF). Such systemic constraints may be overshadowed in the public mind by more spectacular obstacles to social change, like military intervention by the United States, but they are very real.

A conclusion we want to draw is this: although there is little progress so far in building a world where peace and justice would be possible, that does not prove that great progress is impossible, nor does it prove that the methods for changing society already invented will never work. They might still work, if better ways could be found to change the systemic imperatives imposed by the functional requirements of the system.

In this context, the context of looking for what Paulo Freire called the 'untested feasibilities,' the context of looking for feasible ways to change the homeostatic dynamic of a socially created but anti-social reality, the philosophy of Gandhi again becomes a valuable resource. Yes, he showed in practice that ethical action could change history. Yet he also showed, as is less known and less understood, the arbitrary and ethnocentric character of the constitutive rules of modern economic society. In Gandhi's worldview, globalization and neoliberalism are not inevitable because the forces that drive them are not inevitable. He thought outside the normative framework that governs homo economicus. He not only thought outside it, he deliberately lived outside it. For this reason his way of thinking and acting inspires those influenced by him today to think outside the box. In our times, when the options appear to be narrowing day by day, the example given by the life of Mohandas K. Gandhi widens the options. Yes, in some ways he was a wacky guy. As a young man he once tried living on a diet of peanuts and lemon juice. As an old man he went through a phase of wanting to sleep naked near young girls just to prove to himself that he had no sexual desire.[27] His life, he said in his Autobiography, consisted of nothing but his experiments with truth. Humanity needs more experimenters like him, peanuts and all.

In the next chapter we will write about Vandana Shiva, a wonderful Gandhian woman who is, as we speak, widening the options.

* * *

---

27 See Joseph S. Alter, Gandhi's Body: Sex, Diet, and the Politics of Nationalism (Philadelphia: University of Pennsylvania Press, 2000).

CHAPTER 5

VANDANA SHIVA

"Freedom from the first cotton colonisation was based on liberation through the spinning wheel. Gandhi's use of the charkha and the promotion of khadi was both a form of resistance to the British monopoly on cloth and a reminder that it was in our hands to make our own cloth again. Freedom from the second cotton colonisation needs to be based on liberation through seeds."

—*Vandana Shiva*[1]

On almost every page of Vandana Shiva's writings, there are accounts of anti-life disasters driven by the inherent dynamic of capitalism, that is to say, by imperatives of a system whose dynamic is buying cheap and selling dear. In pursuit of profit, genes are patented. To raise prices, seeds are tied to herbicides so that neither the seed nor the herbicide will produce a crop without the other; consequently both must be purchased from the same

---

1 Vandana Shiva and Afsar H. Jafri, "Seeds of Suicide: The Ecological and Human Costs of Globalisation of Agriculture," Sustainable Agriculture and Food Security, ed. Vandana Shiva and Gitanjali Bedi (Delhi: Sage, 2002) 183; hereafter Food Security.

multinational corporation. To create something else to sell, water is privatized. To create more commodities that can be profitably marketed, both indigenous knowledge and the findings of research scientists are redefined as somebody's intellectual property, as—for similar reasons—several hundred years ago, land was redefined as someone's real property. And so on and on and on.... The dynamic of the system overrides ethics and ecology.

We have to be careful with the word 'dynamic.' We do not want to give the impression that we think economics is like mechanics. The founding sin of mainstream (more or less Walrasian) economics is to treat processes governed by social norms as if they were functional relationships between dependent quantities. We want to exorcise that founding sin, not compound it. Nevertheless, we find it useful to say that the modern world has a characteristic dynamic, that it consists of buying cheap and selling dear, and that Gandhi put into practice a different dynamic. The economic law that humans must buy in the best and cheapest market was criticized by Gandhi as one of the most 'inhuman' among the maxims laid down by modern economists.[2]

'Paradigm' is another word we have to be careful with. Many people speak today of 'paradigms' and of the need for a new one, and most of them claim to use the term in a way justified by Thomas Kuhn's demonstration of the importance of what he called paradigms in the history of

---

2 Gandhi, as cited in A.M. Huq, "The Doctrine of Non-Possession: Its Challenge to an Aquisitive Society," Essays in Gandhian Economics, ed. Romesh Diwan and Mark Lutz (New Delhi: Gandhi Peace Foundation, 1985) 79-80. See also note 121 below.

the natural sciences.[3] We use the term paradigm not to refer to any economic model or theory, but rather to the legal framework of capitalism which we, and (we would claim) Adam Smith and Karl Marx, see economic theories as presupposing.[4] Thus only the word 'paradigm' is new to these pages; the concept has been there whenever we have written of the imposition of the property and contract concepts of European commercial law on India by the British. This dominant paradigm frames today's common sense and defines the work of accountants and managers as well as economists.

We do not want to give the impression that a paradigm shift at the level of economic theory would change the world. It is the other way around. Mainstream economics is part and parcel of the pouvoir en place. In Wittgensteinian terminology, the academic disciplines are language-games that are functional parts of the way modern society organizes human action, and human interaction with the biosphere. The reason why the lessons to be learned from Gandhi's practical work promoting the spinning of cotton khadi are today even more crucial than those to be learned from his writings is that today we lack methods for changing the world even more than we lack proof that the emperor wears no clothes, and even more than we lack visions of what a better world would be like.

In this connection Mark Latham, the Leader of the Labour Party of Australia, has astutely observed:

---

3 T. Kuhn, The Structure of Scientific Revolutions, 3rd ed. (Chicago: University of Chicago Press, 1993).
4 See generally, Richards and Swanger, The Dilemmas of Social Democracies. (Lanham, MD: Rowman and Littlefield, 2006).

> *A common Left response to the emergence of global capital has been to denounce market forces by associating the recent period of reform with 'economic rationalism.' The use of this term commonly points to a vanguard of academics and financial interests who have secured a realignment of government policy towards free market forces. It is suggested that strategies of so-called economic rationalism have released undesirable, globalised, market trends. In practice, however, changes to markets have driven changes to public policy, not the reverse. As ever, events have had a much greater impact on policy than has political theory.[5]*

If indeed, the causal powers that move recent history are found more in markets than in political theories or in governmental policies, then it is important to ask how the bad influences of markets can be curbed and their good influences encouraged. We propose to pursue that question by looking at Gandhi's practical experiences promoting cotton spinning and other local economic activities, which he promoted as part of a general philosophy of ethical economics.

Vandana Shiva is not a person who thinks that the solution to all problems is to have fewer markets and more government planning. Sometimes, indeed, she seems to join the chorus of those who say that the policies of Jawaharlal Nehru failed because they were too socialist, or too statist, or too prone to equate socialism with statism. She condemns "three decades of agricultural policy

---

5 Mark Latham, Civilising Global Capital: New Thinking for Australian Labor (Sydney: Allen & Unwin, 1998) 37.

during which this sector was made a state monopoly and run on massive debts and subsidies while ignoring all the ecological imperatives of sustainability."[6] Salvation lies, in part if not in whole, in giving private individuals and local communities material incentives for contributing to the common good, as is implicit in this passage: "Because farmers and local communities did not have any control over trees which they might plant, either they did not plant at all, or when coerced to plant did not maintain or care for them. In this way many community woodlots planted with great physical effort resulted in little gain."[7]

For Shiva, while excessive statist bureaucracy might be called the problem, or part of the problem, globalizing capitalism is certainly not the solution. The solution is a decentralized, ecologically sustainable, and ethical economy along Gandhian lines. The solution is certainly not simply the simple withdrawal by the state from the role it formerly played as regulator of the economy. The latter, the current neoliberal wave of privatizations and budget cuts, is indeed the proximate cause of several current disasters—which include, to extend a bit the list started above, renewed famine and threat of famine, the extinction of the biodiversity on which the future of life depends, poisoning the soil, a wave of farmer

---

6 Vandana Shiva, "Globalisation and Food Security," Food Security 12.
7 "National Conservation Strategy Action Plan for the National Policy on Natural Resources and the Environment, Volume II" (Addis Ababa: National Conservation Strategy Secretariat, 1994) 7; quoted with approval by Vandana Shiva, Biopiracy (Boston: South End Press, 1997) 99.

suicides ...[8] Granting that liberalization of a constructive kind is needed, Shiva condemns the kind of liberalization that is actually happening. More specifically, she condemns the following set of policies, not so much as separate policies, but as elements of the implementation of a coherent malevolent philosophy:

- free import of fertilizers, and deregulating the domestic fertilizer industry;
- removing restrictions on how much land a person can own;
- removing subsidies for water, electricity, and credit;
- deregulating the production of wheat, rice, sugar, cotton, and oilseed;
- downsizing the system for providing food security for the poor;
- removing controls on markets, traders and processors;
- removing subsidies to cooperatives;
- abolishing the general ban on futures trading;
- abolishing inventory controls;
- abolishing selective credit controls on inventory financing;
- treating farmers' cooperatives on an equal footing with the private sector.[9]

Shiva grants that the technocrats who are taking measures such as those just listed have correctly diagnosed the cause of India's agricultural problems, insofar as the

---
8 Vandana Shiva, Monocultures of the Mind (London: Zed Books, 1993).
9 Shiva, "Globalisation and Food Security," Food Security 13.

cause was Nehruvian statism. However, they have prescribed the wrong cure. They have prescribed free trade.

Their prescribed cure is neither logically consistent nor sincerely proposed. Their so-called 'free trade' abrogates a great many freedoms, including, among others, the freedom of farmers to save seeds from their own plants in order to sow them the following season. Nor are their neoliberal policies a sincere effort by the government of India to serve the interests of the people of India. They are a surrender to the power of the World Trade Organization, the World Bank, the International Monetary Fund, and the United States government, all of whom act in the interest of transnational corporations.

But we will not focus initially on Shiva's account of the logical contradictions of so-called free trade. Nor will we focus on her account of the amalgam of technocratic ideology, political and military power, and global movement of investment capital that cements into place the present disastrous course of world history. Instead, we will focus on what the study of Gandhi's experiences can contribute to guiding the alternative course that Shiva proposes. Although her writings follow a consistent pattern across a wide range of issues, we will outline here specifically her proposal for an alternative approach to food security:
- women-centred household food security;
- high nutrition per acre (as contrasted with the profit per acre criterion of agribusiness);
- internal input agricultural practice to reduce debt and the cost of purchased inputs;
- increased use of drought resistant varieties to reduce ecological vulnerability;

- organic methods to improve soil moisture and reduce water demand;
- diversity of crops to ensure balanced nutrition throughout the year;
- use of farmer-saved open pollinated seeds;
- local community food security;
- establishment of community grain banks;
- local procurement so that local producers' livelihoods are protected;
- the cutting of storage and transport costs;
- a focus on culturally appropriate foods for the area;
- the use of locally procured grain for food-related programs of state and central governments, such as food for work schemes, school meals, primary healthcare centres;
- in case surplus exists after meeting local needs, the village grain banks should sell to the states and central government;
- in case of local scarcity, the village grain banks should receive from states and centre;
- the community food banks should have the right to tax to support their activities.[10]

Shiva proposes complementary policies at the state and central government levels to support the household and community approach to food security just outlined.

Her proposals are recognizably Gandhian in their emphasis on local self-sufficiency, and in supporting production in households.[11] They are similar to those made

---

10 Shiva, "Postscript: Starvation Deaths, Overflowing Godowns: How Globalisation is Robbing the Indian People of Food," Food Security 470-472.
11 "If an enterprising baker puts up cheap bakeries in our

by other advocates of green and local economies such as Jerry Mander, Edward Goldsmith, E.F. Schumacher, and others.[12] She differs from non-Indian green economists in more frequently acknowledging her debt to Gandhi, which is to be expected, since in the rest of the world it is possible to think about deliberately encouraging local economies without recalling Gandhi, but not in India.

Given the similarities among the various calls for locally centred and relatively self-sufficient economies (by the way, none of the green economists is a fanatic who would prohibit all long distance trade), it follows

---

villages so as to replace household kitchens, the whole nation, I hope, will rise against such an enterprise." M.K. Gandhi, Young India (17 July 1924), reprinted in Gandhi, Economics of Khadi (Ahmedabad: Navajivan Press, 1941) 89.

12   Jerry Mander and Edward Goldsmith, eds., The Case Against the Global Economy and for a Turn Toward the Local (San Francisco: Sierra Club Books, 1996); Herman Daly and John Cobb, Jr., For the Common Good: Redirecting the Economy toward Community, the Environment, and a Sustainable Future (Boston: Beacon Press, 1994); Paul Hawken, Amory Lovins, L. Hunter Lovins, Natural Capitalism: Creating the Next Industrial Revolution (Boston: Little Brown, 2000); Kirkpatrick Sale, Human Scale (New York : Coward McCann, 1980); Ernest Callenbach, Ecotopia (New York: Bantam Books, 1977); Duane Elgin, Voluntary Simplicity (New York: Bantam Books, 1982); Hazel Henderson, The Politics of the Solar Age (New York: Doubleday, 1981); Ivan Illich, Tools for Conviviality (New York: Harper and Row, 1973); Warren Johnson, Muddling Towards Fragility (Boulder: Shambala Books, 1981); Theodore Roszak, Person/Planet (New York: Doubleday, 1978); E.F. Schumacher, Small is Beautiful (New York: Harper and Row, 1973).

that an objection against one is an objection against all. One of the most obvious and important objections is that Gandhi's schemes that promoted village level self-sufficiency, although they did a lot of concrete good for many individuals, ultimately failed to transform the system. It is important to analyze why they failed in order to determine whether local self-reliance is a hopeless cause; or whether it could be made to work by correcting Gandhi's mistakes, or by trying again in more favourable circumstances.

Gandhi first thought of cotton-spinning in 1908, but it did not become an official program of the Congress until 1921. He conceived it as a way to provide work, and therefore food, for India's semi-starved millions. Most of them were agricultural smallholders or labourers who had no work for four to six months a year. Spinning was a logical choice for a make-work program because India grew its own cotton; because spinning was easy to learn; because it required very little capital; because it could be done at odd hours in between household chores and farm chores; because it contributed to meeting a basic need; because it could help liberate India from dependence on British cloth and drive out the British by cutting their profits; and because it was a tradition which, although it had vanished, had left traces. For hundreds of years before the British came, villagers had earned a livelihood by combining agriculture with spinning and other crafts. Modernization destroyed the crafts by producing cheaper and often better goods in factories. Without cottage industries to supplement earnings from agriculture, the masses were reduced to semi-starvation and to despair.

Gandhi always said that if any other craft could be found that would better serve the function of providing sustenance for the masses, he would promote it instead of promoting spinning cotton to make thread. He in fact founded in 1934 an All India Village Industries Association, which promoted other crafts, as a complement to the All India Spinning Association (A.I.S.A.), which he had founded in 1925.

Spinning was a make-work program. But it was more than that. It was also a means to drive the British from India. On this point Gandhi was a bit of an economic determinist; he reasoned that when the British no longer found being in India profitable, they would leave.[13] They made more profit selling cloth than anything else. If Indians would not buy their cloth, then the British could not sell it. Thus the campaign for khadi clothing had two sides: persuading the villagers to spin the yarn for it, and persuading patriotic Indians to buy it and wear it. Cloth made in Indian mills stood somewhere in the middle of the equation, not as good as homespun, but not as bad as imported. In any case, Gandhi reasoned that the Indian mills alone could not drive out the British, because they did not have sufficient capacity to produce all the cloth India needed.

Cotton-spinning was a make-work program, and it was a means for driving the British from India; but it was still more than that. It was the germ and the working model of the better world of the future, of the world where dharma would reign once again, as dharma had reigned

---

13 Gandhi believed that the global economy was such that if India and China refused to be exploited, the West and Japan would have to change. Economics of Khadi 187-189.

in a partly imagined and partly historical earlier period of Indian history. Gandhi wrote, "It is the greatest delusion to suppose that the duty of Swadeshi begins and ends with merely spinning so much yarn anyhow and wearing khadi made from it. Khadi is the first indispensable step towards the discharge of Swadeshi dharma towards society.... Swadeshism is... a doctrine of selfless service that has its roots in the purest ahimsa, i.e. love."[14]

Gandhi once illustrated the point that spinning promotes cooperation, by describing what he called "the working of a typical centre":

> *At the central office is collected seed cotton for spinners. The cotton is ginned by ginners perhaps at the centre. It is distributed then among carders who redeliver it in the shape of slivers. These are now ready to be distributed among the spinners who bring their yarn from week to week and take away fresh slivers and their wages in return. The yarn thus received is given to weavers to weave and received back for sale in the shape of khadi. The latter must now be sold to the weavers—the general public. Thus the centre office has to be in constant living touch with a very large number of people irrespective of caste, colour, or creed. For the centre has no dividends to make, has no exclusive care but the care of the most needy. The centre to be useful must keep itself clean in every sense of the term. The bond between it and the component parts of the vast organization is purely spiritual or moral. A spinning centre, therefore, is a co-operative society whose members are ginners, carders, spinners, weavers, and buyers—all tied*

---

14 Gandhi, Economics of Khadi 372.

together by a common bond, mutual goodwill, and service. In this society the course of every pice [coin] can be traced almost with certainty as it floats to and fro. And as these centres grow and draw the youth of the country who have the fire of patriotism burning brightly in their hearts and whose purity will stand the strain of all temptation, they will, they must, become centres for radiating elementary knowledge of hygiene, sanitation, domestic treatment of simple diseases among the villagers, and education among their children suited to their needs.[15]

Having described the 'typical centre' he then wrote that the time was "not yet" and that "[t]he beginning indeed has been made," as if acknowledging that what he had been describing had been not so much typical as ideal. We think it is clear that what Gandhi actually described was not an empirically existing khadi centre, but the working of a khadi centre that updated and restored the reign of dharma as it had existed in the ideal Indian village of the past. The key feature of the ideal khadi centre is its lack of conditionality. Instead, the norm is unconditional service to others. The pice (the coin) "floats to and fro"; but the dynamic that drives the ginner, the carder, the spinner, the weaver, and the buyer is not buying cheap and selling dear. Like the medical doctors in Plato's Republic who treat patients for the sake of health, not for the sake of money, the ginners in Gandhi's "typical khadi centre" gin cotton because ginning cotton is their function in the community.

The ideal khadi centre is (or is a central institution of) a true community in the sense given to the word 'com-

---

15 Gandhi, Economics of Khadi 177.

munity' by Daly and Cobb.[16] In a true community: (1) Membership contributes to self-identification; (2) There is extensive participation by its members in the decisions by which life is governed; (3) The community as a whole takes responsibility for meeting the needs of the members; (4) This responsibility includes respect for the diverse individuality of its members. The key item is the third. The community cares for the members. The processes of exchange are shaped to serve the ends of use.

Against Gandhi's swadeshi ideal, and against any proposal for true community, a common objection is that it runs contrary to human nature. It allegedly expects people to be sentimental altruists, when allegedly the fact is that people are rational egoists. Dharma, however, is not sentiment. It is norm. To be sure, in a sense, in Max Weber's terminology, Gandhi is proposing to turn back the clock so that people are no longer modern in the sense of instrumentally rational, but traditional in the sense of being governed by customs (governed by Wertrationalität instead of by a Zweckrationalität that drives them to maximize personal payoffs). But it is hardly open to a Weberian to argue that it is contrary to human nature for people to be governed by conventional norms. According to Max Weber, most people have been so governed, in most societies, for most of history.[17] Indeed it can be

---

16 Daly and Cobb 172.

17 That nascent capitalism was for a long time a minority movement in a world largely governed by traditional customs is a point made by Fernand Braudel, e.g., in the work cited below. The opposite argument, that since human nature evolved over hundreds of thousands of years of living in small tribal bands, it is modern individualism that is out of sync

argued that even now people are governed by what Weber called customary norms; it just happens that the customary norms expect people to be rational egoists. Emile Durkheim's theory that modern individualism is itself the product of a modern conscience collective provides a good fit to the empirically observed facts.[18] Therefore, modern economic rationality is not categorically different from Wertrationalität. It is a particular kind of customary norm.

Nor does serving one's neighbours lack a Zweck. The Zweck, the goal, for Gandhi, is self-realization, as distinct from self-aggrandizement. "While the economists, ever since Adam Smith, preach that everybody doing what he wants will benefit rich and poor alike, the economics of Gandhi is based on a spiritual conviction that by serving the poor we do what we ourselves really need. Self-realization, as against self-aggrandizement, is the ultimate human need."[19]

Further, the rules governing a Gandhian economy can be formulated, not as sentiment, but as rational decision rules, as has been done by the Gandhian economist Amritananda Das as follows:

---

with human nature, is made in Ishmael by Daniel Quinn (New York: Bantam, 1995). See generally Stephen Boyden, The Biology of Civilisation: Understanding Human Nature as a Force in Nature (Sydney: University of New South Wales Press, 2004).
18   Emile Durkheim, The Division of Labour in Society (New York: Free Press, 1984), first French ed. 1902.
19   Romesh Diwan and Mark Lutz, "Introduction" to the book they jointly edited, Essays on Gandhian Economics 16.

> First, let us note that the behavior of individuals within a socio-economic collaborative micro-group is marked by avoidance of economic options by which an individual within the group can improve his economic situation at the expense of the group or without sharing the gains (at least partly) with the group. Second, the group tends to shelter and protect its weaker members from external difficulties and threats, by both sharing of goods and the sharing of work responsibilities. Third, any policy which enriches the group as a whole gets preference over policies which affect part of the group in one way and another part in the opposite direction. Fourth, leadership within the micro-group devolves on the individual(s) who show particular skill in promoting the group interest and who lead in self sacrifice in the interest of the group. Finally the group tends to display a strong community of tastes and a preference for group-oriented leisure and recreational activities.
>
> Quite clearly, such behavior is incompatible with the model of acquisitive-individualist rationality. Yet, there is no reason for regarding such behavior as irrational.[20]

If we are convinced by Das that Gandhi's social experiments were not irrational, and if we are further convinced that his proposals were not contrary to human nature, then we must search further for an explanation of why they did not catch on, spread, and transform society. Our suggestion is that the explanation of Gandhi's failure is

---

20 Amritananda Das, Foundations of Gandhian Economics (New York: St Martin's Press, 1979) 121.

the incompatibility of cotton spinning and other similar schemes with the dynamic of the dominant paradigm. If this explanation is true, then (without a paradigm shift) Vandana Shiva's proposals for food security will fail for the same reasons that Gandhi's projects failed.

Admittedly, this explanation is abstract. Admittedly, it sounds like gobbledygook if one does not already, before reading it, have a clear idea of what we mean. Please be patient. We will draw on Gandhi's concrete experiences with the khadi movement in an effort to make the abstractions concrete. We hope to be able to pour easily understandable meanings into the empty containers designated by the concepts 'dynamic' and 'dominant paradigm.' If we succeed, then the reader will understand clearly why Shiva's writings defending indigenous cultures and advocating women's perspectives, and her attacks on 'the monoculture of the mind' at an epistemological level, are not just frosting on the cake. They are practical necessities. Her food security program will not work without the cultural changes she advocates. Although Gandhi ultimately failed, he too knew that a different dynamic was needed, and he worked hard to practice and to preach one.[21] That is why Gandhi counts as a pioneer of

---

21 Gandhi described the dynamic of modern capitalism, buying cheap and selling dear, as one of the most inhuman of the laws declared by economists: see Huq 79-80. Gandhi's mentor John Ruskin wrote: "[T]here is not in history record of anything so disgraceful to the human intellect as the modern idea that the commercial text, 'buy in the cheapest market and sell in the dearest' represents...." John Ruskin, Unto This Last, quoted by Huq on the same page. Gandhi goes on, in the passage to which Huq refers, to say: "Nor do we always

an approach to peace and justice that in principle would really work. It could be followed, and if it were followed it really would bring peace and justice into existence, in India and around the world.

In its early days Gandhi justified khadi with what he regarded as a slam-dunk argument. In India there were tens of millions of labourers with nothing to do for much of the year. The cost of labour—most obviously in the case of home spinners and weavers who made cloth for their own use—was therefore in a sense zero. India's climate made it easy to grow cotton. Hence the cost of raw material—again most obviously when the villagers grew their own—was therefore small. A spinning wheel is a very inexpensive piece of capital equipment. Therefore, khadi is a way to get something almost for nothing. Its major input has zero cost, and its other inputs are so cheap that their cost can be approximated as zero. Similarly, Gandhi argued that if khadi replaced the sixty crores (tens of millions) of rupees spent annually to import cloth, then India's net gain would be sixty crores. Giving work to idle

---

regulate human relations by any such sordid considerations.... It would be sinful for me to dismiss a highly paid faithful servant because I can get a more efficient and cheaper servant although the latter may be equally faithful. The economics that disregard moral and sentimental considerations are, like waxworks that, being lifelike, still lack the life of living flesh. At every crucial moment these new-fangled economic laws have broken down in practice. . . . We lost when we began to buy our clothing in the cheap markets of England and Japan. We will live again when we appreciate the religious necessity of buying our clothes prepared by our own neighbours in their cottages." Young India (27 October 1921), reprinted in Gandhi, Economics of Khadi 60-61.

hands created a large fund for poor relief. Remarkably, the particular means chosen for poor relief would, in its ordinary daily operations, deposit the bulk of the sixty crores of rupees directly in the pockets of the poorest of the poor.

To be sure, from the first Gandhi enjoined what he called 'sacrificial' spinning as a virtue and as the practice of a religious duty. 'Sacrificial' spinning was done by middle- and upper-class people for free, without pay, in order to set a good example for the poor (following the sociological principle that people tend to emulate those whose social standing is higher than their own), and in order to increase the stock of available yarn. Sacrificial spinning was also supposed to calm the nerves and to purge the soul of disorderly passions. But among religious duties sacrificial spinning had the distinction of being an obligation deduced from a premise that asserted a particular relationship between cause and effect. It was a duty to spin because it was a duty to alleviate the suffering of the semi-starved masses. It was also a duty to spin in order to bring about Swaraj, self-rule for India, which, in turn, would open the way to more alleviation of the suffering of the semi-starved masses. The empirical premise of the theological conclusion was that spinning would in fact cause the effects desired.

An empirical difficulty standing between the recommended intervention, spinning, and the expected effect, money in the pockets of the poor, was that it was hard to sell khadi because it was expensive. According to the argument outlined above, one might expect khadi to be cheap, because the inputs required were, according to the argument, virtually costless. It turned out in practice, however, that khadi was more expensive than mill cloth.[22] The poor people who made it could not afford to wear it. The only way to sell it was to persuade consumers who could afford it to pay more for coarser cloth.

It should not be surprising that manufactured cloth is cheap and of high quality. The dominant paradigm, i.e., the legal framework that governs the global economy, provides for commercial freedom. It organizes market

---

22 Richard Gregg argued that the high cost of khadi is only apparent. Richard Gregg, Economics of Khaddar (Madras: S. Ganesan, 1928). He is certainly right to say that its return per rupee of invested capital is higher than that of manufactured cloth, since the amount of capital invested in khadi is so small. He would more generally be right if a Pigovian tax could be imposed to internalize Gregg's general principle that "when broader social and psychological factors are considered, the slower implements are probably better...." (Ibid. 87) But the principle that decisions ought to be based on true costs all things considered is even colder comfort today than it was when Gregg wrote, since today it is even harder for stationary governments to compel footloose capital to internalize social costs. Gregg argues, correctly in principle, that money prices distort real costs physically measured. See Richard Gregg, A Philosophy of Indian Economic Development (Ahmedabad: Navajivan Press, 1958) 54-69. Similarly, Shiva advocates evaluating agricultural performance in a way which favours small farmers who intensively cultivate their plots, by measuring calories and protein produced per acre. But at this point in history the dynamic of the dominant paradigm, not the engineering criteria of Gregg or Shiva, governs agriculture. Therefore decisions are made on the basis of short-term money-profits per acre.

relationships through the principles of the law of contracts. Nobody has to pay more for coarser cloth. The dynamic implicit in the paradigm drives the entrepreneur to seek the most cost-effective way to produce cloth. What common sense calls inevitable technical progress is therefore guaranteed by the paradigm and its dynamic. Whatever the state of the art may be in any given branch of business, it must necessarily be a technique that makes the product at a cost that allows it to be sold at prices that attract buyers.

Vandana Shiva's proposals for local democratic control of the food supply will not escape the dynamics of the paradigm that ensnared Gandhi's proposals for local democratic control of the cloth supply. Someone will be tempted to buy up grain supplies where they are cheap and sell grain where it is dear. Someone will be tempted to sell food not to those who are most hungry but to those who have the most money to pay for it. Someone will be tempted—as Vandana Shiva is well aware—not to sow grain at all, but to plant their fields in orchids to be exported and sold to the society elite of the first world. There will be demands like those of Cobden and Bright in England in 1830 to cheapen the price of food for the city masses by selling it at free competitive prices that drive the small producer—and the producer who pays fair wages to labour—to the wall. There will be a tendency—the same tendency Fernand Braudel identified as a key to the modernizing process that produced capitalism in the 15th and 16th centuries—to equalize the price of grain across all markets. This tendency will tend to aggregate under the control of big capital the localities and bio-regions that Shiva's plan had disaggregated in order to form true communities with food security guaranteed by local self-reliance and fraternal outside help when needed.[23]

Gandhi's response to the inability of khadi to compete in the market with mill cloth was to appeal to the conscience of the consumer: "Humanity does not search for low prices in a spirit of bargain. The humane in people even in purchases seeks opportunities for service, and therefore wants to know first not the price of the article of purchase but the condition of its producers, and makes purchases in a manner that serves the most needy and most deserving."[24]

Thus Gandhi was a forerunner of today's conscious consumer movement, which promotes fair trade coffee, community supported agriculture (CSA's), and shopping for a better world. A culture shift—perhaps the germ of a paradigm shift. But this does not justify—one must hasten to add— the sectarian conclusion that all of today's conscientious consumers are or should be Gandhians. Some are Presbyterians. Some are Buddhists. Some are Roman Catholics. Some are Anarchists. Some are New-Age people who practice transcendental meditation. It has been plausibly argued that Gandhi's philosophy forms

---

23 "Every time there is a decentering, a recentering operates, as if a world-economy could not live without a centre of gravity, without a pole." Fernand Braudel, La dynamique du capitalisme (Paris: Flammarion, 1985) 90 (translation by Richards).
24 Gandhi, Harijan (2 November 1935) 300, reprinted in Economic Thought of Mahatma Gandhi, ed. J.S. Mathur and A.K. Mathur (Allahabad: Chaitanya Publishing House, 1962) 166-167. Now available in a 1994 reprint by Arihant Publishing House, Jaipur.

a coherent whole, so that his economics is grounded in his view of human nature.[25] Yet one need not accept his view of human nature in order to practice his economics. Not everyone who pays a higher price for goods produced by socially responsible firms is, like Gandhi, following the path of karmayoga set forth in the Bhagavad Gita. With equal coherence people can transcend the dynamic of the dominant paradigm starting from different premises.

The need for a culture shift to orient consumers toward ethical spending is paralleled by the need for a culture shift to orient entrepreneurs—or whoever decides the location of economic activity—toward ethical investments. Gandhi advocated locating production operations in the decentralized rural settings where most of the people of India lived instead of concentrating production—and therefore employment—in urban conglomerations. This issue relates to what Gandhi called swadeshi. Neighbours first.

To illustrate the problems of decentralizing, we will temporarily leave khadi and enter the somewhat different context of the fate of Gandhi's ideas in independent India after his death. We will follow Gunnar Myrdal's account of the failure of attempts to spread small productive enterprises throughout India.

Promoting small-scale and decentralized industry in post-independence India fitted in well enough with the government's plans for economic development, partly because something had to be done to keep people employed until the new jobs expected from industrialization materialized (an expectation which, with the benefit

---

25 Mark Lutz, "Human Nature in Gandhian Economics," Diwan and Lutz 27-53.

of hindsight, we know to have always been a mirage). Thus with a high degree of calculated ambiguity designed to bring dedicated Gandhians into the same consensus with hardnosed modernizers, and including everyone else in between, India's five-year plans, especially the third one, all called for promoting small enterprises in rural areas. But, Myrdal points out, whatever might have been the initial degree of sincerity of the planners, "not only has small-scale industry sought out the big cities but various government support schemes have been adjusted to this trend, often in the face of clear programmatic declarations in favor of dispersion and rural industrialization. In general only the cities can offer industrial enterprises easy access to markets, manufacturing facilities, and external economies."[26]

Thus the problem with bringing work to people instead of forcing people to migrate to cities to find work was similar to the problem selling khadi. Decentralizing did not pay. Someone would have to provide a subsidy to make it profitable to operate workshops at inconvenient locations. The dynamic that drives entrepreneurs to do what pays tends to swell the already overcrowded cities and to impoverish the already impoverished countryside. A better society—such as the sort of society Gandhi and Shiva propose—would decentralize production. Yet on the road between actually existing society and that better society there are many forks. At each of those forks people face their immediate problem, such as the problem of the would-be entrepreneur who wants to locate in a place where she or he can most profitably buy the required

---

[26] Gunnar Myrdal, Asian Drama (New York: Pantheon Press, 1968) 2:1221-1222.

inputs and most profitably sell the products. Shiva (who is a research physicist) demonstrates convincingly that in terms of net physical benefits, and in terms of net physical costs, humanity and the biosphere would fare incomparably better in the kind of society Gandhi envisioned. The better society never comes, though, because at each fork in the road people take the turn that leads back to actually existing society.

Gandhi saw the need for a different dynamic and proposed one. Swadeshi is usually discussed in connection with urging consumer preference for local goods. Thus Gandhi wrote:

Rule of the best and cheapest is not always true. Just as we do not give up our country for one with a better climate, but endeavour to improve our own, so also may we not discard swadeshi for better or cheaper foreign things. Even as a husband who being dissatisfied with his simple looking wife goes in search of a better looking woman is disloyal to his partner, so is a man disloyal to his country who prefers foreign-made things though better to country-made things.[27]

Yet swadeshi has the wider implication of an obligation to act for the good of the community. As applied to those who make decisions about where to locate business, "Employers are to exhaust first whatever pool of local and unemployed workers there is before hiring more suitable labour from other towns or regions. Similarly, the workers would be more reluctant to leave a local employer in spite of more attractive job offers elsewhere. In short, economic agents living together in a community, region,

---

27 Gandhi, Young India (30 May 1929) 183, reprinted in Mathur and Mathur 554.

or country, should first and foremost explore all possibilities to do business with each other before going outside in order to get a better deal. Swadeshi demands the sacrifice of utility for the sake of loyalty." [28]

Thus swadeshi implies a paradigm shift in the sense that Thomas Kuhn gave to the term. The problem is reframed as a problem about loyalty. Something happens that is like a gestalt shift, like neural reprogramming; it changes the formulation of questions and answers.[29] At every fork in the road, people make the choice that is best for the community. Instead of seeing a property-controlling entrepreneur freely wandering the world shopping for the most profitable place to site an operation, through the lens of the new paradigm, there appears a community deliberating on how best to meet its needs with its resources in a sustainable relationship to its environment. The identity of the actors changes. The context that gives meaning to the discourse changes.

A good part of the need for a paradigm shift, not just a change in policy or a new economic model, comes from two reluctances. The first is the reluctance of consumers to pay more for inferior goods. A second is the reluctance of entrepreneurs to forego potential profits by running businesses in the countryside and hiring local people. Given that one needs to be able to see the world differently to propose a conceptual framework in which it would seem at all likely that these and other similar reluctances could be overcome, Gandhi was the man for the job. He was an outsider to modern economic society, quite capable of seeing the world differently. He came

---

28 Diwan and Lutz, "Introduction" 14.
29 Kuhn 140, 204.

from a rural backwater town; his mother was a deeply religious woman who could not read; he grew up in an extended family packed into the rambling rooms of a single large house. Early in his life the vision of restoring ancient India as it was supposed to have been before the British conquest gripped his imagination. He was qualified, as few highly educated people were, to think outside the box. What appeared to be impossible to modern common sense appeared to be possible to Gandhi. On his return from South Africa in 1915 he spent a year touring Indian villages, listening to the people, seeing how they lived. He was uniquely qualified to connect a vision of another possible world to a close empirical study of observed facts.

But we have not finished our account of the paradigm shift we attribute to Gandhi, and we have so far left his swadeshi, or communitarian, paradigm in a non-functional form. A moment's thought will show that the two reluctances described above quickly morph into impossibilities. Over a certain range the conscientious consumer can buy union label garments and eschew sweatshops. Beyond that range, there is not enough money in the consumer's pocket. Over a certain range, an entrepreneur can cut profits in order to put community values first. There is even a considerable upside range over which businesses can make money being local, green, and socially responsible.[30] Beyond a certain point, however, businesses could only site operations at inconvenient locations, raise wages and incur other social costs by operating at a loss, in which case they could only remain in business until their

---

30 There are many examples of businesses making money by being green in Hawken, Lovins, and Lovins.

capital was exhausted. (Gandhi acknowledged this point and held that business owners, as trustees, should take no more for themselves than the workers got, and that they should operate at zero profit rather than pay less than a living wage, but that they were not obligated to operate at a loss.) Similarly, over a certain range putting more money in the pockets of the poor allows them to get a larger share of the available goods, but there is a point—easily reached in India—where the money demand for wage goods exceeds the physical capacity to produce them. Similarly, too, over a certain range of population densities, traditional peoples can feed themselves sustainably generation after generation using traditional technologies. Yet in today's densely populated world it takes scientists like Vandana Shiva to figure out sophisticated ways simultaneously to feed everyone and to preserve the soil for future generations. (Gandhi acknowledged this problem also. He advocated migration from densely settled areas to sparsely settled ones.)

Such largely physical impossibilities plagued Gandhi's khadi experiments, especially in the 1930s and early 1940s. The khadi movement grew slowly. In two decades the movement organized spinning in perhaps 13,000 villages. The number was big enough to make Gandhi the C.E.O. of the largest nonprofit in India, but too small to transform India's estimated 700,000 villages. Since the Congress required that its members wear khadi, the movement had a captive market of people who bought its products as a way of paying dues. But it was undercut even in its captive market by unscrupulous manufacturers who made mill cloth indistinguishable from khadi and passed it off as the real thing at a lower price. Imports of British cloth declined, but not because of competition from indigenous homespun yarn. The British lost out mainly to competition from Japanese mill cloth.[31] In 1935 Gandhi himself had a crisis of conscience. He realized that he was running sweatshops. At the extremely low productivity of hand spinning, poor workers were making two pies an hour.[32] A living wage would be an anna per hour, or eight annas per day for an eight-hour day. He had the same excuse that other people who run sweatshops have: if the spinners did not have the work that the A.I.S.A offered them, they would have no work at all. Women were standing in line seeking opportunities to make and sell homespun yarn even at the miserable wage of two pies an hour. In 1935 Gandhi decided that this excuse was not good enough. After a series of solemn meetings, the A.I.S.A. decided, at Gandhi's insistence, to pay a minimum wage of three annas a day, as a step toward eventually reaching a living wage of eight annas a day. They knew full well that they could not sell khadi at the prices that the minimum wage would force. They also invited another problem which soon materialized: unscrupulous shops sold cloth made from yarn that was indeed homespun, but it was produced by 'private producers' who were paid less than the A.I.S.A's minimum wage.

Sales fell at the new higher prices. One of Gandhi's responses was to put more emphasis on home spinning, which he called self-sufficing khadi.[33] Instead of selling yarn, the villagers would make spin and weave for their

---

31 Gandhi, Economics of Khadi 381, 391.
32 Gandhi, Economics of Khadi 456.
33 Gandhi, Economics of Khadi 478.

own use, and thus become less poor because they would save the money they otherwise would have spent on store-bought mill cloth. But even the home spinners had to buy cotton from which to make their yarn, for which purpose they had no money, or else grow their own cotton, for which purpose they generally had no land. Then they would have to pay a weaver to weave their yarn, for which purpose they also had no money.[34]

The frustrations of the later days of the khadi movement revolved around a central fact: the extremely low productivity of spinning yarn by hand with an old-fashioned spinning wheel. Even with an inexhaustible supply of labour regarded as zero cost, and even with volunteers committed to love and service, there was no way to overcome poverty without producing cloth more efficiently, and also rice, wheat, lentils, and other basic goods.

In the face of the frustration of Gandhian alternatives, and indeed of any alternatives that collide with the dynamic of the dominant paradigm, it is easy to conclude that capitalism is the only possibility. This conclusion appears to follow from the premise that poverty cannot be overcome without increasing productivity, coupled with the premise that productivity cannot be increased without offering material incentives to the owners of resources. Gandhi's experiments with primitive technologies can be consigned to the dustbin along with the 20th century's myriad other unsuccessful attempts to deviate from the dynamic of the dominant paradigm. Thoughts such as

---

34 Gandhi, Economics of Khadi 483-85. Another of Gandhi's responses was to call for a 'science of khadi' which would raise productivity. Of course, productivity had already been raised by textile mills.

these governed India's switch to a Green Revolution strategy in agriculture shortly after Nehru's death in 1964. It is true that India had no choice, since President Johnson of the United States of America had threatened to cut off food aid, leaving India to starve, unless it adopted policies promising larger profits to larger landholders with greater resources and more modern attitudes toward technology. But, quite apart from U.S. pressure, which has been described as "leaning on an open door," many Indians had already concluded that Gandhian and Nehruvian policies were not working, and that capitalist agriculture was the only viable path. Similarly, India took a neoliberal turn in 1991, again with no choice, since it desperately needed support from international lenders, and could only get it by accepting economic orthodoxy. Again, quite apart from the pressure, the logic seemed to many irrefutable: India could not overcome its economic stagnation that was lowering the masses into ever greater depths of misery unless it could produce efficiently, and it could not produce efficiently without liberalizing markets and allowing investors to reap higher profits.

What these and other similar volte faces have in common is that they give up on idealism. They decide to live with the frequently observed empirical facts that business grows, investment in technology grows, efficiency grows, and productivity grows when profits grow. The social price that must be paid to get a larger harvest is that property owners get a larger share of it, while the propertyless become even more powerless than they already were.

If Gandhi's message is identified with the spinning wheel, then it must be admitted that he offers no solution to the problem of increasing production. If, however, his primary message is taken to be dharma, and his primary critique of modernity is that it is adharma, then he does offer a solution. People who follow dharma will increase productivity, and devote the necessary resources to achieving that objective. They will seek simultaneously to achieve other objectives, such as dignity and independence for workers, and respect for all the living plant and animal forms that share the planet with humans. They will do these things for the same reason they do everything else: because it is the right thing to do. Quite apart from Gandhi's decades-long obsession with spinning wheels, there is a non-capitalist way to increase productivity built into his ethic: live simply, work hard, study every problem methodically and scientifically, serve the community.[35] This formula for personal conduct does not circumvent the need to make capital investments in order to increase productivity. It does suggest that the process of stewarding the investments need not be guided by greed. Nor does it imply a world without markets, where nobody buys and sells. It does imply, to use Karl Polanyi's distinction, a world without Markets with a capital M, a world where markets are embedded

---

35 Amritananda Das writes: "[T]he Gandhian ethic of simple living and hard, methodical and organized work in the service of the community, can be utilized to provide the motivation to worldly asceticism in a socialist framework. He [Dr Milton Singer] anticipates that future students of social science will have to study 'the Hindu Ethic and the Spirit of Socialism.'" Das, Foundations of Gandhian Economics 152. He refers to Milton Singer, "Cultural Factors in India's Economic Growth," Agrarian Societies in Transition ed. B.F. Hoselitz (Philadelphia: American Academy of Political and Social Science, 1956).

in and accountable to social institutions, rather than the other way around.[36]

Dharma is duty. For someone else, an ethic of duty might be a conservative ethic. Not for Gandhi. His synthesis of tradition and liberalism exposes dharma to constant reconsideration in the light of truth. It is our duty to constantly seek to determine what our duty is. All institutions are questioned, especially property. Thus Gandhi writes:

Real socialism has been handed down to us by our ancestors who taught: "All land belongs to Gopal, where then is the boundary line? Man is the maker of that line, and he can therefore unmake it." Gopal literally means shepherd. It also means God. In modern language it means the State, i.e., the people. That the land today does not belong to the people is too true. But the fault is not in the teaching. It is in us who have not lived up to it.[37]

---

36 Suresh Desai, "The Role of Price System in Gandhian Economics," Diwan and Lutz 128-142.
37 Gandhi, Harijan (1 February 1937), reprinted in Gandhi, Economics of Khadi 510. A similar idea is found in another ancient Hindu text, the Srimad-Bhagavatam: "Men are entitled to regard as their own just what would suffice to satisfy their hunger. Whoever would appropriate more to himself is a thief, and should be punished as such." Quoted in Huq 79-80. Gandhi's many discussions of trusteeship are critiques of the idea of property too: ". . . I understood the Gita teaching of non-possession to mean that those who desired salvation should act like the trustee who, having control over great possessions, regards not an iota of them as his own." Gandhi quoted by Huq, also at 80.

If Gandhi's message is identified with dharma, then the spinning wheel was only an experiment with truth with mixed results, while its underlying principle, if consistently applied, would result in people cooperating, sharing, and working together to do whatever needs to be done to make the world work for everybody without ecological damage.

Gandhi's principle is a tautology. If every person did her or his duty in a well-organized society, then all needs would be met, insofar as meeting them was not prevented by natural obstacles beyond human control. A = A. Duty done equals duty done. Duty done equals the deeds required by duty performed. In a well-organized society, when the deeds required by duty are performed, all of its institutions are functional and not dysfunctional. Everything depends on answers to moral questions: How do we discern in the light of facts what should be done? How do we educate ourselves and others to acquire the discipline and motivation to do joyfully what we should do? What should be the community's response to trustees who do not act as trustees, but instead put self above service?[38] Concerning this last question, Gandhi gave different answers. Sometimes he called for patience and for the gradual nonviolent conversion of the thief. Sometimes he said that property owners who do not faithfully discharge their duties as trustees of their wealth should be legally compelled to do so by laws defining and governing their duties. Sometimes he said that as a last resort their property should be taken over by the state. This last solution, however, only postpones the problem, since it raises the new question how to ensure that public servants faith-

---

38 "Service above Self" is a motto of Rotary International.

fully discharge their duties to the public. Whatever the answers to these questions may be, when the members of a community are engaged in asking them, and in seeking answers to them, it is a sure sign that they have shifted to a new paradigm.

Although sceptics might doubt that Gandhi's vision of a society guided more by ethics than by buying cheap and selling dear could possibly be brought into existence, no one would deny that it would be desirable to have such a society if it could be brought into existence—except... perhaps... thinkers like Amartya Sen.

* * *

CHAPTER 6

AMARTYA SEN

"Indeed, the nationalist movement in India often summoned these historical traditions and memories to use the past to build the future in a skillful way, and Mahatma Gandhi himself was particularly visionary in this constructive exercise."
—*Amartya Sen and Jean Dreze*[39]

At the end of his book on famines, Amartya Sen writes, "[M]arket forces can be seen as operating through a system of legal relations (ownership rights, contractual obligations, legal exchanges, etc.). The law stands between food availability and food entitlement. Starvation deaths can reflect legality with a vengeance."[40] This is a causal analysis. There is a cause; there is an effect. The cause is

---

39 Amartya Sen and Jean Dreze, India, Development and Participation, 2nd ed. (Oxford: Oxford University Press, 2002) footnote on p. 348.
40 Amartya Sen, Poverty and Famines: An Essay on Entitlement and Deprivation, first published 1981, reprinted in Amartya Sen and Jean Dreze, The Amartya Sen and Jean Dreze Omnibus (Delhi: Oxford University Press, 1999) 166.

modern jurisprudence, which is derived historically from the Roman law of nations. The effect is famine.

Throughout the book Sen refutes empirically the common opinion that famine is caused by the decline or lack of food availability. Instead, he attributes famine to lack of legal entitlement to food.[41] Sen discusses several famines in detail. In the case of the Great Bengal Famine of 1943, which killed three million people and stunted many more, food availability in 1943 was only five percent lower than the average of the preceding five years. The per capita food availability index was nine percent higher than in 1941 when there was no famine. The reason why people starved was that they could not legally command entitlement to food, even though food was physically available. Military and civil construction workers employed nearby in connection with World War II had money and could use it to buy food. This drove up prices. The harvest at the end of 1942 was fairly poor, which drove up prices more. Expecting prices to continue to rise and availability to continue to fall, producers and speculators held stocks in the expectation of further price increases. The speculators turned out to be wrong in that there was a bumper harvest at the end of 1943. By that time, however, starvation deaths had already reached a peak (though hunger-related deaths from malaria, cholera, and smallpox would continue into 1944). The Great Bengal Famine of 1943

---

41   He does not write the ideology critique that would explain why the food availability theory, although false, is nonetheless common. Such an ideology critique is carried out by Arturo Escobar in Encountering Development: The Making and Unmaking of the Third World (Princeton, NJ: Princeton University Press, 1995).

was a boom famine related to powerful inflationary pressures initiated by public war spending, and complicated by public bungling and private speculation. Those who died were mainly poor people who worked for wages or did piecework, who had the misfortune of falling between two price regimes. Rice prices had been stable in the past; around 1943 rice prices went up and thereafter they stayed up, at the historical juncture between the two price regimes, wages failed to keep up with prices. Sen makes a similar detailed empirical case for the legal causes of starvation regarding famines in Ethiopia in 1972-74, the Sahel in 1973, and Bangladesh in 1974.[1]

His study of famines marked a turning point in Sen's work. He had always been interested in the measurement of welfare.[2] Starting with the famine study, empirical studies concerning how to use public action to increase welfare became more prominent parts of his work. We will make some points regarding the measurement of welfare, and then return to famine, and after that go on to compare Sen's concept of public action to increase welfare with Gandhi's nonviolent constructive program.

---

1 Sen and Dreze, Omnibus 55-56, 60, 75-76, 78.
2 We are including in the category of "measurement of welfare" Sen's doctoral dissertation on choice of techniques, his related work for the United Nations on project evaluation, his work on the measurement of equality and inequality, and his essays on ethics and economics, some of which came after the famine study. If we are inappropriately combining disparate endeavours under the same label, then one would have to say that we have chosen a label that does not fairly reflect the breadth of his interests.

Today, after Sen has written so much about the measurement of welfare, always with impeccable logic; always acknowledging and incorporating the valid points of antiegalitarians, sceptics, and free marketeers; it is hard to imagine that just a few decades ago scholars took seriously the claims that welfare could not be measured, and that, consequently, there could be no rational basis for public action to increase welfare.

In 1920, A.C. Pigou, in his Economics of Welfare, argued that an extra shilling in the pocket of a poor person contributed more to society's total welfare ('utility,' i.e., happiness) than an extra shilling in the pocket of a rich person. The rich person would hardly notice the difference; for the poor person, however, a shilling to buy a bottle of aspirin might well spell the difference between being kept awake by a toothache and a night's sleep.[3]

For most (but not all) practical purposes, Sen agrees with Pigou that equality is better. On the whole and with certain exceptions, the same total wealth, the same total income, produces more welfare when it is distributed throughout society with greater equality. Not a dogmatic equality. Not an absolute equality. Not an equality of sameness (on the contrary, Sen advocates more equal capacity to choose to be different). Not equality as a pretext for the violence of a Pol Pot. Not equality pushed to the point where it violates Rawls' difference principle.[4]

---

[3] A.C. Pigou, The Economics of Welfare (London: Macmillan, 1920).

[4] John Rawls' difference principle states that a certain amount of inequality benefits the poorest class in society. By providing incentives to produce more, it results in a greater total social product. Provided that the resulting greater social

Pigou's fundamentally egalitarian approach to social welfare was not extremist, and neither is Sen's.

Pigou was vigorously attacked and, some said, completely refuted. Sen, who was born in 1933, and who entered the debate at a point where the intellectual prestige of Pigou's egalitarian welfare economics was at its nadir, had to deploy sophisticated mathematical and logical arguments, and, later, careful empirical studies like his work on famines, to reinstate the prestige of the general Pigovian ideas that (a) welfare can be measured; and (b) when it is measured, it often implies policy recommendations that aim to augment total welfare by shifting income, wealth, and basic entitlements to health and education toward the middle and working classes.

In 1932, Lionel Robbins of the London School of Economics published An Essay on the Nature and Significance of Economic Science, an influential defence of the position that economists should not make any policy recommendations that include value judgments.[5] In the tradition of David Hume's 18th-century argument that an 'ought' can never be deduced from an 'is' or from any

---

product is then equitably distributed, the consequence of a certain amount of inequality is greater welfare for the poorest class in society, as well as greater welfare for the other classes. The just and fair amount of inequality is that amount of it that most benefits the poorest, and no more. It should perhaps be noted that the single-minded pursuit of exactly the right amount of inequality should not ride roughshod over other ideals. Rawls, A Theory of Justice (Cambridge, MA: Harvard University Press, 1974).

5 Lionel Robbins, The Nature and Significance of Economic Science (London: Macmillan, 1932).

number of statements about what is, and in the tradition of G.E. Moore, who had argued at the beginning of the 20th century that it was a fallacy to define as good any natural property, e.g., being happy; Robbins strictly separated facts from values. Economists were to confine themselves to facts. Facts imply no values. 'Welfare' could not possibly be a concept that is part of the science of economics because the very idea of it implies that it would be good for there to be more of it and bad for there to be less of it.

Kenneth Arrow's impossibility theorem was even more a starting point for Sen than Robbins' separation of economics from value judgments. Contrary to Arrow, Sen argued that rational social choices were possible. Contrary to Robbins, Sen joined the tradition of those who brought economics and ethics together, instead of keeping them apart, a tradition which, in Sen's view, included Adam Smith, Karl Marx, and John Stuart Mill, among others.

Arrow adopted a tripartite division of methods for making social choices, which had been proposed earlier by F.H. Knight of the University of Chicago. Any society makes its collective decisions in one of three ways, or by a combination among them: (a) by the decisions made by authorities, such as kings or priests, or anybody empowered to make decisions for the group; (b) by customs or rules accepted by the group, as Max Weber envisioned when he wrote that traditional societies were governed by custom; (c) by consensus.

'Consensus' for Knight, and for Arrow following him, means rather less and rather more than one might expect at first. It might better be called 'the principle of consent.'

It does not mean that everyone agrees. It does mean that a decision has legitimacy because it can be construed as one to which there was consent. What Knight mainly has in mind is voting and buying—elections and markets. His tripartite theory praises modernity, as modernity manifests itself in industrial democracies. Modern democracies are on the whole better than traditional societies because the untenable concept that someone is smart and good enough to decide for everybody is no longer believed. That there is a right way to do things handed down by tradition is no longer believed either. Modern people do not need to believe much of anything to make collective choices. What they do is vote. To know whether the decision is legitimate it is not necessary to know whether the voters cast their votes for the right reasons. It is enough to know, in many cases, that a certain candidate got the majority of votes. The candidate is then legitimately elected. Knight sees a parallel with markets. To evaluate a product, it is generally not necessary to know its merits, and one should be sceptical about there being any valid way to judge the merits of a product on any scientific or philosophical grounds. It is enough that people buy it. With certain exceptions, the general rule is that people should be allowed to buy what they want, and producers should be allowed to produce what they can sell.

As Arrow applies Knight's ideas, they are indifferent between capitalism and socialism. The voters can choose socialism, as Arrow, writing his doctoral dissertation in the late 1940s, thought that the voters of the United Kingdom had done to an important extent. Socialism was then legitimate in the UK because the voters had chosen it.

One can defend calling such a political process 'consensus' in the strong sense in which everyone joins a consensus even though the vote was not unanimous. Although many voted against the Labour Party, they did so with the understanding that whoever got a parliamentary majority could write the laws. In a sense all consented.

Thus Arrow writes about a Knightian modern world where 'consensus' reigns because social choices are legitimated by individual choices. Individual choice, also named preference, governs society at a level of abstraction where the concept of preference refers both to voting for candidates or laws in a democratic political process and to buying whatever may be for sale in markets, in either a socialist or a capitalist context.

To the objection raised by writers like Maurice Dobb (and, more famously Herbert Marcuse and the Frankfort School generally) that it makes no sense to ground the legitimacy of the social order on individual preferences, because individual preferences are themselves products of the social order, and in particular of a capitalist mass consumption society that socializes its members to be consumers of its products, Arrow has a reply. He classifies such writers as idealists. Idealists start not from the preferences people actually express, but to the ones they would express if the corruptions of the environment were removed.[6] Idealism of any kind Arrow takes to be incredible to a modern mind, and also likely to lead to imposing some people's values on others. The ethical relativism implicit in starting from whatever people's preferences happen to be, regardless of how they came to

---

6 Kenneth Arrow, Social Choice and Individual Values (New York: Wiley, 1951), 74.

be what they happen to be, appears to Arrow, as to most economists, to be the better alternative.[7]

A key problem Arrow set for himself in the 1940s was how to sum individual preferences to get a social preference. This was an updated version of the problem Jeremy Bentham thought he had solved in the early 19th century with his felicific calculus, i.e., calculations adding up different people's levels of happiness. For Bentham a social choice (a decision to adopt certain 'legislation' in his terminology) was correct if it led to the greatest good for the greatest number. Good was defined as happiness, and happiness was defined as pleasure. Each person was to count as one, and none for more than one. Each person was regarded as an expert who knew more about his (presumably also her) own happiness than anyone else. Consequently, as a general rule, free markets in which people chose what they wanted could be expected to aggregate individual happiness to get the greatest total social happiness. Alternative legislative proposals could be evaluated with a felicific calculus that calculated the amounts of happiness each would produce. The one that produced the greatest good for the greatest number was the legislation that ought to be enacted. The reform of British institutions in the direction of more free trade and personal liberty was what Bentham and other 'philosophical radicals' generally advocated. They thought the desirability of free trade was a conclusion that could be demonstrated using the felicific calculus as a method. It was the centrepiece of a utilitarian science of legislation.

As noted above, in the hands of A.C. Pigou and others, utilitarianism, in its crude felicific calculus form, and

---

7   Arrow 85.

also in more sophisticated forms that developed over the years, proved to be a fertile source of arguments for public intervention in the economy for the benefit of the middle class and the poor. In addition to changing its political colours, it was criticized as untenable science, by Robbins in the book mentioned above and also by others. By the 1940s when Arrow wrote, economists no longer thought in terms of happiness, or pleasure, or utility. Happiness could not be observed. Preferences could. To tell what a consumer preferred, it was only necessary to observe what the consumer purchased. Whether the consumer was happy, the economist had no way of knowing. Happiness dropped out as something that could not be ascertained, and which even if it could be ascertained was not necessary to test any hypotheses that economists ought to want to test. Everything economists wanted to say, or at least everything scientific they wanted to say, they could couch in terms of preferences.

Arrow's problem was to formalize rational social choices in modern society. A logical way to deduce social choices from individual preferences would be an explicit scientific algorithm which would make precise what modern people already do in a rough and ready way, namely shape society by their votes and purchases. When the conceptual universe is narrowed to the point where the only possible basis of justification is consent (i.e., choice, i.e., preference) then if society as a whole is going to make a justified decision, that decision has to be justified by some form of consent. If one starts with the Arrovian premise that the preferences of individuals are the unproblematic bedrock on which the foundations of economics can be erected, then it becomes natural to ask

Arrow's question: whether social choices can be justified by summing the preferences of the individual members of society.

Arrow's answer is: they cannot. This is his impossibility theorem. Several premises, each of which is indubitable if you are in a liberal Arrovian state of mind, are required to prove this result. Quite apart from Arrow's formal proof, his result is intuitively not surprising.[8] Once it is granted that the criterion of value is naked preference, which has no justification other than a pure expression of individual will, it is natural to conceive of each individual as a law unto himself, or unto herself. Intuitively, it would not be surprising to find, as Arrow does formally, that a social decision binding all of them could not be made by a group of such individuals. Each individual in the group could only continue to be a law unto himself or herself by becoming a dictator who would impose his or her will on everyone else. An impossible result.

Sen's work on the measurement of welfare patiently led economists back to rational ethics. Sen resisted the tendency to think that if there can be no mathematical and

---

8 The formal proof shows (roughly) that if all we know about individual decision-makers is their order of preferences, and if we want to get a unique social result from summing those preferences, then we cannot simultaneously satisfy the requirements that no individual be a dictator who imposes his choices on the others, that there be a complete ranking of social preferences, that irrelevant alternatives have no effect, and that no individual can by ranking an option higher perversely lower that option's rank in the social sum. For Sen's views see Amartya Sen, "Personal Utilities and Public Judgments: Or What's Wrong with Welfare Economics," The Economic Journal 89 (1979) 537-588.

scientific algorithm for value judgments, then no rational value judgments can be made at all. Like Martha Nussbaum, with whom he collaborated, he adopted the Aristotelian views that reasoning should be of a type appropriate to its subject matter, and that exact reasoning was not appropriate to ethics.[9] Sen mastered the writings of specialists in ethical reasoning and became a professor of both economics and philosophy at Harvard. He did not deny the claims of individual liberty and autonomy to be important human values, but neither was he driven by specious extensions of such claims to the conclusion that there could be no social values.

Sen did not revive the discredited utilitarian view that social welfare could be measured by finding out how happy people were. He did not deny Lionel Robbins' claim that private individuals should be left free to determine their own values, rather than being dictated to by economists in the name of science. Sen accepted much of the libertarian thinking of Robert Nozick, with whom he team-taught a course at Harvard. But he gave Nozick's ideas, and Robbins', a left turn. If freedom is a good thing, then everybody should have it. Freedom is not an empty formula. It is the capacity to do things. It is being an agent. The kind of equality Sen favors is a relatively high degree of equality of capacity to do things. Thus the right of each person to pursue his or her own version of the good becomes a justification for public action to support the opportunities and capacities of individuals.

Seen in the light of Sen's work to answer those who deduced laissez faire from scepticism, his decision to

---

9 See, e.g., Martha Nussbaum and Amartya Sen, The Quality of Life (Oxford: Oxford University Press, 1993).

write a study of famines was a strategic choice. With respect to famines, the proper answer to the proposition that economists should not make the value judgment that they are bad and should not happen is, "You've got to be kidding!" With respect to famines, the proper answer to the proposition that no collective action should be taken to avert and relieve them because there can be no rational basis for social choice is, "You can't mean what you say!" Famine is a topic that lends itself to making it clear that whatever else one may do with one's analyses of the theoretical foundations of welfare economics, one should not use them to paralyze ethical action.

The strength of Sen's case on the issue of famines has a drawback. The drawback is that one might agree with Sen on famines, but regard it as an extreme case, and go on to agree with the sceptics and the free marketeers most of the time. We think it is better to regard Sen's case for public action to prevent famine as an entering wedge, rather than as an exceptional argument applicable only to extreme cases. His arguments for rational ethics and for intelligent public action are general arguments, which just happen to be more obviously forceful in a situation where it is clear to everybody that indifference is morally wrong and that free markets alone will not solve the problem. Although Sen's detailed studies of famine are a reductio ad adsurdum of Pareto optimality (the doctrine that an optimum is reached when there are no more sales between willing buyers and willing sellers), it implies no good reasons for relaxing when there are no famines. In a subsequent book, Hunger and Public Action, Sen and his co-author Jean Dreze lament that it is harder to move people to relieve endemic malnutrition than it is to move people to relieve famine, which suggests that they indeed regard the famine issue as an entering wedge, which is useful to make points that should be extended to other issues.[10]

In that book Sen and Dreze take up again the legal causes of famine. They write:

> ... [I]n the disastrous Irish famines of the 1840s (in which about an eighth of the population died, and which led to the emigration of comparable numbers to North America), the law and order situation was, in many respects, apparently excellent. In fact, even as the higher purchasing power of the English consumers attracted food away, through the market mechanism, from famine-stricken Ireland to rich England, with ship after ship sailing down the river Shannon laden with various types of food, there were few violent attempts to interfere with that contrary—and grisly—process... the millions that die in a famine typically die in an astonishing 'legal' and 'orderly' way.
>
> The legal system that precedes and survives through the famine may not, in itself, be a particularly cruel one. The standardly accepted rights of ownership and exchange are not the authoritarian extravaganzas of a heartless Nero or some brutal Genghis Khan. They are, rather, parts of the standard legal rules of

---

10 Amartya Sen, Hunger and Public Action (first published 1989), 261, reprinted in the Sen and Dreze, Omnibus. Note that the page numbers of the Omnibus are the same as the original page numbers.

> *ownership and exchange that govern people's lives in much of the world.*[11]

Sen and Dreze might have made some further observations regarding the 'standardly'—or regularly—accepted rights of ownership and exchange. They might have gone on to observe that while those rights and rules are commonly accepted today in most of the world, they are far from governing all of the relationships of persons to things on this planet even now, while just a few centuries ago they were confined to Europe. Even now, even in industrial democracies, entitlement to food within families is not governed by the laws of property and contract. Every infant born makes straight for the mother's breast and drinks free milk. If this sort of thing does not happen, the infant fails to achieve what Erik Erikson calls 'basic trust' and is likely to remain emotionally and socially incompetent throughout life. It is only much later, when the grown child leaves home and tries to earn a living, that it sinks in that according to the regularly accepted laws of ownership, if she owns no real estate, and if she can pay no rent, then she has no right to occupy space. If she has nothing to sell that anybody wants to buy, then according to the regularly accepted laws of exchange, she has no right to eat. As long as the child remains under the protection of a functional family, and as long as the entire family is not destitute, that child's right to be somewhere and to eat something is governed by the laws of love, and not by the civil code.

Sen and Dreze might also have observed that the regularly accepted rights of ownership and exchange make

---

11 Sen and Dreze, *Hunger and Public Action* 22-23.

everybody insecure, although they make some people more insecure than others. Sen had noted in his study of famines that in five surveyed villages in the district of Faridpur during the Great Bengal Famine of 1943, 52.4 percent of landless agricultural labourers became destitute, while 40.3 percent of landless agricultural labourers died. Among landlords the corresponding figures were 0.0 percent and 0.0 percent, respectively. In this case the regularly accepted rights of ownership made one class insecure and another class secure.

The arguments of Karl Marx and of John Maynard Keynes, which show that the standard operations of a capitalist economy lead to conditions under which everyone is insecure, can be regarded as consequences of regularly accepted laws. Those laws imply a dynamic. In Marx's terminology (following Adam Smith), the dynamic is called accumulation. In other words, given that the way to make a living in a world governed by regularly accepted rights of ownership and exchange is to sell something, be it labour, services, goods, or whatever, the way essential social functions get moving—their dynamic—is the expectation of profitable sales. Given the way we have organized our economy, it is only the expectation of profit that gets wide-scale production and distribution accomplished. Marx's law of the falling rate of profit shows that this dynamic will eventually weaken, slow, falter, and—for many—stop altogether. Keynes' concept of low-level equilibrium shows that a market is quite capable of reaching equilibrium where supply matches demand while a substantial portion of the population remains out in the cold, unemployed. These standard operations of a capitalist economy, however, are nothing more than the manifested consequences of the legal rules that constitute and govern them. It is the latter, therefore, that can be regarded as the cause of the instability and social polarization that make everyone insecure. Viewed more generally, once it is established that employment is regarded as a species of purchase and sale governed by the laws of contract, it follows that there is no guarantee that everyone will be employed. Whether people are employed depends on whether somebody wants to hire them. Nor is there any guarantee that the products of any business can profitably be sold. Customers are free not to buy. Insecurity, therefore, is a consequence of rights.

Pursuing further the idea that lack of legal entitlements is the cause of hunger might also have led Sen and Dreze to a critique of the use of 'preference' as an explanatory category in economics, which would have supplemented what Sen has written about preference. It is not clear, at least not to us, to what extent Kenneth Arrow thought that preferences of voters were historical causes that explained the regularly accepted rules of ownership and exchange. He seems to assume that in some sense the laws are what they are because the preferences of the populace, expressed in votes, make them what they are. Although his precise meaning is not clear to us, it is clear to us that the direction of the arrow of causation is normally the other way around. Given that the dynamic for getting production underway, which is generated by standard rules about owning things and exchanging them, is profit-seeking, it follows that when profits falter, the economy slows down. In an economy that relies on such a dynamic for its daily bread, everyone suffers when the economy slows down, except perhaps for a few odd characters like bankruptcy lawyers. The basic rules of the system are thus so structured that voters are likely to prefer candidates who successfully manage the system within the standard framework the rules provide. Voters will not prefer candidates who frighten investors. Consequently legislation and policy will be more a consequence than a cause of regularly accepted rights of ownership and exchange.

If Sen and Dreze had followed out these further ramifications suggested by the concept that the law causes starvation, they might have come to agree with the Mahatma Gandhi that the very foundations of modernity are untruthful. Modernity's legal foundations presuppose a lack of community bonds that is incompatible with truth as Gandhi conceived it. People were secure in Ram Rajya, Gandhi's ideal traditional village, because of truth conceived as loyalty; it was everyone's duty to take care of everyone else. With modernity came fewer duties and more rights, less security and more individualism. Sen and Dreze might have followed this Gandhian logic to the point where they would have embraced J.P. Narayan's concept of total revolution, which proposed a communitarian nonviolent transformation of civil society.

Instead, Sen and Dreze refrain from challenging the standardly accepted rules of ownership and exchange. They write:

But when they [the standard rights] are not supplemented by other rights (e.g. social security, unemployment insurance, public health provisions), these standard rights may operate in a way that offers no chance of survival to famine victims. On the contrary, these legal rights [the standard ones] backed by the state power that upholds them, may ensure that the 'have nots' do not grab food from the 'haves', and the law can stand solidly between needs and fulfillment.[12]

Thus for Sen and Dreze, as for the United Nations, for whose Development Program Sen is a leading adviser, the better path is to leave the standard rights inherited from Roman Law more or less intact, and to complement them with economic and social rights. The methods they propose for advancing along this path they call 'public action.'

Public action is an ample concept. It includes state action, the actions of social movements and non-governmental organizations, the electoral and educational work of political parties, and the peace and justice work of churches. It includes as well the cooperative mutual aid projects through which people at the grassroots help themselves and the political organization of the deprived classes; and it includes the work of a free press, which serves as a watchdog and as a system of alarms.

The concept is so ample that it is helpful to proceed toward defining it by saying what it is not. It is not just any state action. In particular, Sen criticizes military expenditures as a waste of resources. He also criticizes official corruption, which often goes together with militarism, or with civil struggles to control the assets of the state. Political parties functioning as patronage machines to benefit their members do not count as doing public action. On the other hand, adversarial politics that aggregates the interests of constituencies does count as public action, even though the motives are not idealistic.

---

12 Sen and Dreze, Hunger and Public Action 23.

Public action is not the standard struggle to earn a living by selling something at a profit. That is private action. For Sen, private action alone is unable to achieve human security or sustainable development, which is why public action is needed. On the other hand, Sen's concepts would seem to imply that private-sector businesses that include ecological and community service goals in their mission statements and accounting protocols are doing public action. It is tempting to generalize that public action is any action by anyone that is oriented toward the common good.

Sen, together with Jean Dreze and other co-authors, deploys an elaborate set of empirical studies to prove that public action as he conceives it—featuring democratic accountability and an activist state intervening to affirm the capacities of its citizens—in fact produces measurable increases in welfare. He is the guiding spirit behind the annual United Nations Development Report, which ranks the nations of the world according to a series of indices of positive freedoms.

One of Sen's claims is that there has never been a famine in a well-functioning democracy. He identifies the mechanisms that produce this empirically observed phenomenon. Adversarial politics assures that no government can allow a famine to happen. If there were a famine, at the next elections, it would probably be voted out and its opponents voted in. A free press assures that no famine can be concealed, and that any administrative bungling of relief will be revealed. Reporters save lives. One of Sen and Dreze's pieces of empirical evidence for the absence of famine in democracies comes from Botswana.[13]

---

13 Sen and Dreze, Hunger and Public Action 152-58.

Botswana is a poor drought-prone country in famine-prone sub-Saharan Africa. It has had no famines. Unlike nearby countries, which have had famines, it has a highly democratic political system and a vigilant free press.

As negative evidence, Sen and Dreze cite Communist China, a country which has made great progress according to many indicators, but which has a highly authoritarian political structure. Notwithstanding its socialist ideology, which was in principle committed to solidarity, there were severe famines in China in 1958-61. The famines appear to have killed 23 to 30 million people, while a controlled press duped both the public and the government with rosy stories. The lower officials did not dare tell the higher officials what was happening.[14]

Although Sen's empirical generalization about famines and democracy appears to be valid, there are other aspects of his empirical claims that are harder to establish. India, his home country, is a particularly hard test case for his theory. A story can be told about India, which, if true, proves Sen wrong. The story is as follows. India has had by now sufficient experience with public action to learn that public action does not work. Under Nehru, India had an activist state, which started the newly independent country with a strong tradition of government intervention in the economy. Because of Gandhi, India has been awash with do-gooders and voluntary benevolent organizations of all kinds. Yet India did not take off economically until 1991 when it left both Nehru and

---

14 Amartya Sen and Jean Dreze, India, Economic Development and Social Opportunity, first published 1995, 75-77, reprinted in the Omnibus. Once again, the page numbers of the Omnibus are the same as those in the original edition.

Gandhi behind, and more fully embraced private action energized by profit-seeking. Even today, India lags behind China, which turned to neoliberalism earlier, in 1979, and which has an authoritarian government. On this account, key elements of Sen's public action approach are discredited: state action, public-spirited voluntary cooperation, democracy, a free press. The winning factors, on this possible interpretation of the experience of his native land are two that Sen denigrates: unsupplemented free markets and authoritarian governments.

We will review eight of the ways Sen defends himself against stories like the one told above, as a way of rounding out an introduction to his views before comparing them to Gandhi's. First, although it is true that prior to 1991, India had a rather slow 'Hindu rate of growth' of about three percent per year, it is not true that India stood still, and one sees quite substantial progress in that time period if one looks at social rather than economic indicators; for example, life expectancy at birth in India was 44.0 years in 1960, 53.9 years in 1981, and 59.2 years in 1991.[15]

Second, Sen regards economic growth that does not produce increases in welfare as a waste rather than an achievement, hardly worth analyzing, certainly not worth emulating. He characterized Brazil, for example, as following until recently a strategy of 'unaimed opulence.' Brazil had one of the highest economic growth rates in the world, but a life expectancy at birth lower than Sri Lanka which had one-fourth of Brazil's GNP per capita.[16]

---

15 Sen and Dreze, India, Economic Development and Social Opportunity 71.
16 Sen and Dreze, Hunger and Public Action 180, 189, 258.

Third, Sen regards China's superiority to India on welfare measures, when the two started out with similar numbers at the time of India's independence, as largely due to the comprehensive health and education programs carried out by the Communist regime prior to the 1979 reforms.[17] He also thinks that in China, as in other countries, having a healthy and educated population laid a firm foundation for future economic growth.

Fourth, since the neoliberal reforms of 1979, China's so-called 'responsibility system' has led to a slowing of improvement on some welfare measures, and slippage backwards on others, notably due to the authoritarian regime's dismantling of most of the health care system.[18]

Fifth, India has yet to translate its post-1991 economic growth into substantial welfare improvements, particularly in the fields of health care and primary education. These basic forms of public action to affirm human capacities were neglected by India's earlier so-called 'socialist' governments, and continue to be neglected in these days of high per capita GNP growth.[19]

Sixth, it is possible to achieve measures on welfare indicators comparable to those of China under Indian conditions, without adopting China's authoritarianism. The proof is the Indian state of Kerala, which actually outdoes China considered as a whole, and to a lesser extent the state of West Bengal.[20]

---

17 Sen and Dreze, Hunger and Public Action 204-225.
18 Sen and Dreze, Hunger and Public Action 204-225.
19 Sen and Dreze, India, Economic Development and Social Opportunity passim.
20 Sen and Dreze, India, Economic Development and Social Opportunity 60, 82, 55-56.

Seventh, Sen favours the expansion of social opportunities by a combination of supportive public intervention and effective use of market mechanisms, a general viewpoint that leads, together with other considerations, to policy recommendations somewhat different from India's past and also somewhat different from India's present. He regards his views as supported by empirical findings worldwide. Consequently, stories about India being benighted until 1991 are not strictly relevant to his proposals, since he is not an unconditional supporter or an unconditional detractor of any of the sets of policies that India has pursued before or after 1991.[21]

Eighth, Sen's defence of the idea that welfare can be measured accepts and advocates the value of people being agents and not just patients. This line of thought lends itself to justifying democracy not just on the basis of what it accomplishes, but on the basis of broadly participatory government by the people playing an active role in whatever the successes or failures may be.[22]

These eight short points do not do justice to Sen's long arguments. They may serve to suggest the sorts of reasons Sen has for believing that his case for public action is not refuted by the facts of recent history. The facts, according to Sen, show that democracy and human rights are complementary to development however it is measured, but especially when it is properly measured. Properly measured, development is the enjoyment of positive freedoms, which makes a people that loses its freedom

---

21 See, e.g., Sen and Dreze, India, Economic Development and Social Opportunity 83-86.
22 Sen and Dreze, Hunger and Public Action 279.

by definition underdeveloped.[23] There is no trade-off that makes less democracy the price of more progress. Economic development without social development is pointless. Security for all in the form of provisions for meeting basic needs is possible at a low level of GNP per capita, as Sen shows in detailed discussions of Costa Rica; Chile at one point in its history; Jamaica; the Indian state of Kerala; and pre-reform China, among others. Although human security at a high level of economic development—what Sen calls growth-led security—is also possible, what really matters is the increase in human welfare, not the GNP.

One cannot help but feel that Sen is philosophically correct, as a matter of economic ethics, but that the dynamics of history are working against him. If history is moving in Sen's direction at all, it is moving that way far too slowly. There is too much uncertainty about whether it is even possible to arrive at the final goal of assuring the sustainable provisioning of food, clean water, sewers, housing, health care, and education, in a world where all enjoy the dignity of being free subjects who are agents shaping their own lives and contributing to society. Although his concept of public action goes some way in the right direction, Sen has not really provided a solution to a problem Keynes diagnosed, the problem of low-level equilibrium. In one of his books, Sen explains why Keynes' proposals for macroeconomic management of aggregate demand never had much influence among Indian economic planners.[24] They seemed to be proposals for solving

---

23 Amartya Sen, Development as Freedom (New York: Anchor Books, 2000).
24 Amartya Sen, Development Planning: The Indian Experi-

first-world problems, not third-world problems. Nevertheless, the problem Keynes set out to solve—that of a market economy that excludes much of the population from its benefits—is very much a third-world problem, and indeed a global problem. As each day passes, the market economies of the 177 or so nations are becoming more and more a single global integrated market economy. As Keynes prophesied, under such conditions it is very hard for an individual nation-state to carry out social policies that benefit its unemployed and precariously employed population.[25]

Sen's theory is more a normative theory than a dynamic theory. While Lionel Robbins proposed to separate facts from values completely, Sen does not separate facts from values at all. The statistics he analyzes are measures of the achievement or lack of achievement of valuable goals. With respect to these measures he analyzes the 'strategies' of each of the 177 or so nation-states in terms of their success or failure in reaching those goals. He routinely, although not always, pays each nation's government the implicit compliment of appearing to assume that it is sincerely trying to increase the welfare of its citizens, and that it has adopted a strategy that it believes will serve such ends. That the global economy as a whole is driven by a dynamic, like the logic of accumulation that characterizes Immanuel Wallerstein's world-system interpretation of history, or like the accumulation on a world scale of Samir Amin or Maria Mies, is not a concept that enters into his country-by-country comparisons of the

---

ence (Delhi: Oxford University Press, 1994).
25 J.H. Keynes, "National Self Sufficiency," Yale Review 22 (1933) 755-769.

relative successes and failures of different development strategies.[26] Sen does, however, offer bits of evidence that even if the relentless logic of capitalist accumulation, as it has been historically aligned with military force and with pride, sets limits to what any government can do, it is not always or perhaps not even usually an immoveable obstacle that prevents public action to increase welfare. For example, he cites a study showing that poor education in parts of India is not so much due to a fiscal crisis of the state induced by the pressures of globalization, as due to lack of participatory democracy that results in a situation where the teachers, although paid, do not show up to teach, and there is nothing the parents can do about it.[27]

If we ask whether a world driven largely if not entirely by the dynamics of profit accumulation can solve Keynes' problem of low-level equilibrium, then we ask a question Sen does not answer. Helping everyone to achieve insertion in the labour market by assuring education and health care for all is not an answer because even though there may be labour shortages in certain fields, the general problem is that the supply of labour already matches the demand for labour with millions still out in the cold. Following the model of a nation that has successfully

---

[26] Immanuel Wallerstein, The Modern World-System, Vol. II, Mercantilism and the Consolidation of the European World-Economy, 1600-1750 (San Diego: Academic Press, 1980); Samir Amin, Accumulation on a World Scale (New York: Monthly Review Press, 1974); Maria Mies, Patriarchy and Accumulation on a World Scale (London: Zed Books, 1999).

[27] Sen and Dreze, India, Economic Development and Social Opportunity 105-106.

achieved high marks on all welfare measures cannot be an answer for everyone. The problem is not that the global market economy has no good examples of people and nations who successfully sell products that other people want and can pay for, and even better examples where commercial success is shared with less fortunate brethren. The problem is that always, somewhere in the system, there will be people who have nothing to sell that anyone wants to buy.

Looking at Sen's writings just as the expression of a normative philosophy, a decline in order of magnitude occurs when they move from theory to practice. At the level of theory, Sen and his co-authors write of positive freedoms. They write about just or nearly just societies where difficult philosophical questions arise because the claims of freedom and the claims of justice are not always easy to reconcile. The level of practice is different. Now the writings are about preventing famines. Then they move to endemic malnutrition, and then on to eliminating illiteracy, and to assuring that as many impoverished girls as impoverished boys are admitted to primary schools where the teachers actually show up and teach them. The practical writings are about eliminating the worst abuses, the ones that could not be justified by any ethical theory.

There may be a connection between a theory of public action with comparatively little to say about the dynamics of the world economy, and a normative theory that in practice tends to focus on the poorest of the poor. It may be that in practice the logic of capital accumulation really does run most of the world most of the time, and that consequently it is not realistic to expect a great deal from public action, defined as action guided by logics other than that of capital accumulation. Given such severe limitations on what can be accomplished, ethics falls in line by relaxing its imperatives. Instead of commanding what ought to be, it sets priorities for the work of the limited power of public action by forbidding the worst of what ought not to be.

Gandhi offers a more radical approach. He challenges the regularly accepted rules of ownership and exchange. He advocates and practices a different dynamic. T.K. Mahadevan said of him, correctly we think, "The core of the Gandhian teaching consists of one concept and no other. It is truth."[28] Many have puzzled over what Gandhi meant by 'truth,' including Raghavan Iyer, who wrote, "He [Gandhi] used the word 'truth' in several senses and it is not always clear which is to be taken in a particular context."[29] We are working with the idea, derived in part from Erik Erikson's study of Gandhi, that for Gandhi the core meaning of truth is loyalty or reliability, and that its context, its Sitz im Leben, is that of an ideal traditional Indian village, in which Gandhi lived in his imagination, and to some extent in his youth, in reality. Truth is about community bonds.[30] Romain Rolland called Gandhi

---

28   T. K. Mahadevan, "An Approach to the Study of Gandhi," Quest for Gandhi, ed. G. Ramachandran and T.K. Mahadevan (New Delhi: Gandhi Peace Foundation, 1970) 249.
29   Raghavan Iyer, The Moral and Political Thought of Mahatma Gandhi (New Delhi: Oxford University Press, 1973) 162.
30   See the discussion of truth in Chapter 2 above, and Erik Erikson, Gandhi's Truth (New York: Norton, 1969). Citing this work, Naresh Dadhich comments that Erikson "traced the historical-psychological development of Gandhi from 'Moniya'

"the man who became one with the universal being," not because he floated off into outer space, but because he stayed on earth and identified his welfare with that of his fellow human beings and all living things.[31]

On such a relational and bonded view of truth, the standard European laws of property ownership imposed on India by the British are untruthful and invalid. Property requires the exclusion of the have-nots from the premises, indeed of everyone except the owner and those licensed by the owner to enter. Truth requires inclusion. Relationship is everything. The story is told that Gandhi once threw a valuable pair of binoculars into the ocean because it had been the occasion of a quarrel between himself and a friend. The point was that the material object was worth nothing if it interfered with what really mattered, the relationship.

The standard European laws of exchange do not work either in the cultural context of a traditional Indian village. The ideal village is animated by the dynamic that animated Gandhi: service. Gandhi specifically disapproved of shopping with a spirit of bargain, seeking to

---

to 'Mohan' to 'Mr. Gandhi' to 'Mahatma.' He has applied his theory of ego-identity to the interpretation of Gandhi's personality. Erikson defines Ego-identity as 'a process located in the core of the individual, and yet also in the core of the communal culture, a process which establishes the identity of these two identities.'" Naresh Dadhich, Gandhi and Existentialism (Jaipur and New Delhi: Rawat Publications, 1993) 53, quoting Erikson 265-266.

31 Romain Rolland, Mahatma Gandhi, the Man who Became One with the Universal Being, tr. Catherine Groth (London: Swarthmore Press, 1924).

buy at a low price and sell at a high price in order to make a profit. He held that even as a consumer, especially as a consumer, one should act in a spirit of service and make those purchases that will most benefit the poor.

Gandhi was not always aware of the problematic character of the everyday common sense of the world he was living in, as it was shaped by the civil laws that frame commercial transactions in a modern economy. He often acted like everyone else, accepting a social reality built around commodity exchange as normal. For example he chimed in with common sense when he wrote "Private property lawfully acquired is entitled to protection." [32] Yet just as often he challenged the premises of common sense with his radical communitarian law of love.

It is obvious that a modern economy, or any economy which might conceivably be created in the future by transforming modern economies, could not possibly function as an ideal traditional Indian village. There have to be markets. There cannot be markets without ownership. There cannot be markets without contracts. Gandhi realized this. He worked throughout his life in a number of practical ways to give an ethical orientation to modern institutions, and to invent new institutions to meet the needs of the time and place. The community bonding imagined to have existed in the traditional village could not be duplicated, but their spirit and intent most certainly could.

One of the ways to carry out such a spirit and intent, in our opinion, is to follow Sen's principle of complementing public action with the intelligent use of market

---

32 M.K. Gandhi, Letter to N. Subrahmanya Aiyar, 17 December 1932, Collected Works 58:222.

mechanisms, regarding markets as "among the instruments that can help to promote human capabilities...."[33] This principle presupposes that the market is an instrument. It presupposes that the market is a tool that can be intelligently employed to serve human purposes, and therefore judged and held accountable by a democratic polity. Unfortunately, it is all too often the other way around. The dynamic generated by the regularly accepted rights of ownership and exchange generates its own imperatives, which democratic polities obey more than they command.

Transforming the dynamics of the global economy is, consequently, a prerequisite to the intelligent use of markets as instruments that Sen advocates. The transformational process requires a questioning and a constructive revision of the regularly accepted rights of ownership and exchange.

* * *

---

[33] Sen and Dreze, India, Economic Development and Social Opportunity 202.

CHAPTER 7

ARUNDHATI ROY

"Gandhi's salt march was not just political theater. When, in a simple act of defiance, thousands of Indians marched to the sea and made their own salt, they broke the salt tax laws. It was a direct strike at the economic underpinning of the British Empire. It was real."
—*Arundhati Roy*[34]

Gandhi's nonviolence was real. Arundhati Roy's implication is that there is some other kind of activism that is not real, or which has some lesser degree of reality.

In several texts Roy gives two examples to show the reality of Gandhi's nonviolence. The one to which the quote above alludes was the Dandi salt march. The British had declared a monopoly for themselves and their permit-holders on the manufacture and sale of salt. Through the monopoly, they burdened salt production with a tax that resulted in higher salt prices for the consumer.

Everyone uses salt. In India's hot climate, where masses of people sweat gallons of salty water through billions of

---

34 Arundhati Roy, An Ordinary Person's Guide to Empire (Boston: South End Press, 2004) 91, cited hereafter as Ordinary Person's Guide.

pores on acres of skin day after day, year after year, many tons of salt are needed regularly to maintain body fluids at normal levels. Salt is easy to manufacture. The raw materials are plentiful. By decreeing itself to be the only legal maker and seller of salt, the British Empire cordoned off for itself a rich source of easy money.

It is not necessarily wrong for a government to cordon off a source of easy money for itself. It may be a good way to raise revenue for public purposes. Most taxes are an even easier source of money than salt making. For most taxes there is no specific government service provided in exchange for the taxpayer's money. To be sure, the government may be expected to use the money to build roads, run hospitals and schools, and abate mosquitoes. Most often, however, it just collects a tax without saying where the money will go. At least the payers of the salt tax got something specific in exchange—namely: salt.

One good reason why the Indian salt tax was, nonetheless, wrong, and wrong from the very start, was that it—and indeed everything else the imperial government did—was imposed on the people by an illegitimate government. The British were masters in someone else's house. Taxation without representation. Government without the consent of the governed. The Indian masses bore the burden. It was they who paid a higher price for salt. They had less money left for rice and lentils because they paid more for salt. Somewhere in India some unknown number of people died from hunger-related diseases because the higher price of salt made the crucial difference between getting enough calories and not getting enough. Although they bore the burden, however, the masses never consented, directly or indirectly, to sacrificing their freedom to make their own salt in order to raise public revenue.

Similarly, we do not want to say that customary norms or legislation should never curtail individual freedoms or raise prices. Certainly Gandhi would not say so. He argued fervently that it was a moral duty to give up one's freedom to buy cheap mill cloth in order to help out the impoverished villagers who eked out their livings making homespun cloth. Gandhi was an advocate of swadeshi (self-reliance) and a protectionist. He supported legislation that raised prices in order to protect the local from the global. An educated and empowered populace might have rationally decided to curtail individual freedoms or raise prices for any number of good reasons—perhaps to raise money to pay for hospitals and schools and perhaps even to reduce salt consumption, since there are medical reasons for believing that most people consume too much salt rather than too little.

What actually happened, however, was that a populace deliberately kept uneducated and disempowered was compelled to pay a salt tax by the superior force of British arms. What actually happened was that the British did not devote the salt money to building schools and hospitals. Most of it went to fund their own military and police. The British raj was a state in the sense Hegel gave the term: an army plus a system for raising money to pay the army.

The Indian masses were thus caught in a structural trap, a double whammy. The only reason the British were able to impose a salt tax on them without their consent was that the British had weapons. What the British did with the money they forced the Indians to hand over to them was to buy more weapons. Gandhi found a way out of the trap. In the salt march, taking a stand against injustice and dissolving the mechanism through which injustice was perpetuated were united. Roy's implication is that activism that does the former but not the latter is not real, or has some lesser degree of reality.

These considerations provide some context for Roy's declaration that Gandhi was a political genius who practiced real nonviolence, not just political theater. Gandhi knew how to bring nonviolence to bear where it would do the most good, where it would transform the fundamental causes of violence, where it would break the links of the chains that held India in bondage.[1] If the Indians would make their own salt, then the British scam would not work. It could not be funded, or it would have to funded some other way, which nonviolent activists would also try to find a way to dissolve.

Roy has unkind words for people who treat nonviolence as political theatre. They may indeed appeal to the conscience of the oppressors and seek to win hearts by self-suffering; they may get attention and dramatize their views; they may go to jail or on hunger strikes. But they do not make salt. It may be, of course, that the same people who are doing 'picture demonstrations' in the morning to get anti-war images onto television screens, are busy in the afternoon running a food-not-bombs kitchen or a collective repair shop for recycled bicycles—in other words, making salt.

---

[1] David Barsamian, The Checkbook and the Cruise Missile: Conversations with Arundhati Roy (Cambridge MA: South End Press, 2004) 136-137, cited hereafter as Checkbook.

The second example Roy gives to show Gandhi's realism is the khadi-based alternative economy, to which Gandhi gave most of twenty-five years of his life, when he was not in jail. Gandhi believed that the main motive that brought the British to India was to make money. He reasoned that on the day when they found that they could no longer make money, but only lose it, they would leave. If Indians were to practice swadeshi, buying their own products, the British would lose their markets, and thus lose the main point of their presence on someone else's subcontinent.

Roy implies that Gandhi wannabes who identify nonviolence with passive resistance have misunderstood him. They should learn from the master and get real. As Richard Deats has pointed out, Gandhi never intended any separation of nonviolence from constructive program.[2] Nonviolence was constructive program. Constructive program was nonviolence. Gandhi always regarded the slow violence of economic injustice as equivalent to the fast violence of war. Nonviolence was their common antidote. The principles Gandhi believed would lead to economic justice—village self-sufficiency, non-possession, voluntary poverty, trusteeship, etc.—were for him every bit as essential to a nonviolent way of life as submitting to the lathi (steel-tipped baton) blows of the police without striking back.

The examples Roy gives to show how Gandhi's nonviolence was 'real,' and her very use of that term, suggest a tendency toward economic determinism—not a strict economic determinism, which would deny that accidents happen and that history is influenced by personalities,

---

2   Richard Deats, Mahatma Gandhi, Nonviolent Liberator (Hyde Park, NY: New City Press, 2005) 61.

and which would deny that political or cultural or military or psychological factors sometimes have weights of their own not reducible to economics, but on the whole a tendency to think that by and large the disasters that are now befalling most of humanity are mainly due to economic causes.[3] For example, she does not think it makes a fundamental difference whether one of the George Bushes is the United States president, or whether someone like Bill Clinton is president.[4] Either way, the United States is locked into playing a military and political role in the world that is the consequence of its national economic interests (although perhaps not in the economic interests of the blokes who wear jeans and sneakers in Michael Moore films).

On the other hand, Roy sometimes seems to deny economic determinism. There is a passage in The God of Small Things where a character who appears to speak with the voice of the author speculates that when all is said and done, it is not the economic laws emphasized by the Marxists, and it is not any of several other plausible candidates for being first in the order of causes, which,

---

[3] See, e.g., Barsamian, Checkbook 140, cf. 117, where Roy also refers to the USA's culture of violence as a contributing cause. At 156-157, Roy sees Argentina being destroyed by the 'checkbook' and Iraq being destroyed by the 'cruise missile' as part of the same market-driven process. She makes the same point in Ordinary Person's Guide, at 34, where she also describes the process as a self-destructive impulse toward global hegemony.

[4] Barsamian, Checkbook 114, cf. pp. 82-83, 111; Arundhati Roy, Public Power in the Age of Empire (New York: Seven Stories Press, 2004) 17-18, cited hereafter as Public Power.

at bottom, determines what happens. It is the laws of love, the ones that say who should love whom, and how much.[5] This suggestion about which cause is the most potent one in human life fits in with a main theme of the novel, which is that all hell breaks loose when a touchable loves an untouchable.

We want to acknowledge that many questions might be asked about what Roy meant when she praised Gandhi's nonviolence as 'real'; and about how the terms of her praise might imply a critique of the ways other people think about nonviolence or practice it; and about how her ideas might apply to any of the multitudes of nonviolent campaigns that Gene Sharp, Sanderson Beck, and others have catalogued. While acknowledging all these important questions that could be discussed, and at some point should be discussed, what we want to do now is to turn to the question, "What is going on when Roy talks of economic causes?" Pursuing this question will help us to articulate some relationships between the way she thinks and the way Gandhi thinks (if we may be allowed to use the present tense for both of them, as if they were talking to each other today).

---

5 Arundhati Roy, The God of Small Things (New York: Harper Perennial, 1998) 33. See also 222, where the love laws seem to be the primal competitors of the war laws. I take the ideas of primal love laws and war laws to be implicit when human nature's demand for ascendancy, structure, and order, is said to fuel violence against those who break history's laws (292-293) and when human nature is said to decimate edifices of the mind (272). See also Arundhati Roy, War Talk (Cambridge: South End Press, 2003) 75.

Roy says in one of her interviews with David Barsamian that militarism has become an economic necessity for the American Empire.[6] We take this statement to be equivalent to saying that economic causes explain American militarism—i.e., that for economic reasons there has to be militarism. She suggests two specific economic causes of militarism. (Elsewhere she mentions several general aspects of the psychology of daily life that are conducive to paranoia, to mad impulses to dominate the world, and to nationalist frenzy, both with respect to Indian militarism and with respect to American militarism. We believe that these are all aided and abetted by the same cultural structures that produce corporate globalization. We do not believe, and we do not believe Roy believes, that there is any bright line separating other causes from economic causes.)

One specifically economic cause Roy mentions is that certain important U.S. industries depend on war sales to keep going. Huge and expensive plants have been built to produce, for example, missiles. They have to sell missiles or else go out of business. Wars are needed to deplete the stocks so that new orders will be placed. The second economic cause is that the United States completely depends on imported petroleum. This second reason for considering U.S. militarism to be a necessary consequence of its economy is by itself a weak reason because the U.S. could buy petroleum without militarily controlling its source, as do many countries which depend on imported petroleum even more completely than the United States does. It becomes a strong reason when it is taken as a premise in a chain of reasoning which also includes other premises

---

6 Barsamian, Checkbook 140.

that people called 'Neocons' hold: the enemies of the U.S. might get control of oil supplies. They might then bring the U.S. to its knees by raising prices or even refusing to sell oil to the U.S. By controlling oil, they might reduce the USA's power to control Europe and Japan, and then the U.S. (allegedly) would be unsafe. Then the conclusion follows: the United States must be militarist.

We suggest, however, that neither the arms industry nor oil provides the strongest argument for the claim that there is a causal link between the USA's economic structure and its militarism. The strongest reason supporting an economic explanation of U.S. militarism becomes visible in the light of a critique of the basic cultural structures that govern modern society. Gandhi's Hind Swaraj provides the needed critique. Like John Ruskin and Leo Tolstoy, Gandhi was a turn-of-the-twentieth-century anti-modernist. He condemned modernity not just for its excesses and inconsistencies but for its fundamental premises (its basic cultural structures). Gandhi was the product of a very traditional Hindu family upbringing. Writing aboard the SS Kildonan Castle while sailing back from London, the young Gandhi gave vent to the horror that made him recoil from the so-called 'civilization' which he had just observed in Europe. Such a so-called 'civilization' was irreligion. It was adharma. If one waited long enough it would inevitably self-destruct.[7]

---

7 Mohandas K. Gandhi, Hind Swaraj and Other Writings, ed. Anthony J. Parel (Cambridge, UK: Cambridge University Press, 1997) 37. The English text says 'irreligion,' which the editor glosses in a footnote as a translation of adharma, meaning contrary to dharma, in the original Gujarati text.

There are many reasons why one might say—and why many people do say—that unsustainability is an inherent feature of the modern European—now global—way of life that Gandhi recoiled from in horror in 1909. If being unsustainable is equivalent to eventually self-destructing, then many people will come forward with many reasons why Gandhi was right. We will make a case for a specific reason why he was right. The rules of an adharma society are the same as the rules of an economic society; that sort of society is one prone to use militarism to keep itself going; militarism in general, and specifically the militarism of the United States at the present time, is unsustainable. Militarism driven by economics is one reason why so-called 'civilization' is unsustainable, or, as Gandhi put it, why it will inevitably self-destruct.

Our case for interpreting Gandhi as someone who offers a key to understanding the economics of militarism presupposes our general thesis that it is the moral side of Gandhi that is fundamental. There has been a tendency in interpreting Gandhi's economics to focus rather too much on the physical side of things. People focus too much on the spinning wheel, as Roy in discussing the economics of U.S. militarism focuses on the unsold missiles lying in warehouses, and on the petroleum being guzzled by the cars that crowd the roads. The strongest justification for an economic explanation of U.S. militarism, like Gandhi's strongest critique of modernity, is not about machines but about social and cultural norms. Modern society is economic society. Economic society is modern society. The legal framework of commerce simplifies ethics in ways that make human relationships inherently violent: its Roman Law concept of property rights (which Gandhi wanted to reform with his concept of trusteeship) is violent because it excludes. The poor are poor because other people possess all the land and most of the other goods. (This is not a characteristic of the land, but a characteristic of the law.) Modern society's market-based human relationships, formalized in the law of contracts, simplify the complex relationships of communal loyalty typical of traditional societies. What is left is the lonely individual, loyal to nobody but herself or himself. What we are saying here is not unique to Gandhi. It was said by Hilaire Belloc, by Karl Polanyi, and by many other critics of modernity whom Gandhi does not cite, as well as by the critics of modernity Gandhi does cite in the list of recommended readings at the end of Hind Swaraj. What we want to do here has as its general context points Gandhi and others have made about the generally violent nature of modernity (which, by the way, are not refuted by pointing out that many or most non-modern societies have also been generally violent). What we want to do here specifically is to fill in the dots between the economics of militarism and Gandhi's nonviolent alternative. This will supply a sufficient, but not the only, justification for using Gandhi's term 'self-destruct.'

Our outline of an argument filling in the dots has three parts:

I. A nation or 'civilization' driven to militarism by its own economic structure will be a threat, a danger, and a plague to the rest of the world, which will lead to its self-destruction, both because of the opposition engendered in the rest of the word and because of the expense.

II. John Maynard Keynes was right in his analysis of the instability of capitalism, and militarism is the main means the U.S.A. (as well as other nations at different points in history) has adopted to escape from that instability. (Hence the U.S.A is a nation described in (I)).

III. The premises of Keynes' analysis are equivalent to Gandhi's analysis of the adharmic character of modernity.

One might object that Gandhi's term 'self-destroyed' provides too negative an image. What is really being proven is that social structure must change because it cannot go on as it is. Looking for a positive image of change, one might instead say, borrowing an image from Roy, that another world is on her way and that on a quiet day I can already hear her breathing.[8] We would like to think that this objection has merit, because we would like to think that benign winds are already filling the sails of positive change. Nonetheless we will continue to refer to the (not necessarily rapid, certainly not instantaneous) process of ending a basic social structure that is unsustainable as 'self-destruction.'

To outline briefly the reasons we would give for regarding statements I, II, and III as true, we begin with I:

I. A nation or "civilization" driven to militarism by its own economic structure will be a threat, a danger, and a plague to the rest of the world, which will lead to its self-destruction, both because of

---

[8] Roy, War Talk 75.

the opposition engendered in the rest of the word and because of the expense.

We would call Arundhati Roy herself as the lead witness. No one has better assessed the deep currents of anger that are now raging.[9] Next we would call Arnold Toynbee, who is one of the historians who has amassed a great deal of evidence tending to show that coalitions of the bullied and the bought are unstable.[10] Rule by military might, as well as rule by military might supplemented by payoffs, if it is to be sustainable, must be supplemented by some combination of charm, belief-system, consent, and enlightened self-interest, sometimes summarized by political scientists as 'legitimacy.'

We acknowledge that there are those who see U.S. foreign policy as fully legitimate. There are those who do not perceive any push toward militarism inherent in the structure of the economy of the United States; there are those who believe that the USA has shouldered the burden of wielding freedom's sword out of sheer altruism, and even some who think it has done so to fulfil Biblical prophecies. The Pentagon itself in its planning documents defines the USA's military posture as protecting a list of U.S. interests that does not include its interest in shoring up aggregate demand in a structurally unstable economy.

---

9   Arundhati Roy, The Cost of Living (New York: Modern Library, 1999) 11.
10   Arnold Toynbee, A Study of History (New York: Oxford University Press, 1972, first edition 1934). For some of the criticisms of Toynbee's views see Henry Lloyd Mason, Toynbee's Approach to World Politics (New Orleans: Tulane University, 1958).

Many still see the U.S. military as the police force of a legitimate world order that still has plenty of reserves of charm, belief-system, consent, and enlightened self-interest, and who do not believe, and who do not want to believe, a single word of what Arundhati Roy says to the contrary. We will not try to spell out letter by letter an ironclad argument that would drag any of the people inclined not to believe her or us kicking and screaming, by the overwhelming force of pure logic and pure facts, to a point where they would be forced against their will to admit that militarism is a structural feature of the U.S. social and economic order. We prefer gentle persuasion. From our point of view, which is admittedly certainly not the only point of view, it is self-evident that at this moment in history the United States has so many enemies that it cannot stop fighting, and that at this moment in history the expense of ongoing wars is so high that it cannot continue fighting. Something has got to give.

In discussing briefly how we would argue in favour of statements II and III, we will outline briefly once again what it is that has to give, according to the point of view we are suggesting—a point of view which, we believe, in the course of time more and more people will regard as a reasonable point of view to adopt. We say 'once again' because to outline the necessary features of a transition from a non-viable to a viable way of life is to outline once again Gandhi's critique of modernity.

Before outlining briefly an argument for statement II, we wish to clarify that we are not contradicting ourselves by saying both that economics can make war unsustainable and that economics can provide a solution to a nation's economic problems. Both are true, and sometime both are true of the same war. Statement I relies on the concept that sometimes war bankrupts economies; Statement II relies on the concept that sometimes war stimulates economies.

> II. John Maynard Keynes was right in his analysis of the instability of capitalism, and militarism is the main means the USA (as well as other nations at different points in history) has adopted to escape from that instability. (Hence the USA is a nation described in (I)).

We would advance two lines of arguments in an effort to persuade people of the validity of this second statement. The first would be an interpretation of the history of the United States in the twentieth century, taking Keynes' refutation of Say's Law as a pivotal concept, and taking the Depression of the 1930s as a pivotal event. The second line of argument would be more abstract and general. It would apply to any nation at any time during the past several centuries. We will briefly sketch only the first here.

Say's Law, which was orthodox economics until the time of Keynes, states that supply creates its own demand. There can never be anything left unsold because the very fact that someone offers it for sale guarantees that someone will buy it, at some price or other. As discussed in an earlier chapter, Keynes, following some suggestions of his father's teacher Alfred Marshall, showed that, on the contrary, free markets left to themselves tend to 'low-level equilibrium,' in which those people who have money to buy have already bought as much as they want to buy, but much remains unsold. In particular, a great deal of labour-power remains unsold, in the form of would-be employees who want good jobs, but cannot find employers who want to buy the skill and energy they have to sell.[11]

Whether it was because of Keynes' superior technical arguments, or whether it was because reality in the 1930s had become so obvious that even professional mystifiers could not mystify it, ideas like those of Keynes (including those of some Swedish economists who thought the same thoughts earlier) became enormously influential in the 1930s. In the United States enormous efforts were made to get the economy moving again by stimulating sales, partly through public spending and lending, and partly through various schemes designed to get people in the private sector to spend, or, what in important ways amounted to the same thing, to invest. Nothing really worked until World War II. The war brought the United States out of the Depression.

When the war was over the tendency toward low-level equilibrium did not go away. Various macroeconomic strategies aimed at staving off a relapse, including the promotion of suburbia by subsidizing home ownership, automobiles, highways, and petroleum. Yet the centerpiece of the vast public sector of the United States, which

---

11 Keynes, General Theory, especially chapters 2 and 3. "The celebrated optimism of traditional economic theory, which has led to economists being looked upon as Candides, who, having left this world for the cultivation of their gardens, teach that all is for the best in the best of all possible worlds provided we will let well alone, is also to be traced, I think, to their having neglected to take account of the drag on prosperity which can be executed by an insufficiency of effective demand." Ibid. 33.

was not dismantled after World War II, but which continued to grow even in the Reagan years, and still continues to grow, has been the military-industrial complex. In the light of Keynes' critique of Say's Law, it can be seen that among its basic functions are providing employment and shoring up aggregate demand; in the context of a socially constructed reality in which employment chronically tends to lag; and in which the work of the sales departments of businesses, selling the commodity after it is produced, is forever the bottleneck that slows an industry down.

We do not know whether this brief sketch of an argument will convince anyone that militarism is the main means the U.S. has adopted to escape from the instability of capitalism. Anyone who is convinced, and anybody who did not need convincing because they were already thinking along similar lines, should see immediately that there is a stronger reason for Roy's claim that the USA is locked into militarism by the requirements of its economy. This is not to rule out the possibility that the United States might have followed Keynes in a different direction, as the Scandinavian countries did, creating an equally huge public sector, and sometimes almost an equally huge (proportionally speaking) public debt, not mainly for military spending but mainly for welfare spending. If such a possibility for the U.S. were to be ruled out, it would have to be ruled out for some reason not immediately obvious. Nevertheless, given the United States as it has historically evolved, and as it presently exists, it needs its military to keep its people busy and its industries humming. Roy was right to point out that the arms manufacturers are a powerful influence in the United States, but she might have gone on to say that each and every citizen of the United States enjoys the benefits of living in an economy that has not fallen back into low level equilibrium. (This was written before the crisis that began in 2008). To be more precise, it has only partially and occasionally fallen towards but not fully into a replay of the 1930s. It has managed to avoid repeating that fate mainly by continuing the same kinds of spending patterns that brought it out of that pivotal depression. Militarism benefits every family in the land, since every family has the assurance that if at age 18 their children have no other promising job prospects, the children can join the armed services, where each will get not only a job with an income, but also subsequent educational opportunities and pension benefits. It is the whole system, not just a particular part of it, that is stabilized by the military-industrial complex.[12]

---

12 Some people have made what at first appears to be a contrary argument: that militarism has damaged the U.S. economy because the taxes needed to pay for it raise the prices of U.S. goods that compete in international markets with goods from countries like Germany and Japan which have smaller defense budgets. But there is no reason why it cannot be simultaneously true that militarism is the U.S. way to compensate for insufficient aggregate demand, and also a handicap in international economic competition. See Fred Cook, The Warfare State (New York: Macmillan, 1962); Seymour Melman, The Permanent War Economy: American Capitalism in Decline (New York: Simon and Schuster, 1974); Phillip Berryman, Our Unfinished Business, The U.S. Catholic Bishops' Letters on Peace and the Economy (New York: Pantheon Books, 1989); Paul Baran and Paul Sweezy, Monopoly Capital, an Essay on

Using this stronger argument to explain what drives the United States to war applies a general methodological principle to the understanding of history: Whatever else happens, people must eat and somehow meet their other basic needs. The system that provides for meeting basic needs is a basic cultural structure. Whatever must be done to maintain it will be done.

III. The premises of Keynes' analysis are equivalent to Gandhi's analysis of the adharmic character of modernity.

In other words, the problems in question could be solved if there were no tendency toward low-level equilibrium in the first place, and there would be no tendency toward low-level equilibrium in the first place if there were not the adharma modern society that Gandhi condemns, and if there were instead the dharma of the idealized traditional Indian village that Gandhi advocates. Arundhati Roy is sufficiently suspicious of traditional values that she can be expected to be reluctant to come to this conclusion, but she nevertheless contributes some of the premises from which this conclusion follows.

---

the American Economic and Social Order (New York: Modern Reader Paperbacks, 1968). The claim that military spending shores up aggregate demand and creates employment is not inconsistent with finding that other American institutions also do so; for example, the mass consumption society built around television advertising, the automobile culture; and more benignly the promotion of home ownership and huge expenditures on health care, on education, and on the care of the aged.

Roy remarks that Gandhi proposes as a social ideal a romanticized traditional Indian village.[13] Our reading of Gandhi is exactly the same as hers and we would go on to add that one of the features of that romanticized village is that everyone there is busy performing some useful social function. Gandhi's ideal village is in this respect like the polis (city-state) that Socrates describes in Plato's dialogues. Socrates says (with the help of Plato, his ghostwriter) that in the well-organized polis every techne (craft, special skill) has its agathon (its good, its aim). The techne of the cobbler has for its agathon shoes. The techne of the farmer has as its agathon food.... The techne of the pilot aims to bring the ship safely into port, while the aim of the physician is health. Buying and selling, which is the subject matter dealt with both by Say's Law and by Keynes' refutation of it, play a subordinate role, according to Socrates as according to Gandhi. Socrates' cynical interlocutors, however, Callicles, Gorgias, and Thrasymachus, see the matter differently. For them the techne, like everything else, aims to serve self. All the crafts have the same aim, namely, making money. Gandhi does not agree with Thrasymachus. He agrees with Socrates.

Adopting the values of Gandhi's village or Plato's polis puts the problem of low-level equilibrium in an entirely different light. The problem that Say mystifies, and which Keynes sets out to solve, is that money, which is supposed to circulate, does not circulate. It stops. Keynes' theory posits several psychological 'propensities' and 'preferences,' which are measures of how much money people choose not to spend. Yet more fundamental than people's propensities and preferences is the normative framework

---

13 Roy, The Cost of Living 11.

of constitutive rules which gives them the right to act as individuals doing what they want to do. Given such a normative framework, it becomes inevitable that some amount of money will be squirreled away under mattresses, or left idle in bank accounts. Since the total sum spent by business people paying wages and purchasing other inputs to production flows out of the coffers of the business people, but does not (viewing the economy as a whole) flow back into their coffers as purchases of goods, it follows, as Keynes says, that some businesses must operate at a loss. So they do not operate at all. In the absence of some ingenious Keynesian remedy, like massive government spending, there is low-level equilibrium.

But for Gandhi, as for Socrates, low-level equilibrium is a non-problem. The cobbler was never aiming at making money anyway. He was aiming at making shoes. Why was he making shoes? Because people's feet hurt when they have to walk on rocks barefoot. The argument of Gandhi and Socrates is even stronger if we assume the cobbler to be female, because motherhood has existed for a long time.

Gandhi moves the argument to the level of the love laws, which Roy says are more fundamental than other laws. If you really want to know why what happens happens, ask who loves whom and how much, and who is supposed to love whom and how much. The modern practices of buying and selling in arms-length markets presuppose, according to the legal norms that frame them, a certain love law: the law that nobody loves you but you. In the ideal traditional village, as in many real traditional villages studied by anthropologists, there are complicated rules prescribing who is obliged to whom to do what and when.

So, what might have appeared to be an ambiguity in Roy's thinking really is not one. When she sometimes adopts a moderate version of economic determinism, and at other times suggests that economics is not first in the order of causes, but rather the laws of love, she is not inconsistent. The love laws (which are, we take it, the norms that define proper human relationships) determine the economic laws.

If all three of the statements for which we have outlined if not a proof, then at least a gesture in the direction of persuasion, are true, then structural change at the level Roy calls the love laws is needed. There is a deeper and stronger reason than the two she mentions for believing that economics drives militarism, and the deeper reason calls for deeper changes. The premises from which running a huge military-industrial complex emerges as a solution to an economic problem are indeed the love laws of adharmic modernity. There is a need for a change in the 'how much' of the love laws. There is a need for a change in norms governing how much people are responsible for each other's welfare. It could be a change to the spirit of service Gandhi put into practice in his own life, but it could also be a change to some other norm with some other spirit. It could be different from one culture to another, and multicultural within the same nation, as long as it solves the problem. The problem to be solved is: the acquisition of the necessities of life must become less dependent on employment that in turn is dependent on the profitability of businesses that in turn is dependent on the sale of products.[14]

Arundhati Roy is among the many people of good will who are not easily persuaded that such dangerous elements of typically non-modern traditions as religion and communal bonding could be cultural resources that could be put to good use filling up the holes in modernity. She is not sure which is worse, traditional society or modern society. She grew up in a small town in Kerala as the independent daughter of an independent mother, a mother who had no man in her life to boss her around and who ran her own business, a school. Mother and daughter were the town rebels, but they made a success of it. Arundhati grew up fearing the traditional norms that would have compelled her to marry.[15] The accounts of Rahel's marriage and Mammachi's marriage in The God of Small Things illustrate what she feared. Later in life,

---

14 Equivalently, the problem to be solved is how to prevent capital flight, which Roy acknowledges to be the worst of the 'spectrum of threats' that hold even well intentioned governments hostage. Ordinary Person's Guide 90-91. Seen positively, the problem to be solved is how to attract capital (or else how to change the paradigm that makes capital investment the main source of jobs). Seen negatively, the problem to be solved is how to keep capital from leaving (or else how to change the paradigm that makes capital investment the main source of jobs). Roy points out that giants in opposition, such as Brazil's Lula and South Africa's Mandela, regularly become midgets in office because of the 'spectrum of threats.' Ibid. 90; Public Power 24-25. On capital flight generally see John Maynard Keynes, "National Self Sufficiency."
15 On Roy's childhood see Barsamian, Checkbook 1-10, 106-107.

though, Roy found that the promises of modernity were also hollow. She found herself among the many people who pick and choose, trying to select the best of tradition and the best of modernity. She calls it a high-wire act.[16] Meanwhile, her enemies destroy her country with a pincer movement that combines the worst of tradition, communalism, with the worst of modernity, global capitalism.[17]

Roy suspects that Gandhi is partly to blame for Hindu communalism. He took Ram and Rahim down from heaven and politicized religion.[18] Sometimes he called his ideal Ram Raj, the rule of God. If one thinks of Gandhi's religious politics as giving a start to ideas that later snowballed into today's mass fundamentalist movements, then one will incline to regard Gandhi as an unwitting accomplice of the Hindu mobs that a few years ago roamed the streets of the cities of Gujarat state, beating and killing Muslims, burning Muslim homes, and looting Muslim businesses.

Gandhi, of course, abhorred communal violence. He died a martyr's death while making heroic efforts to quell it. Gandhi walked a tightrope in a high wire act of his own. Although his commitment to moral politics was part and parcel of his religion, he was an anti-modernist who advocated many modern ideals, including those that today's rightwing Hindu fundamentalists most oppose: a

---

16 Barsamian, Checkbook 126.
17 Barsamian, Checkbook 29-30; Roy, War Talk 104-105.
18 Roy, The Cost of Living 117. Roy points out also, in line with a point we make below, that adverse social conditions make people ready to hear fundamentalist political messages. Roy, War Talk 40-42.

secular state, toleration, the abolition of caste privilege, and the equality of women. If one were to ask the question which of the two, Gandhi or Roy, most passionately opposed fundamentalism, the answer would have to be that a race between the two of them would end in a tie. Roy appreciates Gandhi's good intentions. She suspects that they paved a road to hell.

In defence of Gandhi one might make the argument that liberal religion is not so much a cause of fundamentalism as an antidote to it. Seen as a cause of fundamentalism, liberal theologies open a door legitimating religion in general, through which then pass bigots and assassins. Seen as an antidote to fundamentalism, liberal theologies compete for adherents with violent and reactionary sects. To the extent that the former viewpoint corresponds to the facts, religious views like Gandhi's do more harm than good. To the extent that the latter viewpoint corresponds to the facts, religious views like Gandhi's do more good than harm. (One should not overlook the possibility that somebody might be classified as a 'fundamentalist' by some criterion, but display no proclivity toward violence or bigotry or support for reactionary economic policies. However, such a person would be irrelevant to the present discussion, since she or he would not be a person whose conduct Roy would be worrying about.)

There is, however, a third possibility. It is suggested by scholars who have studied the phenomena of contemporary fundamentalism. One of them, Karen Armstrong, points out that the present upsurge of fundamentalist religious politics began in the mid-1970s, not just in India but in other countries as well.[19] It began at the time when

---

19 Karen Armstrong, A History of God (New York: Alfred

the advantage in the worldwide tug of war between capital and labour shifted decisively in favour of capital. Far from being a medieval phenomenon, which for inexplicable reasons has not died out, fundamentalism is a phenomenon caused by contemporary social conditions, which, for explicable reasons, is alive and well. For politicians looking for vote banks, fundamentalist religion is a commodity that intelligent power brokers know how to buy. For the masses looking for meaning and security in an increasingly meaningless and insecure world, a simple faith is a rock, a place of refuge, an anchor. The church is a fellowship of the like-minded. It gives life conscious purpose. It leads in practice to help in time of need, provided by other members of the believing community. Many churches and communal organizations provide social services that governments increasingly provide badly or not at all: schools, poor relief, even hospitals and orphanages. In the light of this third possibility liberal religion can be seen as an antidote to fundamentalism in two ways: (1) it provides competing theologies that are linked to competing ways to share a meaningful life with members of a like-minded community; (2) it devotes itself to changing the unjust social conditions that make people insecure.

A. Knopf, 1993) 390. See also Karen Armstrong, The Battle for God (New York: Ballantine Books, 2000). Gabriel Almond, R. Scott Appleby, and Emmanuel Siran, Strong Religion: The Rise of Fundamentalisms around the World (Chicago: University of Chicago Press, 2003); Ivan Ivekovic, Ethnic and Regional Conflicts in Yugoslavia and Transcaucasia: A Political Economy of Contemporary Ethnonational Mobilization (Ravenna: Longo Editore, 2000).

A more severe criticism of Gandhi is that his political and economic proposals will not work because people are not good enough. Although Roy calls Gandhi a genius because his nonviolence was real, she also suggests that he is romantic. A society that adopted the principles of Gandhi's idealized traditional village would work (and, for that matter, Nehruvian socialism would work too) if people were good enough, but they are not—not nearly.[20] Roy thus chimes in with the mainstream of western political theory. Political institutions must be designed to cope with the fact that people are on the whole not very good, and not likely to get much better.

In defence of Gandhi, it must be said that he was consistent. If the main problems of society must wait for their solutions until people are better, then the means used by activists to solve problems must be morally uplifting. It is in the long run more important to advance the moral education of the people than it is to achieve any particular goal, even, as Gandhi often said, the independence of India. It should also be said that the line between what is impossible because people are not good enough and what is possible because people are good enough is a moving line. Gandhi thought the general trend of history was decreasing himsa (violence) and increasing ahimsa (nonviolence). His follower, the Reverend Dr Martin Luther King Jr, thought that God acted in history to make freedom possible by creating inner discipline in human souls.[21] In recent decades an enormous amount of empirical research by psychologists specializing in the study of

---

20 Roy, The Cost of Living 11.
21 John J. Ansbro, Martin Luther King Jr.: The Making of a Mind (Maryknoll: Orbis Books, 1982) 63-69.

moral development has undergirded character-building educational programs, at every level from kindergarten to continuing education for adults. Their scientific findings validate what Socrates already knew: thinking about moral issues, and engaging in dialogue about them, tends to improve moral judgment, and to improve conduct.[22] Roy herself is a moral educator, since her writings certainly make people think about moral issues. The predictable consequence of her activity as a writer is that to some extent people will become better.

There remains also the option of not even trying to reform society in any way that requires for its feasibility the general acceptance of norms of social responsibility. As noted above, it is not immediately obvious why the non-militaristic solution to the problem of low-level equilibrium achieved by Scandinavian social democracy in the decades after World War II could not be followed anywhere at any time. The love laws of Sweden, for example, did not change perceptibly at an individual level, but the nation as a whole accepted responsibility for its people. As Per Albin Hanssen, Sweden's great postwar Prime Minister, said, Sweden became a Folkhemmet, a home for all Swedes. There was no need to make the

---

22 See, e.g., the Journal of Moral Education, a periodical published in London by the Social Morality Council; Jean Piaget, The Moral Judgment of the Child (New York: Free Press, 1997) (first French edition 1932); F. Clark Power, Ann Higgins, and Lawrence Kohlberg, Lawrence Kohlberg's Approach to Moral Education (New York: Columbia University Press, 1989); Nel Noddings, The Challenge to Care in Schools: An Alternative Approach to Education (New York: Teachers College Press, 2005).

acquisition of the necessities of life less dependent on employment that in turn was dependent on the profitability of businesses that in turn was dependent on the sale of products; because Sweden achieved full employment at high wages in profitable industries that were able to sell their products. The miracle that happened to the Swedes did not require Gandhian idealism. It only required a well-organized labor movement (with 90 percent of the workforce in unions) and a voting public with a rational understanding of its own economic self-interest.[23]

One of the many people in India who have never considered a welfare state along Scandinavian lines to be a viable option for India is Manmohan Singh, the present Prime Minister, whose views will be considered in the next chapter. A review of the evolution of his thinking will shed light on why he has apparently concluded that Gandhian idealism is needed after all. It will tend to show that no program at all that remains within the confines of standard economics is feasible, neither one that adopts the advice India was getting from western advisors under

---

23 Thus Gunnar Myrdal, one of the principal architects of the Swedish model, wrote that "liberal society was destroyed because people in general started to behave as rationally as its theory had always wrongly assumed that they did." Gunnar Myrdal, Beyond the Welfare State (New Haven: Yale University Press, 1960) 35-36. Of course he spoke too soon. Lecturing at Yale in 1958, he did not expect liberal society to come roaring back as today's neoliberalism. The present authors have analyzed the limitations of Swedish social democracy and social democracy in general in their Dilemmas of Social Democracies (Lanham: Lexington Books, 2006).

the influence of the Scandinavian Way in the 1950s and 1960s, nor one that adopts the advice India is getting now from international advisors who participate in the consensus on a Comprehensive Development Framework articulated by the World Bank under its recent president James Wolfensohn.

If it be granted that when analyzed in strictly economic terms India's current attempt to moderate the rigors of neoliberalism by combining growth with equity cannot possibly deliver on its promises, then there are more reasons to reconsider Gandhi's radical ideas. Perhaps, after all, the adharma premises of modernity are unworkable, modernity unsustainable, destined to self-destruct. Perhaps the dreamers are not those who put into practice trusteeship, a love ethic, nonviolence, and constructive programs. Perhaps they are the realists. Perhaps the people usually thought of as the realists are the dreamers.

* * *

CHAPTER 8

MANMOHAN SINGH

"*Developing countries need a sort of cultural revolution inspired by the Gandhian ideals of trusteeship, non-possession or voluntary poverty on the part of the elite if those countries are going to meet the basic human needs of all their people even with a very low per capita income.*"
—*Manmohan Singh*[24]

We have been advocating the transformation of the basic cultural structures of the modern world.[25] It is not,

---

24 Manmohan Singh, "Sustaining Development in an Uncertain International Environment," The Indian Economic Journal 33/3 (Jan.-Mar 1986) 1-14, at 10. We will refer to Manmohan Singh sometimes as "Manmohan" because he is a member of India's Sikh minority. In that ethnic group everyone takes the last name of 'Singh.'

25 What makes a cultural structure 'basic' is that it defines entitlements to basic necessities, such as food. The 'basic cultural structures' are the economic ones. More precisely, they are the legal foundations of the economy. By using the word 'basic' in the first sentence of this chapter, and frequently thereafter, we acknowledge that there are many people who resist and oppose modern culture, but not in the particular respect we would consider 'basic.' For example, the BJP, the party that

however, at all clear to many people that the basic structures of the modern world should be changed, even if that task could be accomplished.[26] Given that India is a place where numerous attempts at radical change have been attempted, and where they are now mostly rejected by the majority, and also that India is Exhibit A (sometimes in competition with Chile; or in competition with the East Asian Tigers, South Korea, Taiwan, Hong Kong, and Singapore) submitted as proof of the merits of free-market reforms, it is a good site to explore in search of answers to three questions of great interest to the whole world:

- whether there is any feasible method for changing the basic cultural structures of the modern world;
- whether it is desirable to change the basic structures of the modern world;
- whether the advice currently being given to (and sometimes imposed on) developing nations by the main international agencies is good advice.

---

governed India immediately prior to the current government headed by Singh, tends to be very modern in the sense that it is pro-market, but on religious and communal grounds it is anti-modern with respect to what we are calling non-basic cultural structures of the modern world, such as divorce, gay rights, the equality of women, multiculturalism, western rock music, scant clothing, abortion.

26 Many believe precisely that it is misguided attempts to change these structures—most notably Nehru's attempt to establish in India a socialistic pattern of society—that ought to be changed.

1. On Whether Neoliberal Advice Is Good Advice

We will begin with the third of these questions, for those who are giving (and sometimes imposing) the most advice on developing nations would of course answer this question with a resounding yes; they would therefore answer the second question above with an equally resounding no. In the estimation of this group, the best path toward the reduction and eventual eradication of poverty is for each nation-state to pursue its comparative advantage within a regime of international free trade. In other words, the basic cultural structures of the modern world that allow the functioning of capitalism already provide for poverty elimination, if only all the countries of the world would adopt and adapt to them with proper fervor and in the correct spirit.

For these commentators, which, in shorthand, we will refer to as the neoliberal school of thought, 'reform' and 'structural adjustment' mean relying more on markets and less on planning.[1] India is Exhibit A in support of

---

1 The theory of comparative advantage was originated by James Mill (1773-1836) and elaborated by neoclassical political economist David Ricardo (1772-1823). It holds that trade is mutually beneficial, provided that each nation-state, as trading partner, acts in the 'economically rational' manner of (a) specializing its production in goods and services that are cheaper for it to produce, compared to its trading partner; and (b) exporting at least a portion of those goods in exchange for imports of goods and services that its trading partner can produce more cheaply. If a country is relatively heavily industrialized, it is said to have a comparative advantage in capital-intensive goods; if a country is relatively less industrialized, it is said to have a comparative advantage in 'labour-intensive

their case because while following a path of free-market reform, India, at least according to several standard economic indicators, has prospered. Another group of commentators, which we will refer to, also in shorthand, as the New International Division of Labor (NIDL) school of thought, looks at the same facts regarding India's success in the global market and draws entirely different conclusions regarding the reasons they are so. Both schools of thought take the same explanandum (i.e., that which is to be explained), which is India's relative prosperity following its adoption of neoliberal economic reforms starting in 1991; and both use a similar explanans or explanatory mechanism, which is that relative production costs determine global patterns of trade, so industry very predictably migrates toward places where these costs are relatively cheap. The story told on the basis of these same facts, however, differs. In the neoliberal estimation, India is reaping the riches of having found the right niches to allow it to compete most efficiently in the global market; while in the estimation of the NIDL school of thought, India is being rewarded for its preeminence in the patently perverse global 'race to the bottom.' Let us

---

goods' (i.e., its comparative advantage lies in its underemployed workforce and the nation-state should therefore strive to keep wages low in order to attract foreign investment). Although Ricardo's mathematical model said to demonstrate the truth of the theory of comparative advantage relied on the assumption that the factors of production (capital, land, and labour) were always fully employed—as well as fully mobile in the case of capital and labour—and although these conditions have never obtained, the theory is still embraced by mainstream economists.

look at each of these views in turn. While neither those in the neoliberal nor those in the NIDL school of thought take as seriously as we would urge the need for the transformation of basic cultural structures, and while—as will be made clear below—we often agree with critiques of India's Nehruvian socialism, in the end we find that it is the latter interpretation, that of the NIDL school of thought, that is borne out by the evidence from the post-1991 Indian experience.

The current prime minister, a professional economist named Manmohan Singh, was himself the architect of the 1991 economic reforms, in his capacity then as Minister of Finance. Manmohan Singh is a confessed pragmatist and pluralist, who acknowledges that the comings and goings of poverty and its connections with development are the outcomes of numerous complex factors that are not fully understood.[2] Nonetheless we will begin by attributing to him a rather generic endorsement of free market economics, as is found in the writings of his Oxford tutor and admirer Ian Little—who has perhaps greater theoretical clarity and less practical wisdom than his tutee—as well as in his own writings. We take the views in the following paragraphs to be a fair sample of neoliberal views widely held in powerful circles, in India and worldwide. They are theories that hold that the socialistic ideas that, by and large, prevailed in India until June of 1991 actually created poverty.[3] It is important to

---

[2] Manmohan Singh, "Globalization and the Asia-Pacific Region: Challenges and Opportunities in the Twenty-First Century," Asia-Pacific Development Journal 4/2 (1997) 1.

[3] June 1991 symbolically marks the turning point when Manmohan Singh became Finance Minister, although some

note, however, that the acceptance of neoliberalism represented a change in Singh's earlier views toward development. In the late 1980s, Manmohan Singh's career had led him to the job of Secretary-General of the South Commission and to a concept of development that embraced a concept of national self-reliance, although not a fully Gandhian one. Shortly before the crucial moment when he became Finance Minister of India, in his capacity as Secretary-General he wrote: "The South cannot count on a significant improvement in the international economic environment in the 1990s. Maximum self-reliance must therefore be the keynote of its renewed development effort. If only for this reason, the new development strategies cannot be a simple replica of the past."[4] Events

---

neoliberal reforms began at prior dates and although the neoliberal reforms initiated at that time were implemented very slowly and even today have only been implemented incompletely, and even though the pace of reforms has varied state by state in India's federal system. There was no rational attempt to end poverty in India until after June 1991.

4 Manmohan Singh, "In a Changing World: Challenges to the South," Change: Threat or Opportunity, ed. Uner Kirdar (New York: United Nations, 1992) 174-175. Although the book was published in 1992, Singh's chapter must have been written before he left his job as Secretary-General to become Finance Minister of India in June of 1991. The passage quoted continues: "Each country's development strategies must necessarily be specific to its particular circumstances, and related to its stage of development, size, resource base, cultural heritage, and other national characteristics. But a self-reliant people-centred development will need to be guided by certain common principles and objectives. The South must aim at fast and sustained growth, in turn requiring high rates of investment and savings

in India would soon change Manmohan Singh's perspective and convince him that India's development strategy would have to be a replication of the path followed by many other developing nations which had been forcefully persuaded to heed the advice of the international lending agencies.

In 1991 India faced the unthinkable, the intolerable, the yawning abyss. The self-reliance Gandhi advocated had not come to pass, while the dependence he feared had become entrenched. The country could not live without imports. It had overcome the pitiful dependence on foreign grain, much of it donated by the United States, which had been the national shame of the 1960s; but still in 1991 it could not live without imported petroleum, fertilizer, industrial inputs, spare parts, and many specialized products. Yet India could not import. In most of the years since independence India had run deficits, living on borrowed money. In early 1991, the doors to further

---

and the utmost efficiency in the use of resources. At the same time, people-centred development requires a full commitment to equity and participation. This calls for strategies that are sensitive to the social, cultural, and gender dimensions of development. Innovative ways must be found to reconcile the imperatives of economic growth and social equity and to harmonize technical modernization with the preservation of cultural identity." The Common Minimum Programme (CMP), which is discussed below, can be read as another declaration, a decade and a half later, of the desirability of achieving the synthesis of prosperity and equity that Manmohan advocated as Secretary-General. It is a thesis of the present authors that the "innovative ways" that must be found to "reconcile" apparently incompatible objectives necessarily include ways to alter the basic cultural structures of the modern world.

borrowing closed. Commercial lenders, both foreign and domestic, no longer believed that India could pay its debts. India's cash reserves fell to about a billion dollars, enough to pay for two weeks' imports.[5]

The balance of payments crisis led to the fall of the government. The new government, installed in June of 1991, led by Narasimha Rao, named Manmohan Singh as Minister of Finance, and his concrete task as Finance Minister was to prevent default by securing the cooperation of donors and lenders.[6] To gain for his people a new lease on life, Manmohan had to acknowledge before the international authorities such as the International Monetary Fund that India's policies had been 'unsound.' Measures had to be taken to put Indian finances on a 'sound' basis, which, translated, meant that India had to reorganize itself in order to become capable of paying its debts regularly as they fell due.

Imports had to be restricted. Exports had to be encouraged, which was accomplished, in the short run, largely by devaluing the rupee. To deal with the underlying

---

[5] Manmohan Singh, "Economic Policy Planning: The Task Ahead," The Indian Economic Journal 39/3 (1992) 39-40.

[6] "India had an unsustainable fiscal deficit. Our central government deficit was as high as 8.5 percent of GDP. India had an unsustainable balance of payments deficit. The current account deficit was close to 3.5 percent of GDP and there were no foreign lenders who would finance that deficit. Our foreign exchange reserves had literally disappeared, so we were on the verge of bankruptcy, and the nation faced an acute collapse of its economy." Manmohan Singh, PBS Interview, 6 February 2001. The text of the interview is available at www.pbs.org/commandingheights, under Manmohan Singh (cited hereafter as "PBS Interview").

structural causes of the balance of payments crisis, deficits had to be reduced. That meant keeping wage costs down and cutting back also on the 'social wage,' i.e., the benefits provided to the public by government programs.[7] Instead of general food subsidies it was decided that there should be less expensive food programs that would target the very poor.[8]

Deficit reduction also meant turning around public sector enterprises that were operating at a loss, which meant either operating them more as if they were private-sector enterprises, or actually privatizing them. Hiring more people than were necessary to do the work had generated major public-sector losses. Redundant employees were both a source of deficits and an obstacle to privatization, since investors were reluctant to bid for companies that were run more as a source of jobs than as a source of profits.[9] Another major reason for public sector losses was

---

7 Manmohan's Oxford tutor Ian Little and his co-author Vijay Joshi write: "Public employment and wages rose rapidly over the 1980s, aided and abetted by increased indexation. The States were particularly to blame. Arresting the growth of the wage bill will require a freeze on new employment and pay restraint." Vijay Joshi and I.M.D. Little, India's Economic Reforms, 1991-2001 (Oxford and New York: Clarendon Press, 1996) 40 (cited hereafter as Joshi and Little). The authors distinguish between the stabilization measures needed to deal with the crisis, and the ensuing structural reform. This is a distinction useful for their purposes but not for ours. The authors' own analysis of how much deficit spending can be sustained, pp. 24-31, justifies seeing the crisis as having been a wakeup call showing the need for structural reform.
8 Joshi and Little 232.
9 Joshi and Little write: "There is a problem as to whether

that public utilities had been providing electricity and water to farmers at below-cost rates. In this respect two deficit-producing categories, unprofitable public enterprises and subsidies to farmers, overlapped. While deficits had to be reduced, exports and economic growth had to be augmented. This implied augmenting profits. Enter the Programme of Economic Stabilisation and Restructuring, the name for India's 1991 economic reforms.

The Programme of Economic Stabilisation and Restructuring was a solution based on the neoliberal diagnosis of the problem, which held that India's pre-1991 socialistic policies created poverty because they were biased against employment and thus interfered with India's exploitation of its comparative advantage.[10] 'Bias against employment' is a concept in some ways at odds with—and in other ways firmly anchored in—common sense. To understand the concept, it is first necessary to think of employment as a transaction, set within the context of a mainly market economy. Markets are made up of transactions between individual decision-makers. Transactions are sales, from the point of view of the seller, and purchases, from the point of view of the buyer. In an employment transaction, someone sells labour-power, the employee, and someone buys labour-power, the employer. In order for the transaction to occur there must be a willing seller and a willing buyer. That is contract law. A bias against employment operates by reducing the number of willing buyers.[11] In

---

surplus labour should be shed before privatization, or left to the new owners." Joshi and Little 194.

10   Joshi and Little 11, 245.

11   Theoretically, it could also work by reducing the number of willing sellers, but that rarely happens, and it is not recorded

this respect the concept of bias against employment is firmly anchored in common sense, for it is common sense that there are no jobs created without employers willing to hire people.

There are also cases, however, where it is at odds with common sense. One case is the pre-1991 labour legislation in India, which was designed to protect workers and to favour relatively high wages. Common sense might well view such laws as biased in favour of employees, and consequently in some sense biased in favour of employment, especially where the laws provide that the workers cannot be laid off without just cause. Such legislation was thought of by the legislators who approved it as favouring the working classes, and the working classes have often been generically associated with the poor, as the property-owning classes have been generically associated with the rich; but if this is common sense, it is a version of common sense that the concept of 'bias against employment' contradicts.[12] Legislation and labour union action

---

that it has ever happened in post-independence India.

12 Joshi and Little write, "[T]he use of labour has been discouraged by relatively high wages and by over-protective labour legislation." Joshi and Little 220. It is to be noted that neoliberals do not identify the poor with the working class, nor the rich with the property-owning class. In this respect they are in accord with the official statistics, for which, indeed, they themselves often define the criteria that determine who counts as what. Among the very poor, conventionally defined as those who live on less than the equivalent of one 1985 U.S. dollar per day (classified as 'absolute poverty' by the Word Bank), which is the class of people whose numbers in India have now dwindled to roughly 35 per cent of the population, most are unemployed, disabled, too old or too young to work,

favouring workers produces a bias against employment because it gives the workers more rights. Since the sellers of labour-power have more rights, the employment transaction is less profitable for the buyers of labour-power, and consequently, there are fewer willing buyers. In such a case as India's pre-1991 labour legislation, contract law has been modified to lay more burdens on the buyer, often including the burden of keeping and continuing to pay employees whom the employers no longer want.

Labour law was not the only means by which India's pre-1991 governments allegedly created poverty. Indeed, practically everything the federal government did could be construed as creating poverty.[13] Almost any reasonably lucrative economic activity required a permit. Permits required influence, and influence required money. Thus the poor were shut out of the system.[14] India's was a monumentally inefficient bourgeois socialism, which heavily subsidized non-poor elites in both the public and private sectors; it especially subsidized agriculture, through practically free fertilizer, water, and electricity, and then, to top it all off, through supporting agricultural

---

or chronically underemployed. Therefore, the rights granted to steadily employed workers under pre-1991 labour law, and to some extent under still existing labour law, are regarded as favouring the non-poor. They protect workers, most of whom are not poor or not very poor; this protection is described as creating a bias against employment.

13 Joshi and Little 220-221, 245.

14 "Indiscriminate and excessive protection and subsidization must be avoided in order to promote efficiency and technological dynamism." Singh, "In a Changing World" 176.

prices through government purchases of crops; all at the expense of the masses.

Another set of examples of the government creating poverty concerns industrialization. Against Gandhi, India's socialists and quasi-socialists pointed out that an average worker in the United States was 36 times more productive than an average Indian worker, because the U.S. worker was backed by machines that multiplied his efforts. Bearing in mind the Swedish model of a high-wage high-productivity economy, and also the patterns set in the United States by bargaining between the United Auto Workers and the automakers, they reasoned that the way out of poverty for India was high wages, and the way to high wages was in the first place capital investment to raise productivity, and in the second place political clout to make sure that workers and farmers got their fair share of the benefits of productivity gains. Bearing in mind also the rapid industrialization of the Soviet Union, India's Five Year Plans emphasized heavy industry. But as it turned out, industrialization in India did not follow the American path, or the Swedish path, or the Soviet path. As in Japan, India's major private big-business corporations were dominated by a few families. Their private mega-projects were mainly coordinated with public planning, and were often financed with credits from government-run banks and insurance companies. At the same time, the Gandhian heritage remained alive in an attenuated form, in the respect that there was government funding for village artisans, for small business generally, and for many kinds of projects designed to help poor people help themselves. Besides providing funding, the government also directed both private- and public-sector banks to hold certain percentages of their total loan portfolios in priority areas, which included small farmers, scheduled castes (formerly known as untouchables), small business generally, exporters, poor people, and whatever other priority areas legislatures might choose to establish. None of this was thoughtless. India's leaders thought they had good reasons for believing they were on the right track before 1991.[15]

Empirical studies showed, however, that the non-small and the non-poor were usually the beneficiaries of programs and policies intended to help the small and the poor.[16] But the neoliberal critique that led up to the final contours of the Programme of Economic Stabilisation and Restructuring was not just empirical. It was also theoretical: in principle government should not be in the business of directing flows of investment capital. That social function should, most of the time, be left to markets, although government should where necessary regulate markets and promote competition.

Almost everything government and government-directed credit programs had done in pre-1991 India had created a bias against employment, in the sense described above, by promoting capital-intensive production

---

[15] For a sympathetic account of the early planners giving plausible reasons for thinking they were on the right track, see Wilfred Malenbaum, Modern India's Economy: Two Decades of Planned Growth (Columbus, OH: Merrill, 1971).

[16] Francine Frankel reviews and attempts to explain the evidence that Nehru's nominally socialist government in practice favoured the upper classes in her India's Political Economy: 1947-1977: The Gradual Revolution (Princeton: Princeton University Press, 1978).

methods in a country whose great comparative advantage in international trade was its vast reserves of labour.[17] For example, the government created a bias against employment when it promoted cheap loans to help farmers buy tractors. The farmers ended up with tractors that they never would have purchased had they been left to use their own good business judgment in a competitive market environment. Meanwhile, the landless labourers were worse off than ever because such purchases of mechanized farm equipment meant that their ability to sell their labour-power to the farmer had been taken from them.

The anti-poverty theory behind Manmohan Singh and the neoliberal school of thought is, then, in briefest summary, that a major cause of poverty is bias against employment, and that a major cure is to reverse that bias. Restrictions and taxes that make employers less willing to hire should be liberalized or removed altogether. At the same time, the massive subsidies that pamper employers should be reduced or cancelled.[18] By withdrawing

---

[17] "While the labour force increased rapidly owing to population growth, capital-intensive patterns of development and the use of inappropriate technologies created too few jobs." Singh, "In a Changing World" 172. "The use of capital has for forty years been encouraged by interest subsidies.... The search for agricultural self-sufficiency has twisted agricultural production in favour of edible oils and sugar which are relatively capital intensive; and capital intensive methods such as harvesters have been encouraged by cheap loans. Almost all governmental interventions have reduced the demand for unskilled labour." Joshi and Little 220-221.

[18] Manmohan Singh, "Globalization and the Asia-Pacific Region: Challenges and Opportunities in the Twenty-First Century," Asia-Pacific Development Journal 4/2 (1997) 1-7.

subsidies the government can achieve two goals at once: it can reduce its deficits, and it can fund social programs. Prior to 1991 India had no public welfare program at all. Many, especially girls, had no primary education. Public health services were in some cases appalling and in others nonexistent.

India's neoliberalism has definitely, especially but not entirely in theory, been neoliberalism with a human face. Besides funding social programs that directly benefit the poor, the architects of Indian neoliberalism believe the government should fund employment-generating public works, and even fund make-work programs whose justification is the low-wage jobs they provide and not the assets they produce. When in spite of policies that reverse the bias against employment, the poor still have no work, the government should be the employer of last resort, being careful to pay wages so low that the poor do not prefer make-work programs to productive work for a private employer.[19] Today's neoliberals are not Social Darwinists. They do not believe that the poor should ever be left to starve. Manmohan Singh's tutor Ian Little sums up a neoliberal assessment of the most appropriate way of combating poverty:

> *There are only two ways of assisting the poor. One is to transfer wealth to them. This may include the transfer of income, or assets such as land, or the enhancement of their principal asset, that is themselves.... The enhancement of their principal asset, themselves, calls for the increased public attention to and expenditure on health and education that*

---

19 Joshi and Little 235-242.

we have endorsed above. A case can still be made for substantial land reform, but it has proved to be politically impossible, and we do not discuss it. The other way to help the poor is to increase the demand for their services.[20]

Reversing the bias against employment in order to increase the demand for the services of the poor was a large part of what the Programme of Economic Stabilisation and Restructuring attempted to do. According to some indicators, it has been successful. The economic reforms starting in 1991 represented a general opening of the Indian economy. It promoted more exports and allowed more imports. This was entirely in line with neoliberal policy recommendations as expressed by Manmohan Singh:

A dynamic export sector is clearly important for the efficient management of the economy.... Thus, there is certainly a strong case for protection levels to be rationalized in line with perceived long-term comparative advantage and, over time, to be reduced to provide the stimulus of foreign competition in domestic markets. And the anti-export bias implicit in the incentives of tariff and exchange rate systems needs to be removed.[21]

---

20 Joshi and Little 219-220.
21 Manmohan Singh, "Development Policy Research: The Task Ahead," Keynote address at the World Bank Annual Conference on Development Economics, 1989, published in Proceedings of the World Bank Annual Conference on Development Economics (1989) 11-20, at 19.

In accordance with these principles, the government lowered tariffs, lifted price controls, and lifted import quotas from thousands of goods. An overall effect was intended to be widening opportunities for profit for producers of these goods, whether those producers were Indians or foreigners. Taken as a whole, these policies offered benefits to both foreign and domestic producers, although in many cases domestic producers now had to compete with foreigners who previously had been kept out. The government also lowered taxes on businesses and opened previously closed sectors of the Indian economy to foreign direct investment (FDI). In 1993, the Foreign Exchange Regulation Act, which was originally instituted in 1973, was modified to allow 'nonresident Indians' and Indian-owned overseas corporate bodies (OCBs)—i.e., foreign companies that are at least 60 percent owned by nonresident Indians—to buy and own real estate. In general, the reforms carried out in 1991 and soon thereafter opened the possibility for other foreign companies (with the notable exclusion of foreign banks) to own real estate under restricted circumstances. (Rather predictably, real estate prices spiralled.[22]) Together the reforms we have

---

22 Amarjit Kaur, "Labour, Industry and the State in Industrialising Asia: An Overview," Women Workers in Industrialising Asia: Costed, Not Valued, ed. Amarjit Kaur (Basingstoke: Palgrave Macmillan, 2004) 208; Jan Nijman, "The Effects of Economic Globalization: Land Use and Land Values in Mumbai, India," Globalization and the Margins, ed. Richard Grant and John Rennie Short (Houndmills, Basingstoke, Hampshire; New York: Palgrave Macmillan, 2002) 159; Jeffrey D. Sachs, The End of Poverty: Economic Possibilities for Our Time (New

mentioned above have often (mistakenly in our opinion) been seen as the underlying causes of the higher levels of income that have led to India's being Exhibit A. India is Exhibit A submitted to the court of world opinion as empirical proof of the truth of neoliberal theory. New International Division of Labour scholars see the same facts differently, and also in some cases cite different facts. For them India is Exhibit A to prove the truth of a different theory: the theory that in recent years capital has moved its operations to sites where high quality labour is cheap and abundant.

Neoliberals and the New International Division of Labour scholars agree that India has achieved a certain degree of economic prosperity. In the years following 1991, many economic indicators for India were improving, which led both potential foreign investors and Indian entrepreneurs to exhibit considerable optimism about the prospects for profit. Foreign investments poured in.[23]

York: Penguin, 2005) 178.

23 We offer here just a few examples of improvements in economic indicators. In 1996, India's average rate of inflation was 6.3 percent, down for an average annual rate of inflation of 9 percent over the previous ten years. See United Nations Development Programme, Human Development Report 1999 (New York and Oxford: Oxford University Press, 1999) 182. Furthermore, already by 1993, India was tackling its balance of payments problem and bringing exports and imports closer into line with each other. In 1993, India's export-import ratio (i.e., exports as a percentage of imports) was 95. The growth of exports in turn allowed the Indian government to devote a higher percentage of its Gross National Product to debt service, to the great satisfaction of international lenders. United Nations Development Programme, Human Development

Flows of foreign direct investment into India increased from $113 million in 1991 to $1.7 billion in 1995, a more than 1400 percent increase over four years.[24] India's private sector surged forward throughout the decade of the 1990s. Private investment in key parts of the Indian infrastructure expanded dramatically in the 1996-2003 period: private investment in energy tripled; the transportation infrastructure saw an eighteen-fold increase; and private investment in telecommunications a staggering twenty-one-fold increase. These improvements in infrastructure in turn made doing business in India easier. They contributed to India's having what is called (in the idiom of a common meteorological metaphor) a good investment 'climate.'[25] By the late 1990s, India had begun to experience an export boom in the area of information technology (IT) (e.g., the production of software, data entry and data transcription, call centres), and this

---

Report 1996 (New York and Oxford: Oxford University Press, 1996) 137.

24 UNCTAD, World Investment Report 1995: Transnational Corporations and Competitiveness (United Nations publication, Sales No. E.95.II.A.9).

25 World Bank, 2005 World Development Indicators (Washington, D.C.: World Bank, 2005) 271. 'Investment climate' is quantified by the World Bank by asking senior managers about a specific series of considerations for each country and reporting the percentage of these managers who considered each of these factors a 'serious constraint' to doing business. These factors are, in order of their listing: policy uncertainty, corruption, lack of confidence of courts to uphold property rights, crime, tax rates, time dealing with officials, average time to clear customs, finance, electricity, labour skills, and labour regulation. Ibid. 275.

boom has expanded in recent years to include not just traditional IT but also what neoliberal advocates refer to as 'BPO,' business process outsourcing. Since 1991, the Indian economy, as measured by its Gross Domestic Product, has experienced an average annual rate of growth of approximately 5.5 percent; and by 2004, it was growing at a rate of approximately 7 percent per year—a stunning growth-rate by any standard, and one which approached China's phenomenal growth-rate in GDP.[26]

Lest one be tempted to conclude that these nice sounding statistics meant nothing of substance to the poor of India, we would hasten to add that certain socioeconomic indicators show improvement in basic quality of life for Indians over the period in question. The infant mortality rate has dropped from 74 (per one thousand births) in 1993 to 67 in 2002; and the life expectancy rate (i.e., life expectancy at birth) has increased from 58.7 years in 1993 to 63.7 in 2002.[27] The primary school completion rate has increased 3 percentage points over the 1994-2004 period; and the ratio of girls to boys in primary and secondary school has jumped 10 percentage points, to

---

26 Sachs 181-182. Jayati Ghosh, "Macroeconomic Reforms and a Labour Policy Framework for India," ILO Employment Strategy Papers, 2004, 7.

27 Shashi Jain, "Basic Social Security in India," Social Security for the Excluded Majority: Case Studies of Developing Countries, ed. Wouter van Ginnekin (Geneva: International Labour Office, 1999) 41; United Nations Development Programme, Human Development Report 2004 (New York: Oxford University Press, 2004).

80 percent, over the period from 1991 to 2003.[28] Furthermore, while the numbers themselves are much in dispute, most estimates hold that indeed poverty in general has decreased in conjunction with India's increasing economic prosperity overall. Economist Jeffrey Sachs points out that by national measures, the Indian poverty rate declined from 42 percent of the total population in 1990 to an estimated 35 percent by 2001.[29] A different estimate holds that the percentage of the Indian population living below the poverty line had been brought down from 38.9 percent in the 1987-88 period to 35.9 percent already by 1993-94.[30] 35 percent of the population living below the

---

28 World Bank, 2005 World Development Indicators 27.

29 Sachs 182.

30 Jain 38. This estimate takes into account the minimum per capita expenditure and income required to fulfil the most basic consumption needs, and it is an aggregate derived from state-specific poverty lines in India generated on the basis of quinquennial consumer expenditure surveys of the National Sample Survey Organization. This estimate is a poverty headcount ratio (the share of persons identified as poor in a given population)—as is the estimate given by Jeffrey Sachs—which is one of the two most widely used poverty indicators. The other most commonly used indicator is the aggregate poverty headcount, which is the number of persons identified as poor in a population. Sanjay Reddy and Camelia Minoiu identify some methodological problems inherent in these indicators that leave them quite open to manipulation in ways that can either minimize or, on occasion, overestimate official poverty counts. For example, because the poverty headcount ratio depends on the size of the population classified as 'non-poor,' the size of the non-poor population can be altered through redefinition, and the poverty headcount ratio will show a

poverty line would not be a number to brag about for many countries, but for India, which was accustomed to having poor majorities, it is an achievement.

As mentioned above, commentators from the New International Division of Labour school of thought look at the same facts and use them to tell a different story. While they concede that India's GDP growth is quite amazing, and while they concede that poverty is on the

---

reduction in poverty even while consumption levels among the poor may remain the same or even diminish. A problem with the aggregate poverty headcount is that it is insensitive to the size and more importantly the range of income levels within the 'non-poor' population. Sanjay G. Reddy and Camelia Minoiu, "Has World Poverty Really Fallen during the 1990s?" http://www.columbia.edu/~cm2036/sensitivityanalysis.pdf, 28 May 2005 (as of 16 September 2005). Yet another estimate of poverty levels in India—one which makes the important distinction between rural and urban regions—holds that by the year 2000, the poverty headcount ratio in rural India had fallen to 26.3 percent (from 39.4 percent in 1987-88) and in the urban areas of India had fallen to 12 percent (from 22.5 percent in 1987-88). A.S. Deaton and J. Dreze, "Poverty and Inequality in India—A Re-Examination," Economic and Political Weekly 37/36 (7 September 2002) 3729-3748. For a discussion of the debate on poverty estimates in India, see A.S. Deaton, "Measuring Poverty in a Growing World (or Measuring Growth in a Poor World)," Review of Economics and Statistics 87/1 (2005) 1-19; and Abhijit Sen and Himanshu, "Poverty and Inequality in India - I," Economic and Political Weekly, 39/38 (18 September 2004) 4247-4263. This latter article in particular suggests a far more pessimistic interpretation of the rate of poverty reduction in India over the period from 1990-91 to 1999-2000.

decline, the NIDL perspective urges us to pay attention to the ground-level realities driving this growth and to the specific effects of economic reforms upon the poor and the working class. Ground-level ethnographic studies tend to show that some part of India's miracle is an artifact of research methodology. Different methodologies tap different realities. Quantified statistical data of the kinds usually reported tell a story somewhat different from the stories told by qualitative research and by quantitative research with a focus on different indicators. Even though official poverty rates are slowly on the decline, neoliberal reforms have engendered a wider context of overall economic insecurity that is not always revealed in—and is sometimes masked by—official economic indicators. The real estate boom in Mumbai, for example, which was sparked by the easing of restrictions upon foreign ownership of such property, has led to the conversion of more and more property to commercial uses and away from use as residential space, which in turn has driven up prices for living spaces and has made affordable housing for many a far more remote possibility than before.

Furthermore, the NIDL school attributes India's relative prosperity to its offering up of its workforce to the global market in a way that leaves Indian workers unprotected in nearly every way from the global market's future vagaries. Looking at today's numbers, one sees that their wages are higher. But their insecurity may well be greater, because they are now selling their labour power in a global market where competition is stiff and shifts in capital flows rapid.

At the same time competition with India's low wages undermines labour standards in the first-world countries that industries move away from when they move to India. This raises the question whether it should be counted as progress when the poor of one country become less poor by a process that makes workers (or former workers) in other countries more poor.

The removal of price controls and tariffs has contributed to increasing what euphemistic neoliberal language calls labour-market flexibility, which in less euphemistic terms often means losing one's job. Domestic producers of agricultural and manufactured goods are increasingly subject to foreign competition, which often leads domestic producers to fold altogether.[31] This increasingly competitive and unstable environment contributed to the curtailment of the power of the trade unions (as well as to a phenomenon that most often goes hand-in-hand with the curtailment of union strength: an increase in the numbers of people who are [often self-] employed in the informal sector, which we discuss below). At the end of the 1990s, the unionized sector accounted for only 8.3 percent of total employment.[32] The loss of union strength

---

31 On local responses of particular domestic producers facing these consequences of increasing labour-market flexibility, see Patrick Heller, The Labor of Development: Workers and the Transformation of Capitalism in Kerala, India (Ithaca: Cornell University Press, 1999). Heller shows that where the working class is highly organized and where there exist apertures for genuine popular democracy, these neoliberal economic reforms do not necessarily have to lead to the most severe outcomes. We wish to emphasize, however, that although genuine popular democracy and the tenets of neoliberalism never conflict in the realm of rhetoric, in the realm of practical experience they frequently do.

32 Kaur 208. Part of the decline of unionization is a reflec-

means, among other things, that the formal sector is coming to resemble the informal sector in important ways. Most notably, it is the relatively low wages being paid to workers who are fortunate enough to be employed in the formal sector that makes it worthwhile for those U.S. and European firms (in sectors such as medical care, insurance, and banking) to, in the words of Jeffrey Sachs, "increasingly [resort] to the BPO route to cut their costs" by outsourcing some of their operations to India, where labour costs, while having risen slightly over the three preceding years, still in 2003, averaged only 74 cents per hour in U.S. dollars.[33]

---

tion of the collapse of the public sector. For the private sector as a whole, the organized sector accounted for only 2.5 percent of total employment by the end of the 1990s. Ghosh 25.

33 Kaur 208; Sachs 182; Country Data, India, The Economist Intelligence Unit, 25 May 2004. It should be noted that of course not all of the symptoms (e.g., low wages) of the newest labour-market 'flexibility' are being exhibited in the formal sector, for these symptoms are correctly traditionally associated with the informal sector; however, one of the distinguishing features of 'globalization' or the phase of flexible accumulation is that it blurs the line between the formal and informal sectors and makes this line, while still somewhat theoretically useful, just so quaintly twentieth-century. Indeed, India has recently seen great efforts toward organizing in order to bring some formerly formal-sector benefits to informal-sector workers. One of the best examples of this is the work of the Self-Employed Women's Association (SEWA), a registered trade union that has established a women's bank and offers its members social security protection against illness, widowhood, disablement, disasters such as fire and flood, and the like. Jain 54-57.

Even more fundamentally still, however, is the central NIDL argument that any country that pursues an economic strategy whose basis is 'labour flexibility' (i.e., having workforces with low rates of unionization and few if any state-sanctioned protections—euphemistically known as 'disciplined' workforces) is building its house on a foundation of shifting sand, for just as India has undercut U.S. and European production sites in business process outsourcing, so too will India eventually be undercut by some other country or countries whose workers are paid even less. This is the phenomenon that NIDL thinkers refer to as the global 'race to the bottom,' and it should be clear that even if poverty rates are temporarily lowered—by means of temporary job creation—in the country that is the temporary winner in the competition for greatest labour flexibility, in the end not only will the majority in that country lose out, but also the majority worldwide. The ranks of capital are very narrow, bestowing boom conditions at any given moment in time on only quite limited stretches of the planet's surface. The ranks of labour are wide and growing. Even under the relatively favourable conditions of India today, the hardships labour faces are expanding, especially as more and more people are forced into the informal sector.[34]

Evidence abounds that what the NIDL approach predicts is what has been happening in India over the last fifteen years. We will highlight the work of Jan Breman,

---

34 The literature that presents evidence for the 'race to the bottom' argument is vast. One of the best case studies presenting this argument is Jeffrey A. Winters, Power in Motion: Capital Mobility and the Indonesian State (Ithaca: Cornell University Press, 1996).

who has conducted three decades of careful detailed field research among the rural and urban working classes of south Gujarat. Breman's study, published just five years after the first stage of implementation of the Programme of Economic Stabilisation and Restructuring, focuses mainly on the landless workers of this region, the majority of whom belong to the tribal Halpati caste. Although Breman warns against applying his conclusions, without further elaboration, to all of India—since they are based on detailed analysis of local conditions—he believes that the dynamics of south Gujarat have wider validity, "[n]ot least because there are policy-makers, in both national and international agencies, who would like to see in south Gujarat's pattern of industrialization a model for economic growth under the new liberalized regime."[35] Breman started his studies in rural communities in the 1960s, and while much of the region is still rural, agricultural labour is no longer the principal source of income for most families; instead of having access to employment as relatively steady and assured as that in the agricultural sector, families in the region are looking increasingly to whatever opportunities they can find in the informal sector. This fits into a larger pattern throughout the Indian countryside documented in a 1991 report and continuing throughout the 1990s: there has been a shift toward casual work to the detriment of regular work, and there has been a marked increase in the spatial mobility of labour, as people migrate either seasonally or longer-term in search of chances to sell their labour-power. By the mid-1990s,

---

35 Jan Breman, Footloose Labour: Working in India's Informal Economy (Cambridge: Cambridge University Press, 1996), 21.

in both south Gujarat and in India as a whole, the ratio of informal-sector to formal-sector employment in the non-agrarian economy was four to one.[36]

Characteristics of employment in the informal sector—working for one's own account and at one's own risk—include excessive vulnerability and the increasing marginalization of women in particular. These ground-level realities are hardly ever captured in official economic data, partly because people often earn enough cash to be counted among the non-poor, even when their lives are extremely hard, and even when people with less cash officially counted as poor in fact have easier lives.[37] In south Gujarat, some of the main sources of employment in the informal sector include textile-weaving, domestic work, diamond-cutting and diamond-polishing, street vending, and working in the saltpans and in the brick kilns. Breman carefully documents the hardships faced by workers in each of these areas. It might be difficult for certain readers to take to heart the levels of physical exhaustion endured by and the emotional tolls exacted from people who cannot rely upon institutionalized social security programs to any significant extent and who must rely on long daily commutes or even seasonal migrations in order to have any hope of keeping themselves and their families alive, but Breman's fieldwork notes offer a glimpse. He writes:

---

36 Breman 2, 6, 22. The 1991 report referenced is Government of India, Ministry of Labour, Report of the National Commission on Rural Labour (2 volumes) (New Delhi: Ministry of Labour, 1991).
37 Breman 10.

M is a widow and only allows herself to be recruited for brickyards that she can reach from Chikhligam in a fairly short time. That is because her two children have to stay in the village. The eight-year-old daughter is old enough to work together with her mother, but not the four-year-old son. Both thus stay at home where the girl looks after her little brother. The neighbours keep an eye on them. M returns home once a month to put affairs in order and to bring money for the coming weeks. This year she is working near Surat, and travelling back and forth is a heavy charge on her meagre budget. She leaves the brickyard early in the afternoon, reaches Chikhligam in the evening, and then stays until late the following afternoon. In this way she loses as little work as possible. On the other hand, she has no breathing space in which to recuperate. When she returns at the end of the season, M is worn out.[38]

It is important to note that the hardships documented in Breman's study are not confined to the landless or the land-poor, as even those who have stable access to land to farm have been hard-hit by neoliberal reforms.

---

38 Breman 70. The increasing labour market flexibility engendered by India's neoliberal reforms has hit formal sector workers as well. Breman reports that although the Factory Act explicitly stipulates a working day of eight hours maximum, power loom operators in textile mills, paid piece-rate, feel they have little choice but to work shifts that are far longer, in order to make enough money to keep body and soul together and also simply in order not to be replaced by others willing to work the long shifts. Ibid. 124-131.

In the last five years there has been an alarming wave of suicides among farmers in the states of Maharashtra, Kerala, and Andhra Pradesh; the primary reasons given for these include heavy indebtedness (due to neoliberal changes in rural credit programs), inability to meet the rising cost of cultivation, and crop failure.[39] As increased 'flexibility' of labour markets and of policies regarding industrial and agricultural production has translated into an increasing lack of security for families—both security of employment and security of income—burdens shift in ways that move counter to the generally positive trends noted above. Elderly and very young family members are sometimes called to contribute to household income more and not less. As of 2003, 11 percent of children ages 10-14 were counted in the official data as being employed in the urban informal sector.[40]

---

39 Over six hundred farmers in the state of Maharashtra alone committed suicide in the period between January 2001 and January 2005. The Bombay High Court, acting on a public interest petition filed in December 2004, requested that the Tata Institute of Social Sciences (TISS) investigate the causes. The causes listed here are those reported by TISS. Another source of consternation for India's farmers—particularly vexing in a climate of high indebtedness and crop failure—is falling prices for their products. The prices for the following products grown in Kerala state, for example, all declined quite substantially in the 2001-02 period from their 1996-97 levels: rice, coconut, pepper, cashews, areca nut, rubber, and ginger. A.C. George (President, Socialist Party, India), "Comments on the Economic Policies of Manmohan Singh," unpublished letter, 4-5, 7; Anupama Katakam, "The Roots of a Tragedy," Frontline 22/14 (15 July 2005) 43.
40 World Bank, 2005 World Development Indicators 77.

Although reliance upon work in the informal sector does not necessarily contribute to improvements in living standards for a majority of participants in this sector, we should emphasize that this shift in employment opportunities away from the formal sector and toward the informal is something that is clearly foreseen by the international lending agencies recommending neoliberal policies. In its 1995 World Development Report, the World Bank stated:

> *In many Latin American, South Asian and Middle Eastern countries, labour laws establish onerous job security regulations, rendering hiring decisions practically irreversible; and the system of worker representation and dispute resolution is subject to often*

Breman offers a look into the conditions faced by children in the brickworks: "Their labour power becomes indispensable while they are still quite young, and from the age of six they are wakened during the night to carry the fresh bricks made by their father. While wet, those bricks weigh roughly three kilos. The little children run with one brick each, away from the base plate and into the darkness. When they reach the age of about nine, they are promoted to carrying two bricks.... [I]n another brickworks, I found a girl of about fifteen years old who lay on the ground under a couple of jute sacks, shivering with fever. Her younger sister came now and again and shook her gently, trying to get her to go to work, because she was unable alone to carry all the bricks away from the base plate. The labour power of her sick sister is needed to eliminate the backlog. When that has been done, she can lie down again although for no longer than ten minutes." Breman 134-135.

unpredictable government decision making, adding uncertainty to firms' estimates of future labour cost.[41]

In other words, not only were the socialistic policies of the administrations in India prior to 1991 "biased against employment," but such "onerous job security regulations" as those constituting the formal labour market itself also, in this estimation, represent a "bias against employment."[42]

Before concluding this brief delineation of the ground-level consequences for India's working classes of the neoliberal reforms begun in 1991, we would be remiss not to point out one of the most perverse consequences of all. If the neoliberal reforms promised them nothing else, they promised Indian working classes more employment opportunities. Say what one might about the quality of those jobs offered (and we would follow the ILO in emphasizing that much of the new work is not 'decent'

---

41 World Bank, World Development Report 1995 (Washington, D.C.: World Bank, 1995) 35. The World Bank's World Development Report also states: "Policies that favor the formation of small groups of workers in high-productivity activities lead to dualism (segmentation of the labor force into privileged and underprivileged groups) and tend to close the formal sector off from broader influences from the labor market, at the cost of job growth." Ibid. 34. Opening the formal labor market to "influences" from the "broader" (i.e., informal sector) labour market—"influences" such as a drag on wages, shifting costs such as healthcare to individual workers—is, according to this argument, the best way to help society as a whole because making it cheaper for employers to hire workers will undoubtedly mean expanded employment opportunities.

42 Breman 12-13.

work) and say what one might about the rise of the informal sector and the decline of the formal, reversing the 'bias against employment' was at least supposed to mean an increase in the quantity of employment opportunities. Employment opportunities, however, have not in fact kept pace with population growth. Combining 2001 census data for India with data from the National Sample Survey's 55th Round (conducted over 1999-2000) regarding employment and unemployment, ILO economist Jayati Ghosh has calculated rates of growth of aggregate employment, both rural and urban, and found in both these sectors a deceleration of growth rates from 1993-94 to 1999-2000, as compared with rates from 1987-88 to 1993-94: in rural India, growth rates fell from 2.03 percent per year in the earlier period to 0.58 percent in the latter, and in urban India, the rates were 3.39 percent and 2.27 percent, respectively.[43]

A final set of data that favours the NIDL interpretation of the facts concerns poverty reduction prior to 1991. The neoliberal policies instituted after that date cannot be credited with all of India's (in any case somewhat dubious) poverty reduction because most of the reduction in the percentage of the population below India's poverty line happened before they were instituted. The most substantial reductions in poverty rates actually took place prior to 1991, starting in the mid-1970s.[44] Indeed the rate

---

43 Ghosh 10-11. The growth rates during the neoliberal period also represented a decline from the 1983 to 1987-88 period. Ibid. The ILO defines 'decent' work as work including rights and social protections and allowing social dialogue. Ibid. 3.
44 "…while there was a marked decline in both urban and

of decrease of official poverty measures actually slowed a bit right after the 1991 reforms, and then later regained the pace that had set in earlier. This fact further bolsters the NIDL interpretation. India at that earlier time before 1991 was already beginning to reap some benefits from its position in the New International Division of Labour. This fact tends to show that it has been India's status as a vendor of inexpensive high quality labour in the global

rural poverty rates between 1973-74 and 1986-87, there is no sign of anything comparable since." Guarav Datt, "Has Poverty Declined Since Economic Reforms? Statistical Data Analysis." Economic and Political Weekly 34 (1999) 3516-3518, at 3516. On p. 3517 Datt provides a Table I and a Figure I documenting the data for 1973-97; they confirm our claim that poverty reduction actually slowed immediately after the reforms. Datt is a Senior Economist at the World Bank. Part of the story of the decline of poverty in India prior to the 1991 reforms is told by Gilbert Etienne in his Food and Poverty: India's Half Won Battle (Newbury Park, CA: Sage, 1988). "India's economy grew three times as fast during the 1950s and 1960s as during British rule. The food security that Nehru worked for contrasts with recurring famine under the Raj. In just 40 years infant mortality was halved, life expectancy nearly doubled, and adult literacy almost tripled." Ramesh Thakur, "India in the World: Neither Rich, Powerful nor Principled," Foreign Affairs 76 (1997) 15-22, at 15-16. Most scholars find India's progress in reducing poverty since the 1991 reforms disappointing, for example, Guarav Datt and Martin Ravaillon, "Is India's Economic Growth Leaving the Poor Behind?" Journal of Economic Perspectives 16 (2002) 89-108. Some find that poverty actually increased during parts of the post-reform period, for example Abhijit Sen, "Estimates of Consumer Expenditure and its Distribution," Economic and Political Weekly 35 (2001) 4499-4518.

market more than its status as an example of the application of neoliberal theory that has caused its economic growth.

In the two competing stories told about India's relative prosperity in recent years—the neoliberal story and the story of the New International Division of Labour—it is therefore the latter that is most confirmed by the Indian experience.[45] But we want to add a further theoretical reason to buttress our empirical argument. Why in theory can the neoliberal version of the India story (which, after

---

[45] India has been only one of a number of nation-states, especially in the Global South, which, by following neoliberal reforms, have achieved a relative prosperity—as defined by standard economic indicators—that masks continued hardship for the working class and even increasing insecurity for the middle class. Another well-documented example is Mexico. While the North American Free Trade Agreement (implemented in 1994) and the preceding years of neoliberal economic reforms beginning in earnest in 1988 have been credited with having set the stage for economic growth, at the same time Mexican agriculture has been seriously undermined, sending thousands of Mexicans migrating away from the countryside in search of job opportunities. Many find jobs in the in-bond assembly plants (maquiladoras) on the northern border, and many more pin their hopes on crossing the border into the U.S. and finding work there. Many maquiladoras, however, are currently considering moving operations to China, and a number have already done so. This indicates that Mexico might be losing its comparative advantage in cheap labour, which has ostensibly been the main engine of its recent economic growth. See Tom Barry, Zapata's Revenge: Free Trade and the Farm Crisis in Mexico (Boston: South End Press, 1995).

all, is based mainly on the same facts) not be true? Why can it not be true, as good-hearted and well-intentioned neoliberals such as Jeffrey Sachs suggest, that every country's embracing neoliberalism in just the right way will in fact mean the end of poverty? A sufficient although incomplete answer is suggested by the New International Division of Labour critique of the nature of Indian economic prosperity mentioned above: it is not sustainable. It is not sustainable because, as NIDL commentators point out, 'winning' in the global race to the bottom can only continue as long as investors do not find other sites with even cheaper resources, and with equal or greater willingness of governments to do whatever transnational capital may wish.

Further it is also unsustainable because of an inherent instability in the structure of the global economic system into which India has for the time being inserted itself on relatively favourable terms. One of capitalism's greatest defenders pointed this out during the great depression of the 1930s, and although capitalism's current greatest defenders—neoliberal economists—generally do not wish even to hear his name spoken, let alone hear his critiques repeated, experience has confirmed the empirical truth in John Maynard Keynes' theory of low-level equilibrium. In his capacity as Finance Minister and architect of the Programme of Economic Stabilisation and Restructuring, Manmohan Singh apparently actually believed the distinctly anti-Keynesian predictions of his tutor Ian Little, who had stated with confidence that the redundant workers dismissed in the layoffs that accompanied privatization would readily find employment in profitable businesses in the private sector, where they would earn their pay. Little assumes without argument that the normal state of capitalism is a full-employment equilibrium. Yet, the assumption is incorrect. Evidence from around the globe has demonstrated that Keynes was correct when he showed that the normal state of capitalism is what has been called 'low-level equilibrium.' More normal than a state of 'full employment' (defined as an unemployment rate of 4 percent or less) is an equilibrium in which employers have hired as many workers as they wish to hire, but there are still people who want to be hired as workers. There is normally such a thing as involuntary unemployment and also involuntary under-employment, in which a person's primary source of income is informal, part-time, low-pay, and insecure work. Readers in most places in the world need look no further than their own countries to see evidence of this.

The assurance given to governments around the world that a key element of the best remedy for poverty is to take decisions that will increase labour-market flexibility, on the assumption that if wage-rates fall low enough, full employment will be achieved, relies on the premise (the premise known as 'Say's Law') that full employment is the natural point of equilibrium for an economy. Not so. We do not mean to deny that experience has shown that Keynesian prescriptions for curing the economic ills Keynes diagnosed have proven to be inadequate. On the contrary: we hold that the continuing validity of Keynes' diagnosis coupled with the inadequacy of Keynesian prescriptions demonstrates the need for the transformation of the basic cultural structures of the modern world.

Keynes argued, consistently with his view that involuntary unemployment and low-level equilibrium are normal, that it is not wise to pursue full employment by cutting wages because lower wages will reduce effective demand for industry's products, in a world where effective demand tends to be less than optimal even without wage-cutting. On the surface, today's India refutes Keynes: wages in India are low, but nonetheless Indian goods and services sell like hotcakes. We hold, however, that Keynes' wisdom is merely masked, not refuted. The Keynesian principle that sellers require buyers is masked today by the practice of producing in countries where wages are low and selling in countries where wages are high. In a global market, the producers who need customers with purchasing power do not necessarily need to have any buyers in close geographical proximity who have purchasing power. They do not need to sell to their own workers, or to the neighbours of their own workers. Nonetheless, taking the world as a whole, Keynes was not wrong to say:

> [W]hilst no man would wish to deny the proposition that a reduction in money-wages accompanied by the same aggregate effective demand as before will be associated with an increase in employment, the precise question at issue is whether the reduction in money-wages will or will not be accompanied by the same aggregate effective demand as before measured in money, or, at any rate, by an aggregate effective demand which is not reduced in full proportion to the reduction in money-wages [emphasis in original].[46]

---

46 John Maynard Keynes, The General Theory of Employment, Interest, and Money (London: Macmillan, 1954)

Fundamentally, therefore, the advice being given by the neoliberals whose views we have analyzed above is not good advice, for the assertion that full employment will obtain when there is no 'bias against employment' is neither theoretically valid nor borne out by the vast empirical evidence from all corners of the earth. The empirical fact, mentioned above, that neoliberalism has not brought full employment to India, should not be taken as a pretext for drawing the conclusion that even more extreme neoliberal measures should be taken to reach that elusive goal. It should be taken as even further evidence that the real world of capitalism is pretty much what Keynes said it was: a world where unemployment is normal and where the prosperity even of the prosperous is rendered unstable by the drag on prosperity constituted by chronically inadequate effective demand. The five-star hotels of today's New Delhi temporarily mask these facts. They do not refute them.

That these things are so suggests the need for the transformation of the basic cultural structures of the modern world that Gandhi advocated, and which we have been advocating.[47]

159-160.
47 See note 2 above.

2. On Whether It Is Desirable to Change the Basic Structures of the Modern World

The foregoing is only half the story. It is the half about how to interpret events in India since 1991. The other half is about the neoliberal reluctance to acknowledge that it is desirable to change the basic structures of the modern world, the discussion of which we take up now. Here we must say at the outset that although neither the NIDL nor the neoliberal school of thought takes as seriously as we would urge the need for the transformation of basic cultural structures, the NIDL interpretation is held by many people who in fact strongly desire basic transformation. Many in this school of thought, however, seem to doubt that such transformation is possible. Those from the neoliberal school, on the other hand, are not persuaded of any need for changing what we call basic cultural structures and which they tend to call 'economic reality.' India may well have been constrained when it ran out of cash to pay for imports to comply with the requirements of economic reality whether or not it wanted to, but end result, the neoliberals say, was good, not bad. According to this line of reasoning, radicals could better serve humanity by acquiescing in what Francis Fukuyama has called the 'end of history,' resigning as chess players resign when they see they cannot win, accepting as their consolation that the goals they sought to achieve are being achieved, albeit by following other people's theories.[48] Indeed, the neoliberal insistence upon total acceptance of that misguided worldview is such that it is quite common

---

48   Francis Fukuyama, The End of History and the Last Man (New York: Free Press, 2006).

for advocates of World Bank sorts of thinking to dismiss as simply irrational anyone who believes in a Gandhian 'swadeshi ethic' and does not believe in the principle of comparative advantage.[49]

Yet it turns out that the ideas of Mahatma Gandhi are enjoying a revival in India today, even in circles where Gandhian philosophy might at first appear completely out of place. Gandhi was on the whole sidelined, regarded as well intentioned but naïve, by Nehruvian socialism. Now, in our age of free trade promoted by economists who are convinced that people who disagree with their basic premises are not rational, this self-described out and out protectionist, has in some ways returned in glory.

---

49 Thus Ian Little and his co-author write, "It is quite difficult to get people to understand that it is better to import candyfloss if one is not good at making it, and instead to make and export something one is good at making." Joshi and Little 68. See also by the same authors Indian Macroeconomic Policy, 1964-1991 (Oxford: Oxford University Press, 1994) 12. Arundhati Roy dismisses the World Bank with even stronger language than that employed by Little to defend the World Bank: "The World Trade Organization, the World Bank, the International Monetary Fund, and other financial institutions like the Asian Development Bank, virtually write economic policy and parliamentary legislation. With a deadly combination of arrogance and ruthlessness they take their sledgehammers to fragile, interdependent, historically complex societies, and devastate them." Arundhati Roy, Public Power in the Age of Empire (New York: Open Media/Seven Stories Press, 2004) 21-22. For another scathing critique of the World Bank's metanarrative, see Susan George and Fabrizio Sabelli, Faith & Credit: The World Bank's Secular Empire (Boulder: Westview Press, 1994).

Manmohan Singh is an economist who quotes Gandhi frequently, and who, besides presiding over India as its prime minister, also chairs an educational foundation devoted to propagating Gandhi's ideals.[50] In April of 2005, Prime Minister Manmohan Singh inaugurated a multi-media exhibition on the life of Gandhi in Delhi, at the precise site where Gandhi was assassinated, where young and old come to learn about the father of the nation.[51] Although it would appear to be impossible to reconcile mainstream economics with Gandhi, Manmohan Singh is to all appearances making a wholehearted attempt to do so.[52]

---

50 In his radio address to the nation upon assuming the office of Prime Minister after the June 2004 elections, Manmohan stated, "As I share with you the priorities of our Government, I am reminded of the Father of our nation, Mahatma Gandhi. Gandhiji had said that his mission in life was 'to wipe every tear from every eye'. 'Think of the poorest person you have ever seen,' Gandhiji would say, 'and ask if your next act will be of any use to him.' That message of Bapu resonates in our ears as we settle down to the business of government." Quoted in The Hindustan Times (25 June 2004).
51 The Hindu (14 April 2005).
52 One explanation of Dr Singh's admiration of Gandhi, even though he subscribes to economic views much different from Bapu's, would be that at some level of his mind he has acknowledged that a program like the CMP, which proposes to keep India on its high-growth path and at the same time to promote greater equity, is not feasible if it is assumed that people's motives are strictly economic, and that it could only be feasible if it is assumed instead that the ideals like those of Gandhi will influence the behaviour of the people. A second explanation would be that Manmohan Singh thinks of himself

Perhaps change is in the air, and perhaps change can be seen in the evolution of Manmohan Singh's own thinking. Perhaps today the goal the current government of India has set for itself, that of combining prosperity with justice, will be acknowledged to be a goal that can only be achieved by questioning first premises. One way to do that is to reconsider Gandhi. First premises need to be reconsidered because the economic dilemmas faced by India are dilemmas created by cultural structures.

Let us look once again at the dilemma discussed above that faced Manmohan Singh as the new Finance Minister in 1991. On the surface, taking the cultural structures for granted and therefore not seeing them, the choice was simple, practically no choice at all: either regain the confidence of international capital, or let the Indian economy collapse. Yet if we assume that Manmohan Singh admired Bapu as much in 1991 as he does in 2006, we might expect that he would have taken a deeper view, and would have noticed that the cultural structures of the modern world that Bapu condemned in Hind Swaraj (and frequently thereafter) were imposing on India unacceptable dilemmas. One might also have thought that democracy would have tilted the scales toward equality, which would lead to favouring wages over profits rather than the opposite course which pleasing international capital required. One might have thought that a nation with many undernourished people, and with a history of severe famines, would have been obsessed, even to

---

as faithful to Gandhi's ideal of living a life of service to others consisting of experiments with truth, but that in the very interest of truth, he has revised Gandhi's constructive program by replacing ideas that do not work with ideas that do work.

the point of overshooting the mark, with guaranteeing that enough food would be produced, even if that meant continuing the practice of running up deficits by giving farmers cheap water and electricity. But none of these things one might have thought, nor the almost unthinkable possibility of just not paying the debts and declaring the country in default (which actually did occur to Manmohan Singh at the time) was decisive. Instead, the systemic imperatives of the basic cultural structures of the modern world were decisive.

Reconsidering again the crisis of 1991 provides us an opportunity to illustrate here part of the meaning behind phrases like "systemic imperatives of the basic cultural structures of the modern world," which we often use in our writings. We claim that the imperatives built into the congeries of institutions called 'the market' move modern history. India tried to disobey some of the laws of markets. It learned in early 1991 that it could not get away with it. At that point, India changed course, but not because it (or its elites, or its government, or its voters, or its population in general) chose to change. India changed because it had to. Here the compulsion expressed in 'had to' is strong, although not as strong as physical necessity, nor as certain as mathematical necessity. From the point of view of an Indian civil servant, what had to be done beginning in June 1991 was decided not by the will of any individual or group, and not by any philosophy of government, but by the objective requirements of the situation. (From our point of view these 'objective requirements' are systemic imperatives built into basic cultural structures.) These requirements were, by and large, the same as those required of any other nation in the twentieth century.

Details might differ, but the broad pattern was decided everywhere by the same forces des choses.

In the abstract, one of India's choices in 1991 was simply not to pay. It would not have been the first time a debtor did not pay its debts. One of the world community's choices, in 1991 as today, and as Manmohan Singh himself had proposed in his capacity as Secretary-General of the South Commission, would have been to move, as now the world already has to some extent moved, toward an international bankruptcy regime. Such a regime would provide for adjusting interest rates, payment schedules, and the total amounts to be paid as needed, according to the principle that whenever the processes of material life are obstructed by dysfunctional institutions, it is the latter that should be changed.[53] But in 1991, not paying was only an abstract possibility for India. The concrete reality was that life on the Indian subcontinent could only be kept going with the aid of a steady stream of imports, and no fundamental changes of the cultural structures governing life on the planet were in the offing. A moral

---

53 An international bankruptcy regime would count as a change in the basic cultural structures of the modern world. It would modify the fundamental rules of buying and selling, since it would provide that under certain circumstances, which often occur, purchases do not have to be paid for. Manmohan Singh as Secretary-General of the South Commission proposed an international norm providing that however much they might owe, nations should not be compelled to make any payments on their debts that would prevent them from achieving economic growth measured as income per head at the rate of at least two to three percent per year. The bilateral official debt of the poorest countries should be written off completely. Singh, "In a Changing World" 190-191.

command (pay your debts!) had become a physical command (borrow or suffer!).

This illustration illuminates points we have argued elsewhere at greater length and with more historical case studies, and which have also been noted by other writers.[54] The basic cultural structures imply that the costs of production must be kept down. Other social goals must not be allowed to override balancing the books and making a profit (in Marxist terminology, capital accumulation). To reiterate, it is the recognition of the need for keeping production costs down—as a systemic imperative—that drives both the neoliberal and the NIDL interpretations of the global economy. The commands of the market are self-enforcing. Sooner or later, disobeying them will be punished, regardless of what people may choose, say, think, or desire. It follows that a feasible method for basic cultural change must be one that modifies the currently dominant systemic imperatives.

The systemic imperative to lower costs of production has a hybrid epistemic status. There are several things it is not and at least two that it is. It is not a formal mathematical certainty like $2 + 2 = 4$. It is not an empirical

---

54 See Howard Richards, Letters from Quebec: A Philosophy of Peace and Justice (San Francisco and London: International Scholars Press, 1995), especially chapter 8; Howard Richards, Understanding the Global Economy (Santa Barbara: Peace Education Books, 2004); Howard Richards and Joanna Swanger, The Dilemmas of Social Democracies (Lanham, MD: Lexington Books, 2006); Charles Lindblom, "The Market as Prison," Journal of Politics 44 (1982) 324-336; John Dryzek, Rational Ecology: Environment and Political Economy (Oxford and New York: Basil Blackwell, 1997).

discovery, for it is not necessary to conduct studies of experiences worldwide in order to learn that higher price tea cannot be sold in competition with lower price tea of equal quality.[55] It is not a normative principle stating what ought to be, like Gandhi's trusteeship principle, which holds that whoever controls property (whether as owner or as manager in the private or public sector) ought to act as trustee for the poor. Indeed, for Gandhi it is an anti-normative principle, since Gandhi holds that cost of production should not be lowered at the expense of the workers, and that consumers ought to cooperate by paying higher prices for goods made under fair labour conditions. It is unlike Kant's categorical imperative, which was a command of pure reason unalloyed by material motives, for it is an imperative derived from the practical statement of fact that any entrepreneur who does not obey it will not prosper in business and will quite likely become bankrupt. It is, in part, what John Searle calls an institutional fact: it is a fact that is true because of certain institutional arrangements.[56] It is a systemic imperative that would be less imperative if the system were modified, and which might not be true at all, and might not even be meaningful enough to be pronounced true or false, in a different institutional context. It is, however, also an institutional fact with a natural basis, since no society could physically survive if it allowed its costs of

---

55 However, empirical research was necessary to demonstrate the existence of so-called Giffen goods, for which the demand goes up when the price increases.

56 John Searle, Speech Acts (Cambridge: Cambridge University Press, 1969).

production (measured not in money but in things) to rise without limit.

India was expected in 1991 to obey a certain social norm, the norm prescribing that a nation ought to pay its debts. The norm prescribes more generally that a nation, an individual, or any social entity should keep its promises, including the promises borrowers make to lenders when they take out loans. Pacta sunt servanda. Since the command to pay debts is a legal and ethical norm, there is more flexibility in complying with it than there is in complying with physical laws. Gravity cannot be repealed. Disobeying social norms is common. To cite just one example, the United Nations Conventions on Economic and Social Rights, solemnly adhered to by most of the world's governments, enshrined as an integral part of international law, are disobeyed most of the time most places.

We believe that the characteristics of markets that explain their extraordinary power to shape history, and to resist conscious attempts to reshape history, can usefully be called 'systemic imperatives.'[57] Once a people becomes dependent for its livelihood on large-scale commercial exchanges carried out over long distances (with or without advanced technologies) it must obey the laws of markets. It violates their commands at its peril.

Consistently with this belief, we see India (and the rest of the world) as impelled to adopt its present neoliberal posture, not so much by pressure from the International Monetary Fund, not so much by a rightward paradigm

---

57 On systemic imperatives, see also Ellen Meiksins Wood, Empire of Capital (London: Verso, 2003), especially 14, 86, 89, 133, 134, 136, 139, and 157.

shift among professional economists, not so much by swings in the sentiments of the electorate, not so much by the power of transnational corporations, as by la force des choses. India could not escape the systemic imperatives of the global market economy. (This viewpoint explains why we used the word 'structure' in the first sentence and frequently thereafter. The word 'structure,' referring to the patterns of institutional relationships, and here especially to markets and their legal foundations in the laws governing property and contracts, helps to express our view that history is moved not so much by individuals, nations, religions, or classes, as by the rules that constitute institutions.)

Viewing the resistance to change of modernity's basic cultural structures as a consequence of the systemic imperatives of a market economy helps us to outline the requirements of a feasible method to change them. The method must change la force des choses, the systemic imperatives. Consciousness-raising is a good start, since it educates people so that they understand that the systemic imperatives are commands imposed by institutions that have been culturally constructed. Gandhi understood this, for his critiques of the West derive from a clear awareness that the West's dysfunctional cultural institutions were imposed upon India from without; and that not only was another world possible, it had once existed in India and therefore could exist again.

If Manmohan Singh had contemplated in 1962—when he was writing his doctoral dissertation under the direction of Ian Little—the full consequences of following a path that would in principle sooner or later make India dependent on foreign markets to earn the wherewithal to obtain its basic necessities, and which would require India to organize itself internally in order to accommodate itself to the systemic imperatives of markets, he might have concluded that Gandhi's path of self-reliance had been the right path all along. If at independence India had followed Gandhi instead of Nehru, it would have rejected the adharma modern western concept of human relationships based on buying and selling. Work would have been conceived of as part of a spiritual way of life, with the workers owning their own tools, individually or in groups. Service to neighbour would have been its goal. Given driving principles and practices such as these, Gandhian economic structures implemented at the local level would offer an alternative to the misery described by Jan Breman in his ethnographic studies of south Gujarat. There would be a great deal more security and stability for all community members. Whether anything of the sort would actually have materialized if India had wholeheartedly followed Gandhi after independence will never be known. What is certain—and what we hoped to have illustrated not just in this chapter but throughout this book—is that the ideas of Gandhi can serve as a rich resource for progressive social transformation in this dark age when all the paths to progressive change appear to be closed off. Such paths are far from utopian; looking closely, one will see they are well travelled, both past and present.

* * *

Authors

Howard Richards is a philosopher of social science. He is emeritus Research Professor of Philosophy at Earlham College, Richmond, Indiana, USA, a Quaker school where he taught for thirty-five years. He was the Director of the Peace and Global Studies Program there and co-founder of the Business and Nonprofit Management program. Now he lives in Chile where he teaches in the doctoral program in management sciences at the University of Santiago. He is a distinguished fellow of the South African Research Chair in Development Education based at the University of South Africa. As a scholar he has published many books and articles in English and in Spanish. The Evaluation of Cultural Action (Macmillan) was published in 1985, and Letters from Quebec (International Scholars Press) in 1995. Understanding the Global Economy (Peace Education Books) came out in 2004. Another book co-authored with Joanna Swanger, Dilemmas of Social Democracies (Lexington Books), came out in 2006. In 2011 his book The Nurturing of Time Future was published by Dignity Press.

Joanna Swanger is an historian and Director of Peace and Global Studies Program and Assistant Professor of Peace and Global Studies. Joanna served as the Border Studies Program Resident Director for eight years when the program was based in El Paso/Ciudad Juarez. Her research specialty is on labor history and she has produced many articles and essays about the borderlands, including serving as Editor for a special issue of the International Journal of Qualitative Studies in Education on The Border Studies Program: Ethnography as Pedagogy in Undergraduate Education.

Ivo Coelho, SDB earned a PhD in philosophy at the Gregorian University, Rome, for his work on "The Development of the Notion of the Universal Viewpoint in Bernard Lonergan: From Insight to Method in Theology" (1994). He has been principal of Divyadaan: Salesian Institute of Philosophy (1988-90), Rector (1994-2002), secretary of the Association of Christian Philosophers of India (2000-02), and provincial of the Mumbai province of the Salesians of Don Bosco (2002-08). Currently he is Rector of the Studium Theologicum Salesianum in Jerusalem, while continuing to edit Divyadaan: Journal of Philosophy and Education. Among his publications are Hermeneutics and Method: The 'Universal Viewpoint' in Bernard Lonergan (2001), "Hermeneutics and the Inner Word: Jean Grondin's Introduction to Philosophical Hermeneutics" (1999), "'Et Judaeus et Graecus e methodo:' The Transcultural Mediation of Christian Meanings and Values in Lonergan" (2000), and "Lonergan and Indian Thought" (2007). He has recently edited Brahman and Person: Essays by Richard De Smet (2010), and Violence and its Victims: A Challenge to Philosophizing in the Indian Context (ACPI vol. 11, 2010), while Understanding Sankara: Essays by Richard De Smet is in the press.

Acknowledgements

The chapters of this book have earlier been published as follows, and are being reprinted now with kind permission:

"Introduction," Divyadaan: Journal of Philosophy and Education 20/2 (2009) 205-208

"Chapter 1: Gandhi and the Future," Divyadaan: Journal of Philosophy and Education 20/3 (2009) 445-466

"Chapter 2: Jawaharlal Nehru," Divyadaan: Journal of Philosophy and Education 21/1 (2010) 37-64

"Chapter 3: Jayaprakash Narayan," Divyadaan: Journal of Philosophy and Education 21/3 (2010) 379-406

"Chapter 4: Tariq Ali," Divyadaan: Journal of Philosophy and Education 22/1 (2011) 105-122

"Chapter 5: Vandana Shiva," Divyadaan: Journal of Philosophy and Education 22/2 (2011) 217-242

"Chapter 6: Amartya Sen," Divyadaan: Journal of Philosophy and Education 22/3 (2011) 397-420

"Chapter 7: Arundhati Roy," Divyadaan: Journal of Philosophy and Education 23/1 (2012) 99-121

"Chapter 8: Manmohan Singh," Divyadaan: Journal of Philosophy and Education 23/3 (2012) 389-426